DEVIANCE:
Field Studies
and
Self-Disclosures

Jerry Jacobs
Syracuse University

National Press Books

Library of Congress Catalog Card Number: 73-84772

International Standard Book Numbers: 0-87484-224-7 (paper)
                                       0-87484-225-5 (cloth)

Manufactured in the United States of America

National Press Books
850 Hansen Way, Palo Alto, California 94304

This book was set in Baskerville by Libra Cold Type and was printed
and bound by Kingsport Press. Nancy Sears designed the
text and cover and Michelle Hogan supervised production. Alden C. Paine
was sponsoring editor and Gene Tanke was copy editor.

Contents

3.

THE SOCIO–LEGAL MANAGEMENT OF DEVIANCE   91

4.

THE MEDICAL MANAGEMENT OF DEVIANCE   149

Introduction

The following essays will deal with several familiar areas of deviant behavior: prostitution, homosexuality, pornography, drug use and abuse, and the art of conning and "cooling out"[1] the client. They will also be concerned with the question of how the courts and other bureaucratic agencies designed to counter deviance may inadvertently create and perpetuate it. Also included are more exotic settings and forms of deviance that have thus far received little or no attention in the sociological literature—for example, a fly-in whore house and "adult" bookstores. These, and other topics, will be dealt with from an interactionist perspective.[2]

Some of the essays include field notes. These are presented to give the reader a better grasp of how the work evolved, that is, how the researcher attended and interpreted the setting in question. These informal notes (edited for length) are an invaluable source of information when one is trying to understand how, in interpretive sociology,[3] one's formulation of the problem and interpretation of the data is contingent upon one's understanding of the social scene, and conversely, the way in which the latter effects the former. It is the interplay between these two that will hopefully lead the researcher to achieve "verstehen," a stage in the research process that Max Weber sees as a prerequisite for acquiring a sociological understanding.[4]

With the exception of the author's essays, the contributors (two of whom prefer to remain anonymous) are sociology students who have taken graduate or undergraduate courses in deviant behavior from the author. Apart from being students, they have worked as college instructors, lawyers, parole officers, social workers, and are in good standing in a wide variety of employments. The contributors have either studied these forms of deviance close-up and over time, or have themselves been the deviants.

All of the essays are written from an interactionist perspective. By this I mean that they concern themselves with such subjective social-psychological considerations as the individual's intentions, motives, and morals as these relate to the more general sociological problem of establishing the reality of the social scene. This in turn requires that the researcher achieve an understanding of the social meanings of social actions, as these are perceived by members of the social setting, and the way in which these meanings affect behavioral outcomes.

The interactionist perspective contends that the social meanings of verbal and nonverbal communications do not inhere in the words or deeds themselves but are conferred upon one's words and deeds by others. An interpretive process on the part of alter (the perceiving) and ego (the perceived) is an intervening and integral part of defining the situation. The meanings that ego attributes to alter, that is, confers upon alter's words or deeds, depends in large part upon present and past circumstances and the future expectations of the participants within a given social context. The interactionist perspective, while encompassing a wide range of sociological viewpoints,[5] requires above all that the sociologist take this process into account in the study of social phenomena.

The essays or readings have been arranged in four Parts: The Management of Deviance in Public Places, The Private Management of Deviance, The Socio-Legal Management of Deviance, and The Medical Management of Deviance. These headings should be self-explanatory. The reader is asked to pay particular attention to the way in which the readings concentrate on and go about describing the context in which the deviance occurred. The reader's ability to empathize with the deviant will depend upon the contributor's understanding of the social setting he describes and his success in reconstructing for the reader the reality of the social scene.

The readings in Part One are concerned (apart from their different substantive areas) with the question of staging—the ways in which people try to neutralize deviant public activities by offering "front stage" a respectable presentation of self.[6] This attempt at image management is intended to convince others that "nothing unusual is happening,"[7] in order to avoid public embarrassment and injury to the self. The way in which individuals frequenting a fly-in whore house, an adult bookstore, or a homosexual drive-in area are able to succeed in the above undertaking will be dealt with in the readings.

Part Two presents examples of the way in which drug users attempt to neutralize their deviant activities to themselves, and eliminate the need to do so for others, by defining others as incapable of understanding the drug user's experience. The student-user and former user-dealer both undertook to legitimize their present and past activities by offering various moral justifications for their drug habit. The reader is cautioned not to judge these "accounts"[8] in terms of their validity or moral worth, but rather to seek an understanding of the way in which they served to initiate and perpetuate, for the authors, the use and abuse of drugs. The accounts provide, in fact, a description of the socialization process whereby the novice is introduced to and becomes a part of the drug culture. The other essay in this section, Losing, is an autobiography outlining the effects of obesity on one's life-style and describes the way in which obese persons undertake to neutralize the stigma currently associated with this condition.

Part Three deals with the way in which public servants, most of whom are dedicated to the reduction or elimination of deviant behavior, may inadvertently contribute to its growth and expansion. The need to clear court calendars that are backlogged many months (sometimes years) requires that judges and "advocates" favor negotiated pleas. As a result, justice rests not so much upon an accurate appraisal of the facts (tempered with the spirit of the law) as upon the key requirement of bureaucratic justice, expediting cases. What is indicated in these readings is that justice is neither always blind nor equitable. The second essay, which deals with the social organization of a motor vehicle department and the way in which licensers exhibit consider-able license in licensing, shows how the "ad hocing" procedures[9] used by agency personnel systematically create and perpetuate deviant identities and other untoward consequences for many who seek a driver's license. Finally, a study of a social welfare agency considers how worker practices seldom con-form to agency ideals and how this discrepancy puts both bureaucracy and client in jeopardy.

Part Four is concerned with transactions between the consumers and dis-pensers of medical and allied services. While seemingly respectable, the medical contexts in which these interactions occur sometimes lead to the initiation or perpetuation of deviant identities and careers for the par-ticipants.

The first reading treats the process by which experts may label children as severely retarded and later find that some of them appear to have normal or above normal levels of intelligence. The essay also describes the ways in which experts confronted with the above paradox resolve it to their satis-faction, "for the purposes at hand." The second reading is concerned with the kinds of persons who seek the services of quacks for the treatment of incurable diseases, and the nature of doctor-patient interactions in such settings. All of the above persons attempt to present a legitimate self to others and, in one form or another, provide themselves with the moral justi-fications necessary to accomplish this in both marginal and respectable settings.

The reader is asked to pay particular attention to the way in which all of the readings try to interpret the subjective states of the participants and the effects of those states upon an actor's presentation of self in different social settings. One's ability to reconstruct these key features will determine the extent to which one is able to grasp the actor's definition of the situation and arrive at a sociological understanding from an interactionist perspective.

NOTES

[1] "Cooling out" may be described as the artful process of talking a person into a new (and out of an old, previously held) position, status, role or notion so as to minimize (a) the individual's reluctance to give up his prior condition or position, and (b) his predisposition to complain to others for a redress of grievances, when he believes he has been taken advantage of.

[2] The interactionist perspective is held by sociologists interested in the observation, description, and analysis of human interactions (and their problematic outcomes) within natural social settings.

[3] Interpretive sociology refers generally to the sociology that describes and studies the actor's interpretation of his social environment.

[4] Verstehen relates to one's ability to "put himself in another's shoes." It refers to alter's ability to empathize with ego . . . to understand ego's definition of the situation. C. Wright Mills, ed., *From Max Weber: Essays in Sociology,* H. H. Gerth, tr. (New York: Galaxy Book, 1958), p. 56.

[5] See, for example, Howard S. Becker, *Outsiders* (New York: The Free Press, 1963), p. 9; Alfred Schutz, *Collected Papers* (The Hague: Martin Nijhoff, 1962); William Foote Whyte, *Street Corner Society* (Chicago: University of Chicago Press, 1965); Ned Polsky, *Hustlers, Beats and Others* (New York: Doubleday and Co., 1967); and Jerry Jacobs, *Adolescent Suicide* (New York: John Wiley and Sons, 1971).

[6] Erving Goffman, *The Presentation of Self in Everyday Life* (New York: Anchor Book, 1959).

[7] Joan P. Emerson, "Nothing Unusual is Happening," paper read at the September 1969 Annual Meeting of the American Sociological Association.

[8] Marvin B. Scott and Stanford M. Lyman, "Accounts, Deviance, and Social Order," in *Deviance and Respectability: The Social Construction of Moral Meanings,* ed. by Jack D. Douglas (New York: Basic Books, 1970), pp. 89–119.

[9] Harold Garfinkel, *Studies in Ethnomethodology* (New York: Prentice-Hall, 1967), pp. 186–207.

1. THE MANAGEMENT OF DEVIANCE IN PUBLIC PLACES

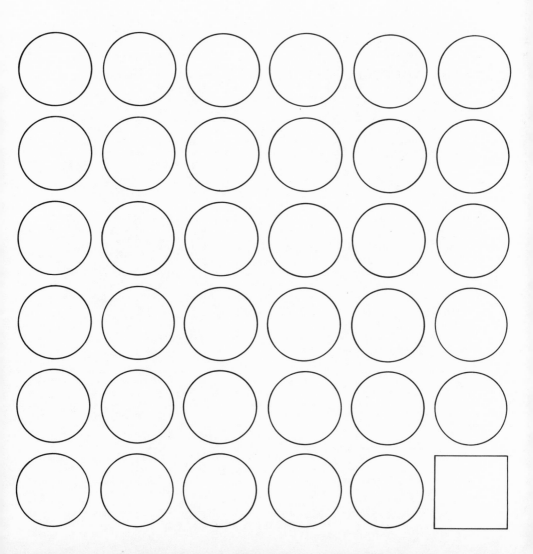

THE MANAGEMENT OF DEVIANCE IN PUBLIC PLACES

1.

Erving Goffman, in discussing the formal features of "embarrassment and social organization," notes that "encounters differ markedly from one another in purpose, social function, kind and number of personnel, settings, etc., and, while only conversational encounters will be considered here, obviously there are those in which no word is spoken."[1]

The three readings that follow, on the public management of deviance, will consider both conversational and nonverbal encounters. While they deal with impression management invoked to present to others a respectable self, all the readings deal to some extent with the social management of embarrassment also. As Goffman notes, "to appear flustered, in our society at least, is considered evidence of weakness, inferiority, low status, moral guilt, defeat, and other unenviable attributes."[2]

Given the settings in which the encounters we are about to consider take place—a homosexual pick-up area, an adult bookstore, and a fly-in whorehouse—the management of embarrassment, especially by the novice, and his attempt to present a self characterized by poise, or "cool" would seem to be a particularly difficult undertaking. Fortunately, the individual is not alone in his desire to avoid embarrassment: "Since the individual dislikes to feel or appear embarrassed, tactful persons will avoid placing him in this position. In addition, they will often pretend not to know that he has lost composure or has grounds for losing it."[3]

While Goffman describes how composed individuals may help one who is embarrassed to overcome or at least control his embarrassment, the same process can be applied in situations in which all members have grounds for embarrassment and in such settings insure that no one loses face. The follow-

*I am indebted to Professor Howard Schwartz, Department of Sociology, Harvard University, for his helpful suggestions regarding some of the ideas found in the Part introductions.

ing readings describe how individuals in a homosexual pickup area, an adult book store, and a fly-in whorehouse attempt to present a nothing-unusual-is-happening stance, and thereby convince themselves and others through verbal and nonverbal forms of interaction that they are morally worthy, competent, and otherwise respectable persons. There is, then, the tacit understanding among the participants that if you don't notice (or discuss) my presence in this marginal setting I won't notice yours. This establishes a pattern of interaction that helps provide for the self-preservation of all concerned.

One's success in establishing this pattern can be viewed with respect to the following features of the interaction: preparation before one's appearance upon the scene, one's entrance, and successful "mixing." These features are dealt with in some detail by Lyn H. Lofland in an article dealing with self-management in urban settings.[4] For example, contributor Ponte, in describing "straight" and homosexual approaches to a men's room where homosexual activities are taking place, notes that the straight approach and entrance is in what Lofland describes as a bee-line style: "With eyes focused on the desired site, he moves toward it, rapidly, purposefully, not turning his head or eyes in any other direction."[5] On the other hand, the approach and entrance of homosexuals to the men's room is better characterized as a delaying tactic: "This involves a minute pause, necessitated by some task in which the individual engages himself; the pause provides him with a few additional seconds within which to assess his surroundings."[6] The first approach may be described as confident, the second as cautious. On witnessing the different approaches of strangers to the men's room, Ponte was able to predict with great accuracy how long the individual would stay in the men's room with others, and by inference whether they were engaged in legitimate or deviant activities.

This form of analysis can be applied equally well to McKinstry's description of a person's approach, entry, and "mixing" styles in an adult bookstore setting, or to Castle's description of persons entering and leaving a fly-in whorehouse complex.

When considering how persons prepare to enter, mix, and manage the problem of embarrassment within deviant social settings, we are dealing with strategies for structuring one's behavior. It can be noticed that these strategies take advantage of the presence of what has been classically called social structures. We might use a term like "homosexual" to indicate a status. Associated with that status is a role consisting of a collection of expected behaviors. Having identified oneself as a homosexual, or a buyer of dirty books, one manages his behavior accordingly. This permits us to observe sociological regularities within the settings to be described in the following essays.

With this in mind it might be interesting to analyze these environments as "social systems" in the sense used by George Homans in *The Human Group.*[7] The nature of the social system in each environment seems to be used by those in the environment as a touchstone for managing their own behavior—for choosing appropriate responses, deciding what to notice and what to ignore, and so forth. From this point of view some interesting considerations emerge. We might describe each of these environments as possessing at least two distinct social systems. One of the regular necessities for the organization of a deviant activity is the establishment of "fronts." Society does not provide recreation centers called "homosexual houses," and one cannot find "whorehouses" in the yellow pages of the telephone book. Certain general ways of organizing a social environment, which the society usually provides, are unavailable in the case of deviant activities. However, a popular alternate organizing procedure is to set up a legal, ordinary, social environment, a "front," and use the physical space of this environment to carry on the deviant activity. This allows the deviant environment access to all sorts of resources provided by the larger society for the organization of any structured social activity—a front can have a phone, a mailing address, advertising potential, an identifying sign outside the establishment, a publicly available entrance, or legal rights such as the right to refuse entrance.

In the following essays we observe deviant activities being pursued in environments that are also respectable settings—bookstores, restaurants, and parking lots. Each of these environments, considered as a social system, has its own distinctive social structure. Most members of society, through ordinary socialization, are aware of the social structures associated with normal social settings such as parking lots. Within this social system emerges another social system associated with the deviant activity and containing its *own* social hierarchy, roles, statuses, and shared meanings. What eventually occurs is that these two social systems have to operate *simultaneously* within the same social environment. In such environments, persons are obliged to structure their behavior with reference to the demands of both systems. It then becomes possible to analyze how the two systems interrelate or how the environment is structured for its members so that these two systems coalesce.

Of special interest in this regard is the deviant social system. We might easily explain a person's knowledge of the parent social system by reference to ordinary adult socialization. But the deviant system, in Ralph Turner's words, needs to "emerge."[8] For example, persons are not taught by parents or schools how a homosexual is expected to behave. Moreover, much of the social structure in the deviant systems, as we can see from the essays, is expressed in *nonverbal* ways. In particular, there were very distinct orientations toward physical space and spatial relations—for example, placing oneself in the homosexual area of the parking lot, or not standing too close to other customers in the bookstore. In fact, it seems that the nature of a deviant activity causes an unusual reliance on nonverbal communication and meanings. Nonverbal communications and systems of meaning have the great advantage that one can use them and always have available the verbal claim that nothing unusual is happening. Ordinary language does not possess a conventional vocabulary for describing the meanings of spaces between people, looks and glances, or the speed or conviction of one's walk. It is hard to arrest someone for a homosexual advance because he entered a certain area of a parking lot or walked toward someone in a certain way.[9]

The manner in which persons learn to interpret and perform such nonverbal activities remains a large theoretical problem. One is not and cannot be verbally instructed, verbally sanctioned, or verbally initiated in these matters. Most theories of socialization heavily depend on a person's access to the natural language as a means of explaining how one learns to conduct oneself in various social settings. In the following cases, such theories are largely inapplicable.

Because of the deviant nature of the new social system and its heavily nonverbal emphasis, the salient theoretical problem for these environments is explaining how a deviant social system comes to emerge under the constraints of non-deviant parent systems, and how subsequent "personnel" participating in these environments become competent socialized actors, when the normal avenues of socialization usually associated with such an undertaking are closed.

NOTES

[1] Erving Goffman, *Interaction Ritual* (New York: Anchor Books, 1967), p. 99.
[2] Goffman, pp. 101–102.
[3] Goffman, p. 102.
[4] Lyn H. Lofland, "Self Management in Public Settings," *Urban Life and Culture,* Vol. 1, No. 1 (April 19, 1972), 93–108.
[5] Lofland, p. 105.
[6] Lofland, p. 102.
[7] George Homans, *The Human Group* (New York: Harcourt, Brace, 1950).
[8] Ralph Turner, *The Social Context of Ambition* (San Francisco: Chandler Publishing Co., 1964), p. 141.
[9] A pioneering work on nonverbal socialization is Arron Cicourel, *Method and Measurement in Sociology* (New York: Free Press, 1964), p. 57. See also Cicourel, *The Social Organization of Juvenile Justice* (New York: John Wiley & Sons, 1968), pp. 1–18.

Life in a Parking Lot: An Ethnography of a Homosexual Drive-In

Meredith R. Ponte

●●● Southern California is frequently said to lead the nation socio-
●●● logically, and one of the most publicized trends has been the
●●■ collective-behavioral phenomenon of "drive-in" institutions.
Service facilities based on the traditional drive-in restaurant have expanded
so far that one can now participate in such diverse activities as going to
church, paying bills at a bank, or getting photographs developed, all without
leaving the car. As another example that "deviance" is but an extension of
"normalcy," I have been observing a homosexual drive-in date center.

I first chanced upon this activity while exercising my dog in a small park
adjacent to a city beach parking lot. Immediately noticeable was the fact
that, although there were numerous cars both parked and being driven, all
were occupied by single males. Women and children were conspicuously
absent. I next observed that two cars which seemed to have been following

each other around the lot drove slowly away, one closely behind the other. I could see them continue to follow each other into the complex of apartments behind me. In the hours I spent there, I saw repeated instances of this behavior.

Later, I was to find that activities here were considerably more differentiated than that described above, but these oddities were sufficient to arouse my curiosity. Having studied homosexuality in several undergraduate courses, I remembered hearing of bars and street corners frequented by homophiles, but encounters by car were something new. For me, then, a parking lot, one of many in the area, of no particular interest or distinction, came to be associated with deviance.

Anselm Strauss suggests that more research be done on the cognitions people have concerning different areas within a city.[1] Impressionistic evidence, he finds, indicates that some parts are seen as places to be avoided. This parking lot seemed to be such a place, at least with respect to the general public. On a subjective level, I felt ill at ease being there and wished to avoid future contact. If Cooley's method of "sympathetic introspection" is valid,[2] then my own feelings as a heterosexually-oriented person were shared by other "normals." As a sociologist, however, I found in the area a rare opportunity to observe first hand the initial stages of a certain kind of illegal encounter.

Besides the aspect of deviance, this social activity was of interest because it represented, in Claud Humphreys' phrase, "impersonal sex in impersonal places," which, along with increasingly impersonal religion and impersonal business transactions, accompanies expanding bureaucracy.[3]

METHODOLOGY

In the early 1930's, the criminologist J. D. Lohman argued for the naturalistic approach to urban community deviance. Specifically, he prescribed concern by the investigator with relationships between the local community and the larger whole and pointed out "the existence of processes pointing to the substantial interdependence of the local and the larger community strikingly divergent as their cultural orders may be."[4] No two social systems could be more divergent than the city police department and the homophile subculture, but although there are frequent police patrols in the surrounding community, the only police activity I observed in this lot took place on a holiday. The significance of this I attempt to suggest in the "temporal" section of this paper. Suffice it to say that there seemed to be at least a tacit cooperation between the police and the homosexual community.

Anthropologist Florence Kluckholn notes some advantages of the participant-observer method including, first, that "It affords access to the data that comes from observation in the current situation in which the community members are involved." She adds that, "if the investigator seeks to gain information by the direct interview, the questionnaire, or the life history, he is creating a special situation, not participating in those which arise within the group itself."[5]

Becker and Geer concur, believing that the participant observer operates "in a social context rich in clues and information of all kinds. Because he sees and hears the people he studies in many situations that normally occur for them, he builds an ever growing fund of impressions, many of them at the subliminal level, which give him an extensive basis for the interpretation and analytic use of any particular action. This wealth of information and impressions sensitizes him to subtleties which might pass unnoticed in an interview and forces him to raise continually new and different questions, which he brings to and tries to answer in succeeding observations."[6] This latter point, the continual raising of and attempting to answer questions, was the fundamental procedure organizing the data in my field notes.

Second, Kluckholn believes that "certain types of data are guarded more closely than other types. Direct questions regarding such information may be met with evasions if not with outright misrepresentations." Certainly, this would seem to be the case in the study of strongly stigmatized behavior.

Kluckholn again: "Ready access to gossip is the third respect in which the participant observation serves to increase the range of data" and also act as a "check on the observations." Often I was able to listen in to conversations, especially those of one group concerning their own activities as well as expressions of disapproval which indicated the patterns of socially approved behavior. For example, the behavior of one person suggested that he was engaged in male prostitution. My suspicions were partially confirmed when someone identified him to friends as "that whore."

And Kluckholn's fourth point: "Participant observation may be of aid in gaining insight into the affective experience of the observed." I noticed that there were fewer persons sitting in a car alone at night than during the day. My own feeling about this activity was anxiety since, should I be approached by the police for example, I would be more suspect than during daytime (when I could ostensibly be enjoying the ocean view, etc.). Hence, my own emotions helped to explain the temporal activities of others.

This last point also leads to the question of the role of the participant observer. A. J. Vidich stresses the effects on the data of the social position of the participant observer, in particular what definition the others make of the participant observer.[7] Schwartz found that when the patients in a mental hospital knew that they were being observed by sociologists (outsiders), they often would "perform" for them and, thus, the patients' behavior was different than that seen daily by the hospital staff.[8] He found that certain problems could best be studied by the "passive" observer, yet within the context of a mental hospital there was little chance to both engage in this role and not be defined as someone "different" with consequent effects on behavior. S. M. Miller found that "active" participant observers' roles had the drawbacks of leading to "over-rapport" or cooptation.[9]

This problem—of being defined as an outsider if passive—was solved for me by the situational context. Within this milieu, it was legitimate for me to sit for hours in my car without making any contact, since that activity was engaged in by the majority of the persons present. Also, as part of the "pick-up process," it was permissible, and part of the norm, to stare at others, more so than in other public places. Thus, I was able to sit in my car and observe interaction without becoming defined as unusual or an outsider and hence arousing suspicions and other definitions which might have affected the participants' routine behavior.

This role also afforded me the opportunity to take on-the-spot notes unobtrusively and by the use of vehicle mirrors I was able to have a full view of activities in all directions. A serious drawback to my coverage of the field was that I was never in a position to observe the sexual activity that transpired between the participants. Thus, much was left to inference.

My own inherent bias limits me as an instrument for gathering data. Systems of analysis common to sociology of knowledge, social psychological studies of perception as well as communication theory, maintain that man's perceptions, especially as they relate to other people, are shaped and modified by his social and psychological assumptions and value judgments. With reference to this study, my biases are those of a heterosexually-oriented individual who has never engaged in sexual acts with another male. The problem here is one common to all studies of deviance. Does one need to experience a particular deviancy to satisfactorily comprehend the deviance?

SPATIAL ORGANIZATION

The way man organizes his space affects his life patterns even though such organization is often subliminal. W. H. Whyte's Park Forest studies delineated this clearly.[10] Spatial arrangements and housing designs initiated at the start of the development were carried on even though the original groups had often long departed. The fact that persons were living in certain houses always led to predictable relationships with others. E. T. Hall notes that obscure temporal-spatial organization permits a high degree of patterning.[11] "One can observe that dogs create zones around them. Depending upon his relationship to the dog and the zone he is in, a trespasser can evoke different behavior when he crosses the invisible lines which are meaningful to the dog." And, "One can tell about where the line is by withdrawing and watching when his head goes down. As additional lines are crossed, there will be other signals, a thumping of the tail, a low moan or growl."[12]

Further, space is not only organized but it communicates. By the very fact of living in a certain house, Whyte's people communicated the fact that they belong to X clique. The parking lot and adjacent beach area is similarly organized by the homophile society. The parking lot has several end-to-end loops. While I sat in my vehicle in the area contained by the loop farthest north, no attention would be paid to me by others driving by. Parking or walking within the area covered by the center loop will get some questioning glances, but I have never been approached while in that area. Upon entering the area on the far south, however, I am immediately aware of slowly cruising cars and the watchfulness of other single males. Even if I am engaged in an apparently "legitimate" activity such as exercising my retriever, I still am defined as someone whom it is reasonably safe to approach. Within this loop, however, is yet another gradation of intensity. Remaining in the area away from the beach will not bring as quick an approach as parking on the strip facing the water. Finally, if I were to park nearest the men's room on that strip, almost immediately another car would pull up alongside mine. (The beach also has a clearly defined gay and not gay area.)

TEMPORAL ORGANIZATION

The nuances of time are somewhat more difficult to describe and harder to perceive, as indicated by the fact that it was not until I had reached nearly the end of my observations that I came to a true appreciation of this dimension.

The twenty-four hour cycle is divided between morning to midafternoon (around 4 o'clock), midafternoon to early evening (until 8 o'clock), and late evening (until about 1 A.M.). The first is the time of the "parkers;" early evening, "society;" and late evening, the "beach watch." The picture is one of an overlap, of ebbing and flowing tides, rather than an all-or-none affair. It is a question of one group's numerical dominance over the others. Week-ends and holidays when heterosexual couples and families invade, the homo-sexual activity diminishes. On major holidays, it is nearly extinct.

My notes for one holiday (a three-day weekend) show that during the day the lot and beach were taken over by "the family at the beach" crowds. A passing homophile couple referred to the whole scene as, "How disgustingly straight!" Returning at night-fall, I waited to observe the beach pick-up activities. As I was sitting in my car, a police cruiser came by. This was the first time I had observed any overt police activity. Later, a police helicopter, with flashing red lights and a searchlight bearing down on the beach and the parking lot, made several passes. This seemed to act as a warning to the "beach watch," as several males returned to their cars and left. Because I had already planned to spend the evening observing and since my wife had also accompanied me, we walked down to the water's edge about 10 o'clock. Shortly, a police jeep came up to us, catching us in its headlights. My wife's straight, waist-length red hair apparently signified to the approaching police officer that we were a heterosexual couple. After exchanging some pleasantries about the evening, he said, "We're here to get some of the faggots that have been running around." It is doubtful that they accomplished their mission since all had been well warned of police activity in the area. This suggested to me the possibility of a tacit understanding between the police and the homophile community that the latter would stay away during those times when the general public is in the area and might complain.

SOCIAL PATTERNS

Parkers.   The first group of whom I became aware were those I called the "parkers." At first, I thought that all homosexual activity in the lot fell within this set, but I was later able to differentiate another major category and a third (numerically) minor category. The parkers are so named because they spend much time in or around their vehicles. Like them, their vehicles connote staid respectability. There were no flashy Cadillac convertibles, souped-up engines, or anything about the car to draw attention to the owner. Emblems and bumper stickers also indicated middle-class respectability, for example an American flag cut from the *Reader's Digest,* stickers suggesting that you "Visit Yosemite" or "See Niagara Falls" and an occasional Mid-Western favorite, "America, Love It or Leave It." Appearances, too, indicated parker status; balding heads, paunches—a physical type the radical-left would characterize as "fat Mr. America in his camper." Clothes too—baggy pants, golf sweaters—tended to be similar to the attire of the suburban "family man."

I have devoted much space to the participants' appearance because I felt that appearance was a key to the social organization of the parking lot. Gregory Stone has done work on how appearance sets the stage for interaction by permitting readily apprehended pre-verbal clues as to the nature of prospective interaction.[13] Clothing was most important, he found, in secondary group relations and declined in importance in primary relationships. All the evidence indicated to me that the parking lot was on the extreme end of the secondary continuum and hence the necessity to stress appearances.

There are three principal activities of the "parkers": 1) Vehicle pick up and contact with hustlers; 2) men's room activity; 3) night-time beach activity.

The Men's Room. During the day, I observed the "parkers" often coming and going between the men's rest room. At no time did I observe any women use their side of the facilities. In one typical three hour duration, I observed that thirty-five men entered and left this place. All spent an average of a half hour inside, except for three persons who entered singly within a period of 15 minutes at the start of my observations and had not left when I discontinued. Of these, two were gray haired and impeccably dressed. The third differed in that he seemed older, had a heavy paunch, and scarred face made more noticeable by a flat-top haircut.

Of the others who entered, most were considerably younger, being the "middle aged" groups described above. Several wore gold wedding bands. All would approach the entrance with a readily apparent wariness, walking with a too-studied, hands-in-pockets, casualness belied by darting, tense glances in all directions, which gave an impression of total incongruity. As a tentative check on the accuracy of my observations, I attempted to predict the length of stay of these persons as contrasted with an occasional other who may in fact have only wished to use the toilet. The latter would, with no hesitation, rapidly park his car and stride, looking in no particular direction or with head down, to the rest room. The first group I predicted would remain inside at least forty-five minutes, while the latter would exit in less than ten. I was seldom in error.

Assuming that this facility was being used as a place to give and obtain fellatio, it is easy to guess, by taking the role of the participant, why that particular room came to be selected. There are no windows and only one entrance. By standing at this entrance, one could view the beach and parking lot and readily notice the approach of law enforcement officials or any "outsiders." Continually, at least one and sometimes two persons were loitering in the area, usually smoking or walking over to the drinking fountain. Yet I never observed any conversation, and in fact they seemed to avoid one another's gaze.

My supposition (guided by Humphreys' findings) is that these were guards who served to warn those within the men's room of impending outside dangers. I also speculate that the older inhabitants were playing the passive recipient roles while the younger were the insertees. This again was based on Humphreys' study coupled with the observation that the older males remained in the facility for such a lengthy time.

The Beach Watch.   The men's room is locked at around 6 P.M. The beach at night is a scene of blackness with three or four areas faintly illuminated by pale yellowish lights surrounding the rest rooms and two small lights attached to a lifeguard stand. This stand is a large wooden frame building with a deck. The restroom and stand act as poles attracting pick up activity.

As you enter the singular half light of night near these areas, the shadows may become briefly illuminated by a flash of a lighter, then the dark punctuated by the red glow of a cigarette. The interaction that follows is almost ritualized: asking for a light or cigarette; asking for the time; commenting on the weather; exchanging general areas of residence (one always seems to live "nearby"); making a proposition to go for a "drink" or go straight to an apartment (or possibly to perform the act on the spot).

Hustlers.   I only observed one individual I could positively identify as a male prostitute. This person was an effeminate appearing young male who spent the afternoons walking a small dog around the lot. Usually he stayed on the beach strip or center strip of the parking lot, thus showing his awareness of the spatial organization. Some days he would not seem to engage in any activities, while on other days I would observe that he was picked up, and a half hour later he returned to be picked up again. During the period of my observations he never missed a day at the lot. Also of interest was the fact that his clientele would not engage in the usual "looking preliminaries" but would drive up, open the door with the engine running, and let him in. Later, I heard him identified as "that whore" by those I called "society."

A second individual, also a member of an ethnic group, was the exact opposite in psychological traits. He drove a powerful "souped up" automobile and, in comportment and gestures, seemed to exude masculine aggression. He also engaged in the same pick up patterns described above. I never saw both at the lot at the same time.

I didn't understand these patterns of behavior and the differing groups that participated until much later, when I had spent considerable time observing from a variety of socially different parking spaces and observation points. Yet, some aspects of parking lot behavior with respect to the parkers were still puzzling even at the end of the research. Day after day I would see persons spend hours milling around in their cars, play the initial encounter games in their early stages and yet not engage in any pick ups. Many times my notes show persons parked here, then cruising, then parked elsewhere, following someone, turning away and parking again. Were they choosey? Often, to quote William James (in another context), the lot was a "blooming, buzzing, confusion." In a later reading, Hoffman's *The Gay World* suggested a possible explanation in that he noted the same milling about in homophile bars and defined the activity as a male unwillingness to be the first to make an approach and risk rejection.[14]

SOCIETY

"Society" does not play as large a role in the parking lot scene, I suspect, because their activities center around bar life and private parties. They differ from the "parkers" in the following ways:

1. Age. They are younger, generally college age;

2. Ethnicity. I observed no blacks or Chicanos in this group (for a possible reason, see Helmer's article on the middle class homosexuals)[15]

3. High status symbols are displayed. Dress was either fashionable mod style or collegiate casual with tight jeans and sandals. They were well groomed, tanned and athletic; and their automobiles tended to be large new cars (often convertibles) or of expensive foreign make.

4. Intensive social intercourse involving leaders, who took the lead in making introductions; gossip, such as "Yeah, I like him as a person, too"; exchanges of news and addresses of parties organized for the evening. Although they were male, there was a Gestalt of femininity different than that I have observed in heterosexual gatherings of males.

5. Contempt for the activities of the "parkers," expressed in various ways: (a) laughing and pointing toward the rest room (which they never enter); (b) looking around at the "parkers" in their cars with disdain and making comments such as "It's sure 'tight' here tonight"; and (c) standing with a portable radio playing loudly; when one of the "parkers" is attracted and walks by, all suddenly stop talking and stare at him; when he approaches, they turn away and ignore him; when he leaves (somewhat flustered), they break out in loud laughter.

6. Overt femininity is firmly put down and "swish" behavior may be met with sarcasm, such as, "You're acting like a silly girl."

SOME SPECULATIONS

David Sonenschein, in a two-year study, ordered a variety of relationships on the basis of two variables, degree of sexual involvement and intended duration.[16] He noted that homosexual society contains a complexity of interpersonal relationships, each with its own expectations of conduct and reciprocity. Settings within the subculture help guide this type of behavior by specifying in advance the behaviors toward others expected in the particular setting. The parking lot is an example of such a setting. Expectations are that the encounter will be both anonymous and brief. The one exception is those encounters among the individuals described as "society." Still, "society" members do not seem to be appreciably different from the older "parkers." For example, although they are college students, they showed little concern, in their conversations, with the intellectual lifestyles or the political questions that many of their cohorts are dealing with. Whereas rejection of the establishment's emphasis on materialism is becoming more widespread in the larger student culture, the people I observed seemed eager to display such symbols as expensive clothes and new cars. The only major difference I felt between them and the "parkers" was one of youth and perhaps youth's contempt for the more settled lifestyle of their elders. On campus, I would have categorized most of "society" as "fraternity Freddies." Similarly, I would have had little trouble visualizing many of the "parkers" turning up year after year to root for their old school football team, with fraternity pins in their lapels and ready comments on the "hippies" in the stands. In short, it is not hard to conceive of the conventional member of "society" of today as the staid suburban "parker" of tomorrow.

Leznoff and Westley found a distinction between secret and overt groups which corresponded to the different modes of evading social controls which the homophiles had developed.[17] When upwardly mobile and growing older, the once overt homosexual stopped participating in an open subculture and began to frequent "street corners and lavatories." Continued participation in the overt subcultures would have threatened the careers of these rising young business executives and professional people. Yet, the desire for homosexual experiences continues to "lead to an interaction on sexual as opposed to a social basis."

My feeling is that if I were to return to the parking lot five years from now, one of my "society" faces would be endlessly cruising the lot in a Buick with an "America: Love It or Leave It" sticker on the bumper.

FIELD NOTES

10:00 A.M. to 3:00 P.M., January 16, 1970, center of parking lot.

10:00 A.M.

As I have arrived there are only three single males sitting in their cars. (Too early, or is the lot no longer a rendezvous?) One is reading a paper and drinking coffee. Another is sitting, apparently doing nothing, and a third is getting out and is standing; looks at me as I drive by. I am parked now behind some palm trees at some distance from where they are. Subjectively, I feel ill at ease. (Because of my ambivalent position as a spy? or is it *anomie*—what do I do if I am approached?) No one is around this area and I'm too far away to observe closely the activities of the people at the other end. I move to first turn facing the beach. A man in his forties pulls in beside me, sits with door open and music playing over radio. He is glancing at me occasionally, but doesn't make any further movement my way. Male age 30-plus drives by in a red VW, circles and comes by again. Exchanges glances with my neighbor. I can observe him by using my rear view mirror, while sitting sideways and can observe my neighbor also. He has apparently lost interest in me and is craning around to look at the red VW as it goes past a third time. Red VW goes down to far end of lot and parks. Blue Lincoln-Mercury with male driver about 40 drives slowly by me; neighbor checks him out in same manner. L-M parks down at far end with red VW.

11:00 A.M.

More cars arriving. Five are driving around. Neighbor checks each one out as they drive slowly past. Some park down at far end. Red VW is driving around again. (Going to pick up my neighbor or is he interested in me?) Can see some people standing and walking at far end, but am still too far away to see what is going on there. (If I get closer will they suspect me as an under-cover cop of some kind? Rationalization?) Male in brown and white Rambler drives by and stops at far end, comes back, drives slowly by again, makes a circle again, comes back, stops by me, on opposite side. Sits awhile, glancing at me but not staring. Gets out and slowly walks over in front of my car, looks at me, looks away, walks toward my neighbor, then turns and looks at me again. I think he sees me writing, he turns around and gets into his car and (faster this time) drives off and out exit. (Will have to be more careful about note taking.) Neighbor pulls away also. Someone is walking down from far end toward me. He has a tense expression as he walks past the line of cars "nosed in" as if he feels everyone is watching him.

Still coming toward me, hands in pockets. Walks by me, stands and lights a cigarette. Inhales then turns and walks back to his car. My other neighbor has returned meanwhile and sits and stares at the pedestrian but makes no move to approach him. Brown pickup drives by, slows by my neighbor. Neighbor cranes around and looks at brown pickup truck. Truck driven by male, balding but with muscular arms, the left one resting out the window has a tattoo of some sort (anchor?). Neighbor cranes around and looks directly at truck. Both drive around circle (no one seems to go beyond this first turn), again, then truck heads out exit with neighbor close behind. (Next time must get ready to follow if same thing occurs and see where they go.)

12:00 P.M.

Lots of cars in the area now—some younger drivers, perhaps high school kids. Roaring of engines as all (count eight) drive by (still around first circle) around the parking lot. Now ten cars are following each other around. One car seems to have gotten between two others. The red Mustang behind it speeds up, cuts in, and re-establishes following pattern. More cars are coming in and parking—lunch break. Some are getting out and walking around. Looks like someone is lighting someone else's cigarette on far end. (Will locate closer down there next time.) *No women. No more than one male per car.* Lots of out-of-state license plates! (How do they know about this place?) Have seen three more following patterns repeated. Some people are sitting on ledge eating their lunch. Both business suits and blue collar dress. One black, in "souped up" VW, stops, gets out, walks around, gets in car, drives around, gets out again. Only ethnic group member I can see.

1:00 P.M.

Some cars are leaving now, and the milling about seems to be settling down. It was like a main drag on a small one-street town except the cars are occupied by males only. One car had three men in it, but the rest were alone. The three looked younger than the rest. They are leaving now. Out-of-state license plates included Oregon, Washington, Illinois, New York. (Are they here attending a convention? Convention center is nearby.) All seem to be clean-cut older types—my beard is definitely conspicuous here. Another neighbor is pulling away now and leaves through the far exit. He hasn't left his car and yet has been sitting here for nearly two hours.

10:00 A.M. to 3:00 P.M., January 20, 1970.

Spot-check of other parking lots on my way to the research area turned up no noticeable homosexual activity.

10:20 A.M.

As I drive into the lot, man in a red Corvair grins at me. He was on his way out the exit but instead backs up, turns around, and follows me. I park and he drives slowly past, circles again and then leaves. Blue VW van and white VW are following each other around lot, they circle twice more and leave.

My location is on the second strip in the first loop (south). My side mirror is focused on the beach strip and I am observing two youthful males on bicycles talking. A man, 30-plus, drives up and pulls in immediately in front of them with a large camper. Gets out. Two with bicycles walk away but continue conversation further south on same strip. Camper owner returns to cab and drives down to south end of lot. There seem to be several persons standing around the rest room at the far end of lot. They are loitering, but I don't observe any verbal interaction between them. Only other male is 40-plus, with flat-top haircut, driving a new Toronado; he cruises slowly by camper owner. Camper owner is standing and smoking and returns glance. Toronado circles again. Parks by me and sits. Camper is once more slowly cruising around. Stares at me, stares at Toronado who gets out of his car and stands. Camper parks near south end (and rest room). (A suggestion for future research would be to note license plates and thus have more info as to age, socioeconomic status, occupation, residential areas, ethnicity of persons who spend time here.) Janitor service parked near men's room. See several people walk away. (Note: later I moved so I could observe entrance of rest room.) On the subjective level, I feel more confident and less ill-at-ease than previous observation. Black in green VW wearing cowboy hat is walking in front of me. He is picked up. Only a few words were passed. Male, bald with a heavy paunch, but prosperous looking, opens door and cowboy gets in. They drive away. I'm puzzled, because the encounter didn't seem prearranged, that is the cowboy didn't seem to be aware of the Olds until the door opened, and furthermore he didn't seem to know the driver. Camper driver is now visible, talking with Toronado. (Jack Spratt and "wife": Toronado is a big, heavy, bull-shouldered man, while camper is very small and slight of frame.) They glance around and get into the camper. Janitors have left. Several persons are walking from car in direction of rest room. Of these, one is old and fat, another is the garbage pail scavenger I saw earlier. A city garbage truck is in the area. No visible notice is taken of the lot inhabitants by operators of truck.

11:00 A.M.

Not much activity. The two have left the camper, and Toronado has driven away. Camper leaves. Not together. (Business consummated?) The two with bicycles are still sitting talking near the south end. South end seems to be the major center of activity. Green MG drives in fast. Blue Jag pulls out and follows. Both single males. Obviously prearranged. Black with cowboy hat is back! (Male prostitution?) Talking to two with bicycle. Cowboy hat picked up again by elderly man in lime gold Buick. Drives up, opens door—cowboy climbs in and they drive away.

11:30 A.M.

Two cars driving around. Bicycle owners still talking. (Waiting for someone or just socializing?) Cowboy pickup is back (gone 30 minutes each time). Interesting check on space supposition: There were two or three persons parked in the middle loop eating their lunch. None of them took any notice as I drove by. But as soon as I entered south loop, all craned their necks and looked at me. I park again on the beach strip, closer to the rest room. I am being cruised. Young man walks past with his hands in his pockets. He has a bent forward, pelvis-out posture. He directs a sharp look at me as he walks past. Continues on past me and turns and looks back. I pretend not to notice. He turns and walks over to the rest room.

12:00 noon. Rain, stops in 10 minutes.

The camper is cruising around. The only major activity seems to be at the rest room. A fat man in blue shirt parks and walks into rest room, the second time today for him. Looking for someone special? The black minus his cowboy hat walks by. He has a singular gait: holds body rigid, hands in his pockets, and walks with a quick movement of the legs with short steps. Gets into VW and roars off—radio playing loudly. A young man (Chicano) somewhat more effeminate than the others, is feeding a little dog. The dog walks away and he calls after it in a feminine voice. He runs after it, his wooden clogs falling off, grabs the dog, and spanks it.

Camper again!

Lots of men milling around in their cars, parking in different spots and then moving away again.

New pink Cadillac pulls up by young man with the dog. The Chicano walks over and apparently exchanges a few words. "Yeah it's all right," is all I can get. He gets into the Cad. They sit, apparently talking—then drive off. Gold-green Cougar with "Love It or Leave It" bumper sticker arrives. (Note: next time take an inventory of bumper stickers and other identity symbols.) Driver is noticeably different from others. Very effeminate in manner and gestures; has bleached "styled" hair. Goes into rest room. Pink Lincoln-Mercury pulls up beside me. The driver is fairly young; he looks at me, then looks away with a smile. He sits drumming his fingers on the dash. He has just driven around the lot several times. A hip-appearing man and another standing talking: "He should be back in a little while, he just went to the liquor store." Other nods. "You going back in there?" "Yeah."

Second man walks back to rest room. The camper again! I notice someone is always loitering around the rest room area. (Why? Will watch and see if can observe a pick up.) Couple, with kids, park down at second loop. Don't seem aware of, or at least are not interested in, lot activity.

1:00 P.M.

Spot check—no activity at other lots or rest rooms.

1:35 P.M.

I am stationed where I can observe the rest room entrance, as well as part (the south loop) of the parking lot. I am on a street, outside the lot. An old grey haired man, well dressed, is strolling in a leisurely way around the rest room. He enters, then comes back out, looks at me, takes a drink of water, and goes back in. Another hip man and two very hip girls (girls are bra-less) are loitering around the rest room. I believe they came up from the beach. (Do they have any connection with homophiles?) A man in an Australian racing suit (very brief), well-tanned, comes out of rest room (stripped for action). Hip group were apparently only resting in the shade. Now they have crossed the street and left the area. A man in a pink shirt and purple tie has been loitering around the rest room. Another man, dressed in a charcoal suit, goes into the rest room and then almost immediately comes back outside. He loiters and smokes in much the same manner as Purple Tie.

2:00 P.M. Same location.

Haven't seen the older man come back out of rest room yet. Purple Tie has disappeared inside. Charcoal Suit is walking around over by me—crosses street to liquor store. He returns and resumes loitering. Purple Tie comes back out, goes inside, immediately comes out—leaning against wall smoking, walks over to other side pacing back and forth slowly. Suit is inside. Two men with beards(!) exit from rest room. One walks away, second loitering outside. No conversation with Purple Tie who is also still loitering. Purple Tie enters the rest room again. Camper enters lot again. He has now been here a total of six hours! Chief lifeguard car parks near me. Leaves.

Interesting mixture in rest room: "Heads" (recognizable by long hair and boots, according to Tom Wolfe's *Electric Kool Aid Acid Test*), and an "America: Love It or Leave It" advocate, judging by his bumper strip. Still no exit by America or by elderly man, both of whom have been inside for about an hour and a half.

3:00 to 7:00 P.M., January 30, 1970.

I am parked in lot near rest room hoping to note which persons come from restaurant and which from apartment house area. The restaurant is closed at this time. I will note who drives in and who walks in for a period of 30 minutes. My assumption is that pedestrians are from the apartment area nearby, while those in cars could be from anywhere. I observe a male acting in the manner of some type of cop. He is dressed in a business suit and tie, and has a crew cut. He is walking in the two-loop area, looking into empty cars as well as glancing at persons in the area. The lot is sparsely populated. Some straight couples are parked in the second loop. An old Ford pulls up and an elderly, shabbily dressed man gets out. A man in his fifties, who has been standing nearby, gets in. He is dressed nattily in a sport coat with a sporty hat.

3:30 to 4:00 P.M.

[A tally of persons who walked in and drove in. Walk-ins: 3 single men, college-aged; 2 bicyclists, of college or even high school age; 1 single man, college-aged; 1 single man between 20 and 30; 1 man under 20. Drive-ins: 5, all over 40, in fact 3 appeared to be in their 50's.]

6:00 P.M.

It is immediately noticeable that there is a different group from the daytime. Of the persons I have been observing before, the majority were well over thirty, and, if they were younger, their dress and manner suggested working class youth. The dominant group at this time are similar in dress and manner to the men I see daily on college campuses. If older, they suggest, superficially at least, white-collar and young professional status. They are generally well groomed, and a few have surfer-type bleached hair but it's not styled. There are only three persons sitting in their cars, and no one is around the rest room. The restaurant seems to be serving very straight, middle class, heterosexual couples. All the gay life there is centered around the phone booth or in the liquor store. (The liquor store is popular with the general public as well.) To make the contrast clearer, the persons I have been observing during the day tended to have ex-football player frames and short haircuts. Their clothes, if casual, were sloppy, and if they were formal they were also baggy. The crowd I am now observing gives the (admittedly fleeting) impression of upper-middle-class status. The daytime crowd generally is vaguely middle-class respectable, or else working-class (blue-collar) sloppy.

7:00 P.M.

The parking lot is practically empty. One or two persons are parked, and there are no college-aged pedestrians.

12:00 P.M. to 5:00 P.M. and 6:40 P.M. to 11:00 P.M., February 6, 1970.

I am on the major thoroughfare, facing the restaurant. No activity there; the restaurant is closed during the day. I am now parked by the turn of the first loop. I was cruised by a black VW. I notice the black man with the cowboy hat walking away and getting into his VW. He leaves. A group of younger men I had observed the other night are standing on the beach strip, talking and joking. There are a large number of parked cars occupied by single males, and about fifteen cars are milling around. A man and a woman on bicycles ride into the loop area. I can see them looking around at all the males in the area. (How can you miss?) The man and woman look at each other and laugh. The man makes caricatured feminine gestures and then guiltily looks around. The group talking on the beach strip is checking out each car as it goes past. They have become the locus of interest of five cruising cars. Much laughter (joking about the cars?). I am sitting nearby. I overhear conversation about a party in Westwood in drag. They turn to look at cruisers and then turn back to one another and laugh. All are casually dressed in London Fog type jackets and jeans. One is a black, nattily dressed in pants and sport coat. Picture an endless number of cars of all types driving slowly around, their drivers craning their necks at each other, some stopping, some starting, but no observable conversation between them, contrasted with the group described above laughing and talking. Some of the cars are very sedate, but others are souped up—with loud pipes, and their radios blaring in teenage courting style, they are honking at those on the strip. There is endless, apparently random, movement of vehicles. Moving your car into the stream, you become caught up in a world of questioning stares and counter looks. Even going out the exit, there are exchanges of glances between those leaving and those coming in, and the glance always includes a smirk or broad smile.

Kept a tally of bumper insignia observed: 13 patriotic, 13 state and city college, 3 Naval shipyard, 4 miscellaneous, several AAA, 1 "support your local police." Majority of cars have no bumper stickers, however. Chicano terrier owner (minus his dog) has been picked up by a black Mercedes (new). The Mercedes stopped, there was some hesitation on the dog owner's part as if he didn't know the driver, and then he entered and the car sped away.

1:45 P.M.

I parked where I could observe clearly the sole entrance to the rest room as well as liquor store activity. Three men were standing outside on the men's side. I made a tally of persons entering the men's rest room and remaining for more than thirty minutes between 1:45 and 4:45 P.M. Thirty-four men entered. Of these, seven returned once after having totally left the premises. Two others returned more than twice in the three-hour period. No women were observed entering their side of the rest room.

During the observation period, there were, except for a few minutes at most, at least two persons always loitering in front of the rest room. (Guards?) Often the interaction proceeded as follows: a man would enter and a second man would exit, look around and then go back inside. Their dress and appearance were vaguely middle class or working-man style: suits, casual slacks and sports shirts, slacks and sweat shirt, etc. Generally the clientele are older. Three older men entered as I started observing and have not left as I am leaving. One was grey haired, with the florid complexion that you associate with the stereotype of an alcoholic; he was expensively dressed. Another was fat and old and wearing tight pants, and the third was nondescript except for his age. (Do the elderly perform fellatio for younger persons?)

In summary, an overall characterization of men recorded as entering the rest room is that they are equally divided between middle and old age with a minority of under-thirty persons (not more than four). Length of stay could be positively correlated with age, and may indicate the amount of waiting necessary to engage in a sexual encounter. Have also noticed that guard positions seemed to be exchanged among younger members. These persons will stand or walk in such a manner that they can observe both sides of the rest room.

6:40 P.M.

I am parked on the lot near the beach. I note that the Chicano dog owner has been picked up again. His clientele has larger cars and they are often expensive foreign cars. Today he is getting into a Jaguar. The parking lot is almost empty. (Too early?) The parking lot is used by heterosexuals returning from work to park their cars, but they generally avoid the first loop area and quickly park and walk away in contrast to the homophile community's studied casualness.

A possible reason for the scarcity of male persons sitting alone in a parked car at night ("parkers"): it is too suggestive—a male sitting alone is too liable to fall under police suspicion. At least this is my thinking, and I find myself working on possible explanations to a questioning cop. I also feel I am conspicuous to passing heterosexual couples. The lot is too well-lighted for inconspicuous sitting.

8:00 P.M.

I have seen two separate, seemingly prearranged, rendezvous. Activity seems to have shifted almost totally to a younger crowd—what I think of as the "society" crowd. Dress, which is "surfer" jeans and bare feet, is noticeable. Beards are noticeable for the first time. Activities center around couples and combinations built on couples. Some couples have one obviously feminine member, but this doesn't seem to hold true for all couples. Some affect surfer dress but others wear sport coat and tie or mod styles (bell bottom trousers, etc.). The more masculine members of couples are dressed in suit and tie.

9:00 P.M.

Judging on the basis of spatial grouping, I can observe cliques. There are two at the present time, all "society" types. One clique has four members and one has about six. The larger is generally more youthful in appearance, their dress being jeans, bare feet, and fairly long hair, while the second clique has no one in bare feet; they are wearing bell bottoms and mod colors or else what is formal dress for the other clique: sport coat and tie or sweater and tie. Both cliques are collegiate in appearance.

10:00 P.M.

All Society has left and the parking lot is relatively deserted. When men arrive they park and sit a minute, and then walk onto the beach. (Pick up activity on the beach? Fellatio there?) I am standing on the beach in the shadow of the lifeguard stand. Visibility is nil except for two faint lights. A male is approaching who has been standing in the shadows. He lights a cigarette and I can briefly see his face. I remain where I am. The man approaches; he continues to stand near me and smokes. I move away. I am on the opposite side of the lifeguard station, and it is extremely cold. A second man is walking up from the water. He doesn't notice me and walks to the other side of station. Now talking to the other man.

"Have a light?"

"Yeah, here you go."

"Chilly, tonight."

"Sure is, I've been standing here for about an hour and the wind is going right through my coat." [Pause.]

"Live around here?"

"Yeah, over behind X restaurant. You?"

"No, I'm out of town. Is X bar any good night life?"

"Yes, pretty [can't hear] over on X street. Think I'll get a drink," pause, "and warm up." Pause. "You?"

"Sounds good." (Note: this conversation is not verbatim. It was too dark, and it would have been too obvious to take notes.)

This is the only pick up I heard although I stayed until midnight. Several men were standing around but did not chance upon any further interaction. Estimate five other persons were on the beach as I left. No police activity. All were standing within a certain section of the beach and you probably could draw parallel lines from the lot and rest room to the ocean's edge and have the general outlines of the homophile "hunting" territory.

8:30 A.M. – 12:00 Noon, February 19, 1970.

8:30 A.M.

A police helicopter with flashing red lights has begun patrolling the beach with a high-powered spotlight. Conversation by "society" not interrupted.

"Where's that yellow [car]?"

"Over there. . . ."

"No, not that guy."

"How about E–– and E––, will they be here tonight?"

"They're going to [city in Orange county]."

"Those bitches—why can't they be here tonight? That guy in the Mercedes is got a party in [town]."

"It's sure tight here tonight" (gestures toward some non-Society sitting in cars).

"Meet me here at 10 o'clock." Then he calls out as one is walking away, "and we'll all go out there, to his place."

The first person speaking is an organizer. I saw him two weeks ago. His typical activity will be to talk with a group and then run over to some car that pulls up or go over to someone obviously unacquainted and link arms and bring him over to the group. Introduces other persons to one another. Party wheel. Also spends considerable time walking hurriedly between lot and phone booth at liquor store. Dressed tonight in bare feet and jeans and shirt with tail hanging out. He appears to be young, and I could easily mistake him for a high school student. Although he has quick flighty movements, there is nothing overtly feminine about him. His fellows are dressed in latest fashion, that is, Prince Edward suits, bell bottom trousers, colored shirts and matching ties. Bathroom crowd seems to be almost entirely on the beach and the lot is dominated in numbers by "society." After passing of police plane, several have come off the beach and have left. Police activity doesn't seem to have concerned "society." No apparent traffic between restaurant and beach at this time. Also, there are a considerable number of heterosexual couples in the area. (It is a holiday weekend.)

10:00 A.M.

Several males together in cars have come and gone. Lot is quiet now, almost deserted.

10:30 A.M.

A few parkers in their cars, including some who have come off the beach earlier. Some are walking along the beach strip. Movements when walking are unnaturally quick, betraying tension, I believe—jerking of head around, etc.—even though the attempt is to portray casualness. (Business as usual, nothing much is happening.) A parade of five to six cars is racing around the area several times; now all have parked. Nothing is happening in the way of interaction.

All continue to sit. Some shift positions. Interesting note: previously heard Society refer to others as that guy in yellow Mustang, that guy in Mercedes, no names.

12:00 P.M.

Lot is empty, beach seems empty, no activity at restaurant. I conclude that it is not connected with the parking lot social scene.

5:00 P.M., February 22, 1970, Sunday afternoon. My wife is with me.

Previous spot checks of lot area indicated little homophile parking or rest room activity during Saturday daytime. "Society" is present, however. Radio playing loud. Snatches of conversation ("What's the address? Who's going to be there?") indicate that arrangements are being made for the evening activities elsewhere. Person I had before tentatively identified as a social leader or organizer briefly embraces a friend. The friend turns away, embarrassed. One interesting observation of "society": they seem to accept the 1950's status system. For example, cohort members on university campuses tend to wear blue jeans and similar attire, and their cars are old beat-up VW vans or sports cars; but the symbols manipulated by this group involve being well dressed, always with a tie (attire for the majority), expensive buckle boots, and new cars, the larger the better, such as Cadillac convertibles. Even when styles are beach casual, they differ from the college undergraduate majority in being expensive.

5:50 P.M.

Police helicopter.

6:00 P.M.

Rest rooms locked up.
Police car! First time. Activity doesn't disturb "society." I can hear snatches of conversation of two sitting in a car:
"Yeah, he is *really* a great guy, he's got a good attitude toward the gay life."
"I really like T-- as a person."
The man I suspect of being a homosexual prostitute comes by and talks briefly with these two. He leaves and shortly they leave.

7:00 P.M.

Few cars about. Dull night.

8:00 P.M.

Wife and I are sitting on the beach facing water. See a vehicle's lights coming rapidly toward us on the beach. Sees us. Stops. Two cops; one stays in the car and the second approaches.

"How are you doing?" Pleasantries exchanged concerning the night. "You haven't been bothered, have you?"

"What?"

"We're down here to catch some faggots that have been around."

We left at 9 P.M.

3:00 – 4:30 P.M., February 24, 1970.

I am on the second runway, first loop. Beach patrol is driving on the sand. Interesting interaction between it and a man who had been cruising on beach. While the man had been looking around in typical cruiser manner as the jeep passed, he suddenly became interested in the sand and continued looking down until jeep had gone well past. Then he resumed his cruising posture.

Typical mode of interaction has occurred between "society" and "parker." "Parker" drove up to where "society" is sitting. "Parker" looked once at "society" to see if he got any encouragement. "Society," after a measuring glance, looked straight ahead, apparently taking no notice. If he decides to persist, a parker gets out of his car and stands near "society," walks past, and turns around and looks back. "Society" will continue to look in other direction. "Parker" will keep his cool and return to his car and leave.

10:00 P.M. (Ex post facto notes)

After about an hour's wait, a man came toward me. I believe I had seen him sitting in the lot as I went down. In the darkness, he lit up a cigarette. He gave the appearance of being middle aged with a fairly athletic figure. After standing near me and finding that I didn't move away, he asked: "Say, do you know the time?"

"No, I don't."

"Cold tonight." I nod noncommitally. "Cold breeze, coming off the water." I nod again. Pause. "Well, I'm going to get a cup of coffee." Pause; he loses interest and walks away.

Apparently, my presence on this beach, in the dark, labeled me as someone desiring to be picked up. When I failed to respond or to keep the conversational gambit alive, the man lost interest. Later, two individuals who had been sitting on the lifeguard stand deck jumped apart as I approached. Both males. (Fellatio?) My approach didn't more than momentarily disturb them; I looked back and could vaguely make out that they were huddled together again.

Other snatches of mumbled conversation I have heard indicate that a formalized interactional code exists involving asking for a light and a determination of where the "action" will take place.

NOTES

[1] Anselm Strauss, *Image of the American City* (Glencoe, Ill.: The Free Press, 1961).
[2] Charles H. Cooley, *Social Organization* (New York: Shocken Books, 1962), p. 7.
[3] Claud Humphreys, "Impersonal Sex in Public Places," *Transaction*, VII (Jan. 1970).
[4] J. D. Lohman, "The Participant Observer in Community Studies," *American Sociological Review*, II (Dec. 1937), pp. 891-898.
[5] Florence R. Kluckhohn, "The Participant Observer Technique in Small Communities," *American Journal of Sociology*, XLV (Nov. 1940), pp. 331-343.
[6] Blanche Geer and Howard S. Becker, "Participant Observation: The Analysis of Qualitative Field Data," in Richard N. Adams and Jack J. Preiss (eds.) *Human Organization Research*, (Homewood, Ill.: Dorsey Press, 1960), p. 118.
[7] Arthur Vidich, "Participant Observation and the Collection and Interpretation of Data," *American Journal of Sociology*, LX (Jan. 1955), pp. 354-360.
[8] Morris S. Schwartz, "Problems in Participant Observation," *American Journal of Sociology*, LX (Jan. 1955), pp. 343-353.
[9] S. M. Miller, "The Participant Observer and 'Over-Rapport'," *American Sociological Review*, XVII (Feb. 1952), pp. 97-99.
[10] W. H. Whyte, *Organization Man* (New York: Simon & Schuster, 1956).
[11] Edward T. Hall, *The Hidden Dimension* (Garden City, N.Y.: Doubleday Co., 1969), p. 73.
[12] *Ibid.*, pp. 146-147.
[13] Gregory P. Stone, "Appearance and the Self," in Rose (ed.) *Human Behavior and Social Processes* (Boston: Houghton Mifflin, 1962).
[14] Martin Hoffman, *The Gay World; Male Homosexuality and the Social Creation of Evil* (New York: Basic Books, 1968).
[15] William J. Helmer, "New York Middle Class Homosexuals," *Harper's*, CCXXVI (1963), pp. 85-92.
[16] David Sonenschein, "The Ethnography of Male Homosexual Relationships," *Journal of Sex Research*, Vol. 4, No. 2 (1968).
[17] Maurice Leznoff and William Westley, "The Homosexual Community," *Social Problems*, Vol. 3, No. 4, 1956, pp. 257-263.

The Pulp Voyeur: A Peek at Pornography in Public Places

William C. McKinstry

While private forms of sexual deviance may provide certain kinds of satisfactions, other forms of satisfaction can only be negotiated in public. When pursuing sexually deviant activities in public, we quite naturally seek to maximize our privacy in order to minimize the possibility of detection and public denunciation.

An excellent but little researched example of a public setting for deviant behavior is the pornographic book shop. [The homosexual drive-in lot was another.] "Pornographic" is not used here in a legal sense, nor is it intended as a value judgment, but rather as a term that would still be used by the majority of the public to label the material available for public consumption in "adult book shops."

The store where adult or girlie books and magazines can be found has been in existence for years. Many newsstands, book shops, liquor stores, and even drugstores, have offered, and still offer, such merchandise to their patrons. Over the years, however, this material has tended to be rather mild by international standards, and real pornography was either kept on a high shelf at the back of the store (closely watched over by the clerk), or sale of it was left to the clandestine dealers on the street.

Recent court rulings have changed this situation drastically. In photography, all but the culminating sex acts themselves have now been brought into an area that can be legally defined as art or culture. In California, as of this writing, two nudes of the same or the opposite sex, can be photographed fondling each other on a bed, and as long as the genitals are not directly involved magazines or books containing these photographs may be legally sold to adults. Whether this trend will continue or whether it will be reversed is a matter of conjecture. One thing is obvious however, and that is that American free-enterprise has stepped in to fill this newly opened economic niche.

Stores specializing in pornographic material generally refer to themselves as adult stores or adult book stores. Because of their specialized nature they provide an ideal setting in which to study one of the best examples of borderline deviants—the pulp voyeur. Here, otherwise upstanding members of the community must acknowledge their sexual deviance to a limited sector of the community in order to gain their voyeuristic satisfactions. What makes it easier, of course, is that other members of the community are doing the same.

The purpose of this study, then, was to seriously consider the public world of the pulp voyeur and the ways in which he negotiated his public display of deviance. In addition to shedding light on a little known portion of this world, it is hoped that the results of this study can be to some extent generalized to other forms of essentially private behavior which, for various reasons, must be partially negotiated in public. [For example, many of the techniques used by bookstore customers to neutralize their deviant activity are invoked by those frequenting the front region of the fly-in whore house described in the next reading.]

METHODOLOGY

The study was carried out in two stores in adjacent cities of approximately one hundred thousand people each. Both stores were of the most avant-garde type, that is, almost one hundred percent of their merchandise dealt directly with sex. There were other stores that sold pornographic material in these cities, but none that matched the two study stores in either the amount of merchandise carried or in the degree to which they stretched the limits of the law.

Both stores were owned by the same man. This feature of the study was not built in. It simply happened that the most avant-garde stores in the area were owned by the same enterprising individual. The reason for studying two stores instead of one was not to detect the difference the style of store makes in the customer's behavior, but rather to detect any differences in type of customer that might result from the store's geographical setting. The differences in the two stores and their neighborhood are discussed in the next section.

The principal method used in this study was participant observation, though much was learned from long discussions with two of the clerks, John and Gil, who were much more than simply sources of information. Without their full cooperation the role of participant observer would have been difficult or impossible to carry off. By allowing me to pose as a clerk, or at least to reside in the counter area, they enabled me to observe the floor area without having to adhere to a key background expectancy of customers of the store—keeping your eyes off the other customers. Had I been obliged to conduct my observations from the sales floor, it would have substantially limited my ability to conduct the study.

In addition to being free to observe the whole store from the counter area, my role as pseudo clerk allowed me to watch in detail the interaction between the clerk and customer. It seems to have been more-or-less accepted by the customers that I was entitled to the same confidence shown the clerks.

THE STORES

As previously mentioned, the main difference in the stores is their location. Store A, which is slightly larger than Store B (approximately 20 by 35 feet), is located on one of its city's main boulevards. The block on which the store is located is unlike any other block in the city. While the city as a whole could be considered the archetype of a modern suburban community, this particular block has a distinctly big-city flavor about it. Though it is something of an exaggeration, one could almost say that the block has a Bowery atmosphere. On the same block are located a bar, a pawn shop, a liquor store, the Greyhound bus depot, and a small movie theatre showing nothing but triple-X-rated movies.

Store B, which is also on one of the city's main boulevards, is in a very different type of neighborhood. On the same block are located a jewelry store, a wig shop, and a finance company. In addition, an elementary school and a junior high school are located a short distance away. The clerk in Store B informed me that several local businessmen had come into the store since its opening six months ago and told him that his establishment was not appreciated in the neighborhood.

The exteriors are fairly innocuous. The stores are almost entirely glass in the front, and in both cases the glass has been painted an opaque forest green. A large plastic sign above Store A proclaims "Market St. News, Books, Magazines, Tobacco." On the window in small white letters is written "Adult Books & Magazines, 8mm Film, Novelties, Tobacco, Gifts, Party Items." In much smaller white letters, written directly on the door, are the words "Adults Only, Must be Over 21." Upon surveying the interior of the "Market St. News," one cannot help being struck by the fact that, apart from several homophile and underground newspapers, the only other newspapers sold are the local paper and the *Los Angeles Times*. These are on a rack pressed into the corner behind the door. There are no other newspapers or popular magazines for sale. Strung across the front of the store is a rope with a large rectangular banner on it spelling out, "Movie Arcade," referring to the machines in the small room at the back of the shop. Except for the store name, the front of Store B is almost identical to Store A.

Inside, the stores are much the same. The floors are carpeted and the fixtures are of the latest design. Almost the entire stock of both stores is directly related to sex. The stores are stocked and arranged in much the same way. Running along the side and rear walls are seven-foot high racks containing paperback books. The books are usually arranged by publisher, although there is some attempt to group them by subject matter as well. The only exception to this are the books for male homosexuals. These tend to be grouped into one sector, though even this pattern was beginning to be broken by Store A.

Other grouped subjects besides male homosexuality are heterosexual couples, heterosexual group activity, lesbianism, virginity, sado-masochism, orality, and anality. Almost all of the books indicate by title or cover picture the general subject of the book: *Hot Pants in Paris, Mass Orgasm, Lure of the Lash, Amish Love, Kiss of Leather*. In addition to the fiction, there are nonfiction books masquerading as "pop sociology" but in fact dedicated to erotica, for example, *Sex in Female Prisons*.

Out on the store floor are racks containing picture magazines covering the same general categories as the paperback books. The titles are generally more abbreviated, for example, "Lesbo," "Broadside," "Naked Now." The magazines are encased in clear plastic covers with small round stickers covering the genitals of the models in the cover photos. The clerks told me that the covers keep the magazines clean and increase sales. The fig-leaf stickers, they said with tongue in cheek, were included so as not to offend the public's moral sense.

In the glass counter at the front of the store and on the wall behind the case are a large assortment of novelties and apparatuses, including dildos (latex penises) in all shapes and sizes, scented and flavored douches and vaginal creams, tickler prophylactics, battery operated stimulators (phallus-shaped), packs of photographs, nude playing cards, humorous towels and wall posters, 8mm films, and sex position manuals. Under the magazine racks around the store are various types of newspapers, almost all of them having something to do with sex. There is also a line of humorous greeting cards sold in the store. These are on a circular rack near the counter. In both stores there is a small sign taped to the front of the cash register advertising the local "swingers" club (wife swappers), with a phone number to call.

In a separate room at the back of the store are five to seven coin-operated movie machines. These machines run a color film approximately twelve minutes long. Upon the deposit of a quarter, the machine will run for approximately two and one-half minutes, whereupon it suddenly stops. Another quarter must be deposited before the machine will run for another two and one-half minutes. This room is dark and quiet, the only sound being the periodic dropping of a quarter and the low hum of the machine.

On my last visit to Store A I was surprised to find that a new product had been added to the inventory of the adult store, a product of an entirely different class than any previously sold. I realized immediately upon entering that something new had been added. There, hanging from the ceiling four feet above the counter, was a nude female mannekin in a "Love Basket" (manufacturer's name). The Love Basket, priced at three hundred dollars and powered by a large, well-made electric motor, is designed to move a real woman in an up-and-down and circular fashion while she is engaged in sexual intercourse. I cannot say for certain whether it was the first mass-produced item of its kind, but to the best of my knowledge it represents a great leap forward in aggressive merchandising.

While neither of the stores had been open for more than a year at the time of the study, there was the promise of stability. The owner took little risk in selling his wares. Only individual books can be court tested, and all legal maneuverings are handled by the publisher. According to John (the clerk at Store A), the owner of the stores dealt only with well-established and reliable publishers for this very reason.

Both stores seemed to be doing a very good business, excellent, in fact, for the investment in stock and overhead. According to the clerks, approximately 50 percent of the sales are accounted for by paperback books, 30 to 40 percent by magazines, and 10 to 20 percent by novelties, mostly tickler prophylactics. Store A in particular seemed to do a good business in novelties. Regarding the content of the material sold, one clerk estimated that approximately 75 percent of the books and magazines were about heterosexual couples or heterosexual groups. The balance was made up of approximately 20 percent Lesbian type (up to this point, bought exclusively by men) and 5 percent male homosexual type. More particularly, books dealing with orality, virginity, and teenage sex were mentioned as being especially popular.

As for the clerks themselves, John and Gil, whom I got to know quite well, and Don, with whom my acquaintance was briefer, all tended to fall into a somewhat similar pattern. All are in their thirties or early forties, single (two had been divorced), very articulate, and all look upon their jobs as only temporary. In addition, all three have a very libertine attitude toward sex. This, of course, is to be expected considering the nature of the job. However, even when allowing for this, their libertine outlook seems more loose than necessary. This probably has a net effect of increasing business, as each clerk seems to enjoy helping the customer, particularly those shopping for, and inquiring about, the novelties. While enjoying his work, each is careful to be serious when discussing the merchandise with a customer. The customers are never given the "knowing smile" that one might expect in such a situation. In fact Gil's bedside manner is so professional that customers frequently discuss intimate sexual problems with him, asking him to recommend store items that might be of help. Once again, the clerks are always careful to handle customers in a serious and businesslike fashion, especially if the customer is buying or looking for something of a more deviant character. John, for instance, on being handed a male homosexual magazine at the cash register, would always be careful to keep the magazine face down as he slipped it into a bag, thus respecting the customer's privacy.

In contrast to the serious and businesslike manner of the clerks, the counter area itself has a light air about it. This is partly due to the humorous towels and posters hung behind the counter and partly due to the labeling on the boxes in which some of the novelties are stored. For instance, tickler prophylactics are labeled "Latex Party Items." This labeling is probably necessary to meet legal requirements, but it nevertheless has the effect of "laughs, not erotica," and "just harmless fun." This atmosphere no doubt serves to put our borderline deviants at ease.

THE CUSTOMER

The typical adult book store customer while almost always male, ranges in age from 21 to 60. He tends to be ordinary looking and is often married. Men who come into the store, whether in the day or evening, are usually off work (judging by the length of time they stayed) and though some wear business suits, most are informally dressed. Customers are almost always neat and clean. In addition, it should be noted that some are "repeaters" who return to the store quite frequently. These men would often become rather friendly with the clerks. Most of the men making purchases are by themselves. The number of customers belonging to minority groups is quite small, even in proportion to their ratios in the total population. Minority customers are more often Chicanos than blacks and they frequently spend their time browsing.

Women, who seldom enter the store, are never alone. They are either with another woman, their boyfriends, or their husbands. When making a purchase (which is done only when they are not with a man) they almost always choose one of the funny greeting cards, novelty towels, or otherwise purposefully humorous items.

Many of the people who come into the store only browse. There are no restrictions against browsing in the store except for the protective plastic covers and fig leaves on the magazines, and many men stay for as long as an hour. The browsers typically resemble the cash customers, except that they tend to be slightly younger. Occasionally underage boys would try to come in (almost always in groups of two or more). They would be asked for identification, and then politely asked to leave. The proportion of men coming into the store whom the clerk felt it necessary to ask for identification was very small, even allowing for his strict enforcement of the age laws. Underage persons generally presented no problem.

As mentioned earlier, Store A is located on a block with a mild Bowery atmosphere. Though this did not change the caliber of customer, it did slightly affect the cross-section of browsers. This was especially true in the evening, when the number of transients in Store A (customers not from the neighborhood) exceeded those in Store B.

Customer's Patterns of Interaction: Before discussing the tacit understandings that are binding within the store itself, brief mention should be made of behavior outside the store. Fully one-third to one-half of all the men who walk by the store alone take notice of it, either by turning their heads and slowing their pace or by actually pausing in front of it. One young man, who appeared to be of age, came to a full stop in front of the door of Store A one evening, looked at the store for a couple of seconds, started to walk toward the door, paused, turned and walked on. People actually going into the store are usually more direct, though even they sometimes pause and quickly glance about before entering.

Most individuals coming through the front door do so as if it were any other store, pausing to look around and then moving toward the merchandise. However, some attempt to cover their deviance immediately. This is typically done by acting as though they came into the store by mistake. This is not always a cover, of course, but it happens often enough to be question-able. For instance, one afternoon at Store B a very well-dressed and respect-able looking gentleman about fifty-five came in. He immediately looked at John, and without so much as a glance at anything else in the store asked if the store carried chewing gum. John said no. The man nodded an acknowledg-ment and very slowly began to look around at the store. As soon as John looked away, he slowly moved off toward the magazines. He stayed in the store for about a half hour.

The dominant norm of the store is obvious upon entering, and few people have any trouble falling in line. It is almost as if they had anticipated it. The password is silence. Though there may be as many as fifteen men in the store, spaced not more than three feet apart, there is hardly a sound to be heard from the floor. The contrast between the floor and the counter area is often startling. None of the clerks make any effort to talk in anything but a normal tone of voice. Since some are quite talkative, especially John, their voices could often be heard booming across the floor. This behavior did not seem to bother the customers, nor did the clerks seem to think anything of the contrast.

The second norm of the store is physical separation. Individuals are espec-ially careful not to come into close contact with one another. Though this is common in most public places, it is particularly adhered to in the adult store. Even on those days when the store was full of men, a good degree of separa-tion would be maintained. Another feature of the store's interaction pattern commonly adhered to in public settings (but more stringently enforced within the adult store) is that of not looking at the other patrons. Both browsers and cash customers are especially careful to avoid each other's glance. Even when moving between the magazine racks or from one side of the store to the other, customers did not remove their eyes from the merchandise.

A last major feature of interaction patterns within the store is that of not showing any facial expressions, particularly expressions of pleasure. No matter what magazines or books he picks up, if he is alone, the customer will always maintain a poker face. This holds even if he becomes engrossed in the reading of a book (each book invariably has an erotic passage every few pages). I found it amazing, in fact, to stand in my place by the counter for long periods watching the sales floor, and not see a single change of expression, not even the short nod of approval or slight grimace of disgust that is common in other stores. It should be remembered that many of the books contain sado-masochistic passages (even when not hinted at on the cover of the book) that can be rather shocking by conventional American moral standards.

The one blatant exception to all of the above is the conduct of groups in the store. Groups do not usually frequent the store and they stand out when

they do. They tend to stick close together, quietly showing each other magazines or books they have found or pointing out novelties to one another. Their
general attitude is one of humor. They frequently snicker as they point out
items to one another and occasionally even boldly talk and laugh out loud.
However, even group members are careful not to look at, or get close to the
other customers.

As noted above, women seldom come into the store. When they do come,
they come in groups or in mixed pairs, and generally follow the same pattern
as the men, though they rarely pick up the books and magazines, but only
point to them. Women usually avoid the main counter and novelty section
entirely and their stay in the store is relatively brief. When they are in the
store, they do not outwardly affect the single men who are browsing. The
men's poker faces are maintained, as though "nothing unusual is happening."

Incidents that occur in the store (and these do not occur often) generally
have to do with groups and mixed groups. For instance, one afternoon I
observed that a young couple—no wedding rings—came in with an older
man. The older man was quite drunk, but even so appeared embarrassed and
bashful about the merchandise in the store. Apparently it was his first visit
to the store and the young couple seemed to take delight in showing him
around. Before they had left the store the older man, at the prodding of the
young couple, had bought twenty-six dollars worth of dildoes and other
novelties.

Another unusual incident happened with a couple on a quiet weekday
afternoon. A handsome young man and woman in their mid-twenties came
in (neither wearing wedding rings) and proceeded to quietly browse through
the magazines together. Theirs was not the usual pattern of snickering, but
was rather one of quiet conversation. After spending a short time looking at
the magazines, they went to the back of the store where they spent a long
time watching the movies.

The pulp voyeur, after staying in the store for as long as he likes, must
come to a decision. If his desire or curiosity has been satisfied, or if he wishes
to minimize his deviance, he may choose to leave without making a purchase.
This he does with as little fanfare as when he entered. If his desire is not satisfied and he wishes to carry on his voyeuristic activities in a more private setting, he must approach the counter, book in hand and thus formally admit
his deviance to others. All kinds of rationalizations may be offered as to why
one enters an adult store. They become far more scarce, however, when one
actually buys a book, magazine, or novelty.

Though many men are able to maintain both their silence and an adult
presentation of self when at the counter, a great many, perhaps a majority,
revert to a little-boyish approach. One has the distinct feeling when watching

them that they feel guilty about doing what they are doing, are putting themselves at the mercy of the clerk, and want to get the whole thing over with as soon as possible. Though they often utter no more than is necessary to complete the transaction, they frequently try to make distracting comments, for example, "Warm outside today, isn't it?" Again, this is not an unusual activity in any store. But in the adult store it has an awkward and hollow sound about it.

One thing did seem unusual. This was the comparatively large number of men who act slightly surprised at the sales tax. Such comments as "Oh, that's right, Ronnie [California's Governor Reagan] must have his," are common. Though this may have been just another distracting device, it could have also indicated surprise at the government's involvement in such a deviant enterprise.

The clerks in the adult store were extremely careful not to upset the customer's cover. This was especially true of homosexuals, who would invariably wait until the counter area was clear of other customers before approaching it. The clerk would quickly complete the transaction by slipping the book or magazine into a bag, face down.

While at the counter, many less bashful customers (and browsers) peer at the novelties in the glass case or on the wall behind the counter. It is not unusual for men to express their amazement that such things actually exist and are on sale in public. If a customer or browser shows the slightest interest in a particular item, the clerk (this applies to all of them) opens the case, places the item on top of the counter and begins to talk about it. Though this action has the potential of driving the customer away, the clerk's subtle and businesslike handling of the situation usually keeps this from happening. A brief discussion ensues that often ends by including other pieces of merchandise. These discussions are almost always kept on a superficial level, that is, detailed questions about, or descriptions of, the actual purpose or use of the item are not asked for or given. The conversation is carried on, it seemed, with the tacit understanding that the customer knows best how to use the product in question, that he knows what his needs are, and that he is the best judge of the worth of the product in fulfilling these needs. There were apparently good grounds for thinking this way. None of the clerks ever received any feedback as to how their products worked out.

After being put at ease by the clerk, some customers became quite friendly and talkative. After getting the clerk to give him a run-down on most of the items in the glass case, the customer often launches into a superficial discussion of the sociological or psychological aspects of sex. A frequent line of conversation is the changing morals of the American people and why this change is occurring. Often the customer takes a condescending attitude as he discusses the strange sex quirks that one finds in our culture. This may be a way of attempting to neutralize his own deviance, since it is frequently the case that the customer has just bought something of his own.

The "regulars" are usually the store's most friendly customers. These men come in as often as several times a week, establishing rather informal acquaintances with the clerk. Though they often buy books or magazines, the strongest drawing card is probably the movie arcade. Two new movies a week are screened by the management in an attempt to satisfy the insatiable curiosity of the pulp voyeur. Fortunately for business and the profit margin, these efforts proved unsuccessful.

CONCLUSION

What are we to conclude from the above description? If it were not so pronounced, the behavior pattern within the adult store—characterized by silence, physical separation, inattentiveness to others, and a lack of facial expression—would seem typical of thousands of other mundane human settings. This is, of course, exactly what makes the adult store remarkable—everything is "business as usual." The norms of the sales floor contribute to this atmosphere, as do the innocuous behavior of the clerk and the "just harmless fun" aura of the counter area.

All of the above allow the borderline deviant to maintain his privacy, without which he could not gain the satisfaction he desires.

The voyeur brings with him to a public place the conditions necessary for his satisfaction. He has been socialized into the norms of the adult store even before stepping inside the door. Hence, the store is able to maintain its semi-respectable appearance over time even though its incumbents are constantly changing, and the borderline deviant can maintain his privacy, without which he cannot gain the satisfaction he desires.

In addition to showing us how norms develop to protect privacy in a public place, the adult store has afforded us an excellent chance to see how the borderline deviant handles his deviance. Rarely does the pulp voyeur develop a concept of himself as a deviant. This is due almost exclusively to the fact that most of his voyeuristic activities can be pursued in secret, provided, of course, he has bought a book or a magazine. On occasion, however, he must replenish his supply of viewing material. When these occasions arise, he must confront his fellow voyeurs and the store personnel.

Ash Meadows:
A Fly-In Brothel

Robert M. Castle

●●● Ash Meadows has been for many years a fly-in brothel. It is located
●●● in Nye County, Nevada, near the eastern boundary of Death Val-
●●■ ley, sixty-five air miles from Las Vegas. One can drive to Ash
Meadows, but most of the trip is over secondary highways and the last few
miles are by way of a dirt road.

Ash Meadows Airport appears on the current Las Vegas Sectional Aero-
nautical Chart which is published by the U. S. Department of Commerce. The
1969 AOPA Directory, an official publication of the Aircraft Owners and
Pilots Association, contains the following notation:

> "Lathrop Wells–Ash Meadows. Mount Whitney Sectional. Lat:
> 36-22, Long: 116-18. Elev: 2210; 7-1/2 mi NE of Death Valley
> Junction; Tel: (702) 969-2611. Runway: 15-33/3300, gravel.

Ground trans: courtesy car. Food: restaurant. Lights: beacon, runway (hours of darkness). Unicom: 122.8. Storage: tiedowns. Services: rest rooms. Hours attended: 24. Lodging: Ash Meadows Lodge (2611/150'/yes). Resorts nearby: Death Valley."

There is an image in the flying fraternity of Ash Meadows, an image somewhat in the Heffner-*Playboy* tradition: the airport windsock is supposedly a pair of pink panties; on arrival the pilot is met by a pink jeep, trimmed with lace, and occupied by two or more Bunny-type females; all is lighthearted, festive, and gay, with no room for conscience, guilt, shame or other outcroppings of middle-class morality. Ash Meadows is seldom referred to as a whorehouse, and the girls are not characterized as whores. Ash Meadows, as the delusion goes, is different. The narrow line between wholesome fun and sinful deviance has somehow been transcended there.

Questions immediately arose in my mind. Why a fly-in brothel? Why a brothel sixty-five miles out in the desert? Why Ash Meadows when Las Vegas offers brothels and many other activities along with more acceptable explanations for being there? Are the interactions between the performers at Ash Meadows other than they would in a different setting? Are those interactions somehow a function of the means of transportation by which the customers come and go? In the pages that follow I have answered some of these questions, while others have proved to be more than my somewhat limited research could fathom.

My first trip to Ash Meadows was on Sunday, January 14, 1970. Flying in over the general area of the airport, I was unable to locate any signs of human habitation. I began to entertain a suspicion that I was the victim of a federally condoned, masterfully planned practical joke—an adult snipe hunt. I continued to circle. Wherever I looked I saw nothing but desert plains surrounded in the distance by rugged mountains. I was contemplating my return to Redlands when I looked directly below and saw the words ASH MEADOWS painted in large yellow letters on a roof top. Then I clearly saw an airport runway scraped from the sparsely vegetated desert. I subsequently learned that others had suffered the same difficulty in locating the site.

Partly as a release from tension, and partly to show off a little, I made an unauthorized pass over the area before landing. This, too, turned out to be commonplace for the pilots who flew in and out of the airport.

While landing I noted with some dismay that a conventional windsock had replaced the pink panties which rumor had led me to expect. My disappointment deepened as I taxied into the aircraft parking area. The jeep did not appear. There was no sign of life of any kind. No other aircraft were in the area.

Ash Meadows consists of a three-building complex on the south side of a dirt road and two mobile homes and a building on the north side. The latter is surrounded by a high wooden fence so as to be all but out of sight except from the air. It is situated across from the other buildings and is down the road about seventy-five yards. The buildings are located near some ponds which are fed by springs. There are many trees, which for some reason do not show up plainly from the air. These provide a good deal of privacy so that one cannot see the building on the north side of the street while in or about the south side complex.

The south side consists of the airport facilities (runway, lights, taxiway, and parking area), a small motel unit (which does not appear to be used by transients), a large motel unit for the overnight guests, and a building which houses a restaurant, a pool room (two tables), and a bar. A swimming pool adjoins this building on the east. To the west is a large pond which covers an area about equal to that of the large motel and restaurant. The southside buildings are architecturally similar to the Spanish-California ranch-style houses one sees in the Santa Barbara area—concrete brick, red tile roof, and large verandas. The large motel unit has approximately ten units facing the pond on the north and ten units facing the airport area, which is obscured by trees, on the south.

Every time I noted the motel area, there were three to five cars (California or Nevada license plates) parked in front of the south-facing units. I was informed that frequently such groups as county or state survey crews would bunk in the motel while employed in the area. Guests were charged from $10 to $20 a night for a room that, except for the bed, was sparsely and cheaply furnished. I saw no evidence that the motel rooms were used for prostitution; in fact, apart from a black maid, I did not see any woman in the vicinity of the large motel units. I was unable to establish what the small motel was used for.

The restaurant was clean but cheaply furnished. Western paintings adorned the walls. The tables were closely spaced and covered with worn white table cloths. A den-sized bar was separated from the restaurant by two rows of slot machines. The radio equipment for the airport (unicom) was located behind the bar and was operated by the bartender. The pool room adjoined the restaurant on the west.

The brothel, the building on the north side, is of a different style of architecture. When I first observed it I thought it was a warehouse. It is set on pilings so that the floor is three or four feet off the ground. Over the door, which faces to the west, is a red light which apparently burns night and day. The street on which it is located dead ends about fifty feet past the entrance. The dirt road that leads from Death Valley Junction to Pahrump appears on the map to go through Ash Meadows, but actually circles it to the north. Unless one knew the road, he might well drive into Ash Meadows and end up at the brothel.

The brothel consists of a waiting room connected by a hallway to about eight bedrooms. In the center of the waiting room, which is about ten by twenty feet, is a post which supports the main ceiling beam. A juke box sits in one corner. There are neither chairs nor sofas, only a bench which goes almost entirely around the room. The bench is constructed so as to prohibit two seated people from being in physical contact with each other—there is a raised box-like structure as wide as a seat between each seat. All lighting is provided by red lights that hang from the ceiling. The main entrance is guarded by a small see-through opening and a strong chain. The walls are adorned with good-sized, tasteful, sepia-toned semi-nude photographs, about four in all.

Among the staff operating the south side is a woman, in her late thirties, who manages the place and may own it. She made no attempt to interact with any of the male customers but was quite sociable with the various employees and neighbors who came in from time to time. There were also a cook, who freely mingled with everyone who entered his domain; an off-duty and an on-duty bartender; and two black maids. All of the employees, except the bartenders, appeared to have drinking problems about which I overheard the manager complaining on several different occasions. The bartenders were very capable and neither gave nor took offense easily.

The prostitutes were, judging by manners and appearance, of working class or lower middle class origin. Description is quite difficult because of the different roles they played depending upon which side of the street they were on.

Upon arrival, the first time I was there, I entered (actually, I sort of sidled into) the restaurant, attempting to be as unobtrusive as possible. This form of entry proved to be typical of whorehouse customers. Every effort was made to insure privacy. On the other hand, tourists and neighbors who dropped in, usually during daylight hours, for a drink or some food, would enter briskly. They immediately exchanged loud greetings with the cook or bartender and established the nonsexual purpose of their visit so that everyone could hear. I later learned that many of the whorehouse customers are repeaters, but this was not easily discernible from their interactions with others.

On one occasion, a Mustang Airline Cessna 206 landed with two passengers, a woman in late middle-age and a younger woman who appeared to be in her twenties, and a man, the pilot. The older woman, an authoritative type, made a theatrical entrance exchanging conversation with the pilot as she did, in such a manner as to tell everyone in the room that she and the young woman were not part of the surroundings into which they had been thrust by the circumstance of an airline schedule. She then swept the room with her eyes, stopping her glance at each male to verify that the message had been received and understood. Most of them avoided her stare.

If the entrance of the male customers, whether "drive-in" or "fly-in," could be characterized as sidling, their exits were stealthy. An absence was usually noted rather than a departure. In the same way, customers would seem to reappear out of nowhere. This phenomena must be considered in light of the fact that most of the individuals who were in the restaurant had arrived in the company of two or three others. Trips to the north side were usually made separately and sequentially. If the disappearance of one of a group was noted by the others, no reference was made to it. If anything was said by either the one who had made the trek or by the one who had remained, the statements were of a vague and ambiguous character and did not pinpoint where the absentee had been or what he had been doing.

There appeared to be a routine for the fly-ins. They went first to the bar and had a drink, then they ordered dinner. After dinner they went into the pool room. If one of them wanted to play, he would put a quarter on the table. His turn would be determined by the order in which his quarter was placed on the table. He would play the winner of the preceding game. Some members of a party could be playing pool while their companions were otherwise occupied.

There seemed to be a distinct difference between the drive-ins and the fly-ins with respect to the amount of alcohol they consumed, both before and after their arrival, and their ability to unobtrusively hold their liquor. Such drunks as appeared during my observations were drive-ins.

Except for a rare comment by a drive-in, usually drunk, one could be at the restaurant for a number of hours without even being aware of the prosperous and active business that was being transacted across the street. There was absolutely no hustling. The staff made no effort to interact with the customers. The normative structure that emerged through the interaction between customers, and customers and staff, was one of calculated avoidance of any reference, direct or indirect, to the place across the street. There was an apparent team effort by persons in the restaurant to define the situation as normal, that is, totally respectable. No one was guilty of anything, and there was no carefree abandonment to licentious, wanton, and lascivious conduct. In fact, the customers tended to be somber. When an occasional statement or act occurred which might upset this front, withdrawal by all but the transgressor, and perhaps the crowd of which he was a member, was immediate and surprisingly effective.

I did not witness any direct sanctions by the management, although I was constantly aware of its non-directive attempts to control the situation, particularly in the adept management of drunks by the bartenders. No one was "eighty-sixed," but I heard two drunks complaining to each other that their drinks tasted as though there were no alcohol in them.

If one of the employees was having difficulty with a customer, the woman manager would appear. As previously indicated, she was a woman who appeared to be in her late thirties. She wore Levis, and her appearance was that of an overweight Joan Crawford. She would ask the employee, usually the bartender, a question which might well have been coded in view of its general irrelevance to the immediate situation. Upon receiving an answer, she would return to her office, about thirty feet away at the south end of the pool room, where she could have telephoned for help if she had desired. To what extent potential trouble-makers were aware of this, I could not tell. However, no real trouble materialized while I was there.

Although I have made frequent reference to drunks, there was little drunkenness, in fact, there was relatively little drinking. This observation drew support from the fact that although there might be twenty to thirty people in the restaurant at one time there were only six stools at the bar in a barroom about the size of a family den.

The slot machines also saw little action and no other gambling paraphernalia was noted. The food was expensive and not very good, and a tough steak served by the cook cost $6. It was obvious that eating, gambling, and drinking were supporting activities of little consequence to the economic goals of the establishment. These were things the customer could do while waiting for a friend or his courage.

In my talk with the cook about problems of maintaining law and order, he made statements from which I inferred that problems incident to the nature of the business and its isolation kept the employees aware of the potential for violence. He said there were eight guns immediately available—one, I guessed, for each of the employees. The cook also advised me that there was a deputy sheriff on call who could be there within fifteen minutes at any time of the day or night. He described the deputy as being a real nice guy but tough, the type that wouldn't put up with any nonsense from anyone. The deputy appeared one evening while I was there. He sat with his coffee and chatted for forty-five minutes or more with the manager, cook, and a woman who appeared to be the madame. He looked tough. How nice he was, one could only guess.

The cook told me that several weeks ago there had been an occasion when all eight guns had been drawn. The culprit was a Negro who had been refused entrance to the brothel. In the cook's opinion, the real bad guys were the whites who brought Negroes to the place, knowing that they would not be admitted.

I asked if minority groups were excluded from the brothel, and he said that they were. However, a little later he mentioned that the brothel would do a good business on the next evening because between twenty to thirty Mexican day workers would be receiving their pay that day. When I asked if the brothel admitted Mexicans, he said, "Sure, they never cause any trouble." (Apparently blacks were the only ones defined by the bartender as "minority groups.")

On two occasions I ate dinner in the restaurant while six to eight of the prostitutes were also dining. The cook placed three or four of the tables together so that the girls could eat as a group. They also walked to and from the restaurant as a group. There were no stragglers. There was one, older in appearance by at least fifteen years, who appeared to be in charge. When she directed the girls to do something, they did as they were told. Sometimes one or another of the girls might screw up her face or make some other minor gesture of unhappiness, but I did not see a refusal or hear a rebuttal.

The girls were always neatly and completely dressed while in and about the restaurant. They all wore slacks and blouses of a type that can be purchased at Penney's or Sears Roebuck—none of the clothes were expensive, stylish, or sexy.

The girls talked with each other and did quite a bit of laughing, the only sign of any self-consciousness on their part. The conversational tone was subdued. Sitting twenty feet away I could hear only an occasional word. There was no conscious attempt on the part of any of the girls to draw attention to themselves. They totally ignored the other customers and exchanged only occasional remarks with the male employees.

The customers self-consciously ignored the presence of the prostitutes. They also ignored each other's presence for the most part, except during games of pool. There would be some conversation within groups that came in together; otherwise, customers appeared anxious not to recognize others or be recognized by them. Even the regular, and more boisterous, drive-ins observed the house norms which protected other customers from being classified as deviant.

Notwithstanding this presentation of self, many customers had come to Ash Meadows in search of deviant forms of sexual expression. This conclusion is in part based on estimates I received from the cook and the bartenders that probably half of the customers were married. Informants who were acknowledged customers stated that once you paid for a girl's time, anything went. I had heard that the girls charged for units of time rather than by the customary trick—the customer could try whatever occurred to him.

Only once during the study was my presence in the restaurant questioned. A group of well-dressed young men who announced themselves as members of the Las Vegas Junior Chamber of Commerce, and who had been engaged in a golf tournament at Furnace Creek, came into the restaurant about 11:00 P.M. on a Friday evening. They had driven the sixty or seventy miles from Furnace Creek. They were very drunk. The most garrulous of the group became curious about my presence there (he was also angry at having lost to me at pool). Finally he asked in a loud voice, "Are you here for a little swordsmanship?"

On an occasion when there were only three other men in the restaurant another atypical interaction occurred. These three were all proudly from Oklahoma and laborers. They were in their early twenties. All of them were seated at the bar and drinking when one made a statement to the effect that he was going across the street for some of that "sweet-stuff." One of the others told him he didn't have the nerve. When the one who had indicated his intention to go across the street got up and went, one of the others, after a few minutes wait, checked to see if he had entered the whorehouse. Upon returning, he announced, "Well, I'll be dammed, he went in. I didn't think he would." The conversation then turned to how the remaining two had falsified their driver's licenses to buy liquor before they were twenty-one. They kept referring to the bartender as "Curly." He was completely bald. All in all, their behavior was exceptional.

During one of our conversations, I asked the bartender if there was any age limit for entering the brothel. He said it was entirely up to the girls, but they didn't usually take anybody that looked under sixteen. "After all," he said, "the boys have to find out what life is all about sometime. It's better that they learn here than knock up some young girl."

On another occasion, the bartender had told me (when he and I were alone in the restaurant) that people didn't ask questions when they were at Ash Meadows. I had been asking general questions about the number of airplanes that flew in and out, what type of men came in the aircraft, how people behaved generally when there, and so on. We had talked particularly about an aircraft that crashed into the mountains when returning to Las Vegas from Ash Meadows about a week before. He pointed out that the six men who were killed were all real gentlemen, and that three of them earned at least $35,000 a year. He concluded by telling me that neighboring families and tourists came there to eat and drink and often brought their children with them. "Why they don't think anything more about the place across the street than if it were a church."

The cook vacillated between being friendly and totally ignoring me. He was drinking continually. There seemed to be an understanding between the cook and the bartender that the latter's drinks would be controlled so as to prevent him from passing out prior to the end of his workday, which must have exceeded twelve hours. I saw him cooking at 6:00 P.M., at 1:00 A.M., and then saw him getting breakfast at 8:30 A.M. the same morning.

On one occasion when the cook felt like chatting, I inquired about the number of fly-ins and drive-ins that came and went. He said that he had heard there were as many as twenty-four airplanes there on one occasion but the most he had ever seen was seven. He didn't want to be tied down, but figured that over half of the men who came into the restaurant were between 30 and 60 and married. Most of the customers drove in, and that most of them, especially the Mexicans, did not use the restaurant. Finally, he told me that he was going to Spokane to get married on Sunday. When I asked if he was coming back, he said that his fiancee had two children and that while Ash Meadows would be a nice enough place to bring a wife, it was no place for children.

On my last trip to Ash Meadows, I decided to make an on-the-site inspection of the whorehouse across the street. I walked up the stairway and rang the bell. After waiting about two minutes (everybody seemed to have to wait), I was admitted by a woman whose entire appearance was that of non-identity. After peering at me through the peep window she partly opened the door to take a better look and then removed a chain which latched on the inside. As I stepped inside, six girls were lined up in a column to my left, the tallest in front and the shortest in the back. I wondered if this grading was accidental. The doorkeeper then introduced me to each. As each was introduced, she smiled and moved as though about to step forward, but she didn't. After the introduction, there was an awkward pause. One said, "Which one do you want?" When I said that I wanted to think about it for awhile, three immediately disappeared down the hall. The other three took seats in the waiting room.

There were two other men in the room. One of them was the drunk Oklahoman whose entry into the whorehouse had surprised his friends. The other was a young soldier on leave. He never said a word, but just sat there with a smile, laughing if and when anyone else laughed.

One of the girls told me to hurry up and make up my mind. She nodded to the other two men and said they had already been back in the bedrooms and were "recharging their batteries."

The Oklahoman was occupying their attention. He kept showing them a big roll of bills and asking one of them to go with him to Las Vegas. When she would ask to hold the bills, he would get angry. He started apologizing to her for being a bad lay. After awhile she told him that he was really a good lay, one of the best. At this point he started telling her that she wasn't so hot. She told him that if he wasn't careful she would get her glasses and see what he really looked like.

About every two minutes one of the girls would tell me to hurry up and make up my mind, and that if I was sleepy I could take a girl and go back to a bedroom and get some sleep. I was not approached physically. Their salesmanship was anything but seductive. Each was dressed in something that appeared to be halfway between a Baby Doll outfit and a bikini. It was not long before one of the girls asked what I was doing there. I said that I had flown in earlier in the day and would spend the night. My statement was verified by one of the other girls. It became obvious after I had been standing there for about ten minutes that unless we transacted some business, I had overstayed my welcome. I excused myself saying that I was going back to the bar to get another drink.

I went directly to my motel room, where I remained for about thirty minutes. When I returned to the restaurant, I saw the brothel doorkeeper drinking coffee with the cook and some of the other help. Apparently she had told them of my behavior on the north side. Subsequently, the attitude of the help was more aloof and guarded. There was little doubt that the employees at Ash Meadows felt more comfortable when a visitor has proven himself to be a cash customer at the whorehouse. My failure to negotiate any business across the street had set me apart. My deviant behavior while there—that is, the lack of it—may have left them with the impression that I considered myself better than they were or that I was an investigator looking for someone or something. (It was my opinion that most of the help had done time.) It could also have been a subtle hustle. One thing was clear, until I went across the street, I was accepted; when I returned, I was an outsider.

Ostensibly there was no connection between the restaurant on the south side and the brothel on the north side. The girls were permitted to eat on the south side if they behaved. After the dinner hour, the girls did not return to the south side. If they wanted food, they ordered it on an intercom. Obviously, they could call for help in the same way. On one side of the street the girls were well-behaved young women. On the other side, they were whores. The south side appeared to be a staging area for the customers. The behavior of the customers and staff was somewhat like that of a group of soldiers going into combat on a troop carrier, with each absorbed in his own thoughts.

There seemed to be some effort in the restaurant to idealize the women and to create some tenuous relationship with the prostitute that was more than just physical. All of this was recognized and acceptable on the south side. In the brothel, however, the whores were not interested in being idealized or in having to interact with the Johns, except sexually and for cash in advance. It was also apparent that there was a considerable amount of sub rosa communication between the two areas, and customers were freely and openly discussed by the staff when not within earshot.

Finally, the organizational structure of Ash Meadows did not divide or segregate either the customers or the girls in terms of customer status. So long as all customers were cash customers, one was as good as another.

I cannot see that Ash Meadows is different from any other whorehouse. What is unique is that the customers will fly or drive fifty to three hundred miles to get there. Such gains as might be made by a customer in terms of secrecy would seem to be lost because his purpose in being there is clear. One can get the same type of service in Las Vegas, notwithstanding the fact that prostitution is illegal in Clark County. One is, of course, more apt to be seen in Las Vegas, but one's presence there can be explained in terms of the shows, gambling, or even business. Not so with Ash Meadows. If your presence there is noted, no one doubts your purpose. Ash Meadows is a one-industry town. Its existence would be easier to understand if the traffic were limited to those who flew in, a sort of private club motive. But such is not the case. As long as you are over sixteen and not black, you can trade at Ash Meadows.

2. THE PRIVATE MANAGEMENT OF DEVIANCE

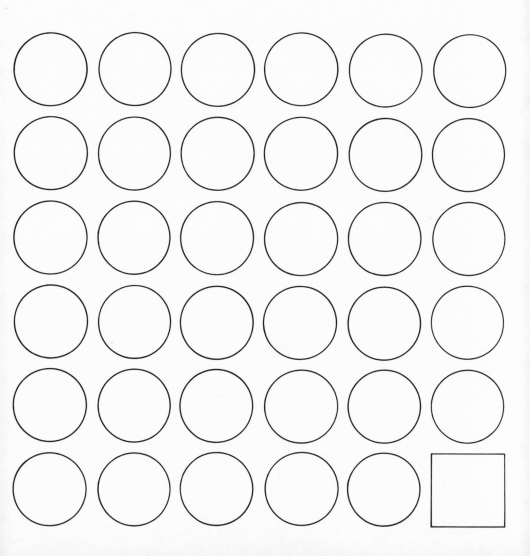

THE PRIVATE MANAGEMENT OF DEVIANCE

2. The essays in Part Two highlight an important difference between the Durkheimian perspective and that of interpretive sociology.[1] The former takes social categories, such as "addict" and "obese" person, and attempts to convert them into objective and measurable sociological concepts. By using common-sense knowledge of the society, operational definitions, and technical measurement procedures, the sociologist attempts to arrive at a concept that can be reliably and validly employed to classify persons into social types. Then rates of prevalence and statistical associations of such types with other variables can be calculated and analyzed. As objective social facts occurring in the society, the existence and prevalence of such social types can then be explained by the use of appropriate sociological theories.

In contrast, the interpretive sociologist does not attempt to take over social categories used in everyday life, repair their definition and their use, and convert them into objective, measurable concepts. Instead, he asks how these concepts are used in the natural social settings of everyday life. Since persons do not invent and use such concepts for the purpose of doing scientific sociology, what purposes *are* these concepts serving for them? What social uses are these concepts being put to? How do they figure in the practical affairs of social actors?

The readings in Part Two will permit us to begin to answer some of these questions. In particular, they will help extend a classical concept in interpretive sociology, George Herbert Mead's concept of the "generalized other."[2] This notion refers to one's ability to be "self-critical"—that is, his ability to perceive himself as another member of society might see him and govern his actions accordingly.

These chapters will show persons engaged in long internal dialogues with themselves concerning aspects of their social identity. The authors have done more than construct an idea of how a generalized other will see them. They have deduced which categories of people will notice these aspects of them-

selves, under what circumstances and with what consequences, and many
other matters connected with their social situation. The materials found in
these essays should therefore be helpful in producing theories about how
members of society construct Meadian self-images, that is, theories about how
they arrive at beliefs concerning other's perceptions of them. We will also
see some of the actual social uses of categories such as "addict" or "obese"
person. We will see how persons use these categories to assess their social
situations, how they govern their actions with others in the light of such
categories, and how they use these categories to reason about actions and
their consequences as they occur in everyday life. Each of the three chapters
that follows will be concerned with two aspects of privacy—the deviant
activity itself as a personal undertaking that is not open to public scrutiny,
and the essentially private nature of the coping mechanisms used by the
deviant in his (or her) attempt to "pass." We will read how two heroin
addicts (one a practicing addict and the other a former addict) and a girl
who has been obese since childhood have attempted to neutralize their
deviance for themselves and others.

The first reading, "Shooting Up: The Autobiography of a Heroin Addict,"
is a study in how a "straight," white, middle-class girl became an addict, and
the ways in which she sought to convince herself and others of her continued
respectability. For example, she has been a heroin user for some time but
does not consider herself an addict; she considers herself to be an occasional
user, "a weekender." Accepting this definition has helped her keep her self-
image intact. To further reinforce the contention that she is "normal," she
tells us that, when forced to stop using heroin because of serum hepatitis,
she did not experience the withdrawal symptoms that "true addicts" undergo.
On the other hand, she has vowed on several occasions to quit heroin but has
thus far been unsuccessful in doing so. Indeed, she tells us that she needs
heroin to live, considers its use "adaptive," and if forced to give it up, she
might very well turn to suicide. Quite apart from having to provide a moral
justification to herself (and to the author, since she knew me as the recipient
of the paper), she has the added burden of coping with the "mental illness"
that one might infer from her forced visit to a psychiatrist. This she does by
reflecting on the "idiocy" and general incompetence of doctors (on two
occasions she has to diagnose her own illness for them in order to receive
proper treatment). She is also concerned that she might not only consider
herself deviant but that others might learn of her visit to the psychiatrist and
consider her "sick." In fact, she is so concerned about this that she considers
the possibility of stealing her case record from the hospital. While troubled
by the private management of her self, she has been very successful in her
public presentation of self. The general public does not suspect that she is

anything but a bright, pleasant, well-behaved, middle class college student.

The second reading, like the first, deals in a formal sense with the same problem, stigma neutralization. The task here is to define obesity out of existence and, failing this, to "cover it up." The elaborate ways in which the author of this piece contrives to cover her obesity (even to her parents) and arrange her life so that there seems to others to be legitimate cause for her physical inactivity and social isolation, are ingenious. However, so pervasive are the effects of her obesity upon her "life chances" that all of these efforts at stigma neutralization ultimately fail. In fact, when years of attempting to cover up fail, and she finally succeeds in losing weight, all of her worst fears are realized. She is still isolated from meaningful social relationships, and it now seems to her that it was her "self" and not her "body" that had been rejected all along. This definition of the situation has left her discouraged, feeling that there was not much point to the entire enterprise of losing weight, which was for her a life's work.

The third reading is by a former heroin addict. Like the first essay, it is autobiographical, an outline of the socialization process experienced by a heroin user and the rationalizations used to initiate and perpetuate heroin use. These two stories differ, of course, because the storytellers are quite different. For example, one is a respectable white, middle-class girl who has never been arrested, while the other is a lower-class Chicano who has "done time" and been "rehabilitated." Apart from this, there is the crucial fact that in the first case the story is told from the perspective of one who is still using heroin, whereas in the second case, the events are related after the subject gave up heroin use. This leads the addicts to two different accounts of the drug experience and its efficacy.

In the first case, the addict sees heroin use as her salvation, as "the only way out," apart from suicide. In the second account, heroin is viewed as a sure route to marginal employment, false hope, "bad faith," and ultimate ruination. Both describe a drift into drug use. However, the first addict sees her ability to cope as dependent upon her "occasional" use of heroin, while the second attributes his former inability to function to the same cause. Insofar as he has defined "shooting up" as his undoing, the former addict is careful to define this practice as not of his own making—in his view, he was a "victim of circumstances." On the other hand, the girl, viewing her use of heroin in a positive way, tends to see herself as instrumental in her drift toward acceptance of heroin.

The reader is urged to keep these features in mind. They will help him to understand the derivation of the "definition of the situation" held by the participants, and why their respective interpretations of events are crucial in understanding their behavior.

NOTES

[1] For the differences between the positivistic sociology of Durkheim and interpretive sociology, see Jack D. Douglas, *The Social Meanings of Suicide* (Princeton, N.J.: Princeton University Press, 1967) and Jerry Jacobs, *Adolescent Suicide* (New York: John Wiley & Sons, 1971).

[2] Anselm Strauss, *The Social Psychology of George Herbert Mead* (Chicago: University of Chicago Press, 1959), pp. 86, 232.

"Shooting Up": Autobiography of a Heroin Addict

Anonymous

An autobiography implies gross egocentricity, as if I thought I were a terribly interesting person or something; but after considering the alternatives, this, nevertheless, seems to be the most valuable approach to my subject. If I were to restrict my discourse to general statements about the addict groups I've known, my ideas would have wider applicability, but the paper would be nothing more than a superficial description of addict subculture such as has been arrived at a dozen times already by sociologists through interviews with inmates. By writing subjectively, I can give a better description of what shooting-up feels like. All the objective descriptions I have read don't get anywhere close to the reality. No wonder professionals have such a hard time explaining heroin use if the best reason they can think of is euphoria or simply "pleasurable effects." The biggest disadvantage of the autobiographical approach is that I am not a typical

case; therefore, I'm explaining little except my own case. I will specify what
is atypical about my case:

I am a [white] university student who has achieved some small success
in school: I'm close to graduation and usually get A's. And I am from an
upper-middle class background: both my parents are professionals; I was
raised in the North End; I attended private schools. This is a big contrast
from most hypes I know. They're exceptional if they got through high
school, and most of them were raised in Eastside, which is the worst slum
in Smogsville. To give you some idea of what Eastside is like, you can go
down there any night and see drunks in the street and girls looking for a
pick up—they seem to be promiscuous by about age thirteen. I don't think
I'm exaggerating when I say that the major leisure-time activity of young
guys is stealing. You can buy smack on almost every block, or just cruise
around for a few minutes until you run into someone on the street you know
can make connections. I have never met anyone from Eastside who didn't
use smack. Incidentally, no one in Smogsville except policemen and people
from the adjacent lower-class neighborhoods have ever heard of Eastside.
People from Eastside have a strong identification with their neighborhood
and use the term among themselves, but they don't use it to outsiders because
they know you won't know what area they're talking about. It's just a few
square blocks, practically a community in itself.

Second, I'm atypical in that I've been using smack for almost a year and
haven't gotten strung out. This is unusual. Most of the hypes only last a few
months on the street before they go to jail for awhile. In short, my pattern
of use is different.

The obvious question now becomes how a straight-looking girl from the
North End ever managed to get familiar with Eastside, considering that Eastside is a closed society and people down there don't even know how to talk
to someone from the middle-class world, and they automatically dislike them
besides. To answer that question is to tell how she started using smack.

I learned Eastside and smack from a boyfriend who grew up there. Unless
a girl wanted to change identities and become one of them herself, which is
to say become a scuzz, the only way she could get in would be through a
boyfriend. I met the guy on a farm in Oregon. I was the cook and he was a
farmhand. I was up there because I was on the road and he was up there
because he busted out of juvy hall and had relatives in Fallsville. I'd been
traveling around the country for a couple of years, but that's another story.
Because of a fortuitous combination of circumstances I ended up back here
in school, the guy followed, turned himself in, did about a year, and got out
with the intention of turning middle-class. He and I and a buddy of his from
Eastside used to go around together a couple of nights a week, usually not

doing much except getting loaded—smoking marijuana or maybe dropping reds or rainbows—none of which I much liked except that it was a rather different social activity.

Then the buddy got a girlfriend who was a hype from way back. She was 28, an ex-hustler, and a veteran of many habits, especially coke. I never knew anyone who took so much dope. All she cared about was getting loaded and that's all she ever did. My boyfriend and I often dropped by their pad after the library closed. One night they had just bought some smack and offered us some. My boyfriend demurred but I said, "Hell, yes, I want some," just because that's about the only thing I'd never done. Everyone was rather surprised at my willingness (there was another hype there with really awful tracks on his arms), but they shrugged, advised me that I might heave or get sick since it was my first time, discussed who should fix me up (I can't remember which one they decided on), and described the procedure to me. One guy took off his belt and tied me off, another cooked the stuff and hit me.

The rush was terrific. I wasn't expecting it. The others were asking me if I felt it yet, since they hadn't been sure how much to give me and thought they were erring on the short side instead of the heavy side. They gave me plenty though, because I stood up, maybe to unkink or flex my arm or something, since finding a vein on my arm takes some probing, and when the rush did hit me it practically knocked me off my feet. My head reeled so I could hardly even sit up, let alone stand or walk. I hadn't expected such an overwhelming experience, but I thought it was fun, a really wild sensation. The others were checking, asking me if I felt okay, and I assured them I felt better than fine. My attitude was like, "Wow, this stuff sure does it to ya! Spectacular."

I suppose I might have been a little worried if anyone else acted like there was something to be worried about, but they were all very casual about shootin' up, like they did it all the time. Their mood was happy and light, and as soon as the rush passed and I could be aware of something besides my body, then my mood was happy and light, too. Mostly, I was having fun. It was a big adventure. I kept thinking how daring I was. The only one that wasn't too happy was my boyfriend. He didn't think I ought to be taking any smack and he was nervous just being around the stuff. He got jumpy every time he was around something that could put him back in jail because he hadn't been out long enough to feel comfortable or secure on the streets.

I was very high for several hours. After the rush, smack feels a little like reds. I feel talkative and warm towards the people I'm with. I like everything and everybody. I dry heaved a couple of times, but it passed. In retrospect, I guess I was nodding. I think I would recognize the feelings as such now.

Nodding means spells of floating; surges of sensation flow through the body and for a few moments you can't think, only feel. Everything is suspended while the person is absorbed in his body. To an observer it looks like he's falling asleep—and if he's had too much he might almost pass out. (Just a little bit more than the passing-out stage is an O.D. or overdose.) After awhile I just settled down to a super-relaxed state and went home and went to sleep. I was still loaded the next day. This has often happened to me if I take a really big hit. It takes a day or so to wear off. The biggest effects of the wearing-off stage are a pleasant weakness, slowness, and numbness. You can't feel your feet touch the ground; walking feels like springing along; every movement is a sensation—again, floating is the closest analogy.

I went to school in the morning, preoccupied with what I was feeling, self-conscious, and tickled because I knew I looked the same as I always did: there I was, going among ordinary people and activities as if I were part of it all, when really I was experiencing everything on a different plane, in a new mode. I got a kick out of dissembling, acting straight; like I was playing a trick on everybody.

I didn't think I'd ever use smack again. I thought it was a chance incident. I was kind of proud of my distinction. How many girls from my background have run into the things I have. (But I see now that kids nowadays, especially middle-class kids, know a whole lot about dope.) But a couple of weeks later one of the hypes I knew wanted to borrow a hundred bucks to make up enough to buy a piece and go into business. I lent it to him, got the money back within a week, and a couple of balloons for my cut. Incidentally, getting any money back from a hype is a rare occurrence. A balloon is literally a balloon, like kids play with, only it has a spoon of smack in it. It costs $25 and yields about 10 good hits for someone like me who doesn't have a habit. Someone with a bad habit might get two or three hits out of it.

About the same time I got an apartment out in the sticks, very safe. Within a few weeks the couple I first shot up with were both using heavy. They had to give up their apartment and move in with his family since they were spending all their money on smack. The girl was the big force behind our increasing use. She was always engineering a buy. They needed a place to shoot, and I had an ideal place. So at least once a week they came up and they always brought me a hit. We got into kind of a routine where they'd come every weekend and babysit while I worked. I don't think we especially liked each other, but we got along, and anyway, we had a reciprocal arrangement worked out: my apartment for their smack. I liked to get loaded every weekend and if I couldn't I was frustrated and mad.

After a few weeks I got serum hepatitis and quit using for about six weeks because I was just too sick to want it. Besides, I was taking 20 units of course work at school and it was all I could do to keep functioning. I was exhausted all the time and knew that if I used any drugs it would be my ruin. I didn't have any opportunities to shoot during that time anyway because my people had gotten badly strung out and couldn't spare any stuff. They quit coming over also because they heard I had hepatitis. Also, we'd had a falling out over an imagined insult (the girl was wearing one of those mod floppy outfits and I thought they were pajamas).

But during midterm week of first quarter, my boyfriend by chance had some stuff. We shot up and it sure was nice. I realized what a beautiful feeling I'd been missing. I was ready to start shooting regularly again, like once a week, and my boyfriend always seemed to make sure to have the stuff for me. He must have sensed that the only use he was to me was as a connection, and he'd settle for anything. I got so disgusted with him I got rid of him once anyway for two weeks, smack or no smack. He begged and pleaded to see me for just a few minutes, though, and was tactful enough to bring a fix. So that period of abstinence didn't last long.

Our sources of free smack ran dry about this time, since all our people were desperately strung out, down, raunched out, and writing checks for a living. I started sending my boyfriend to buy smack and I spent $50 in two or three weeks. Putting out that much money really hurt and I firmly resolved I'd never spend another cent. By this time our people were in jail and I figured that was the end of that episode in my life. I'd seen enough of it. Simultaneously, I realized I was getting hepatitis again. I went and had the lab tests run, and of course I was right. I still fixed up once, though, because I felt terrible and didn't want to study. I got so sick so fast that I couldn't even make it back to the doctor. He'd told me to come back in a week because he thought I just had a little touch of infectious hepatitis. But when I got up enough strength to go—five or six days after my first visit—they put me in the hospital.

The doctors couldn't figure out what was wrong with me. The tests showed my liver was 90 percent destroyed and people just don't get that sick from infectious hepatitis. They don't get infectious hepatitis twice in five months either. They never thought of serum hepatitis—I look too much like an average housewife. They must have thought I had cancer because they were going to do a biopsy. I was exasperated. Those ding-a-ling doctors would have run around in circles forever, so I just told the specialist what I had. I don't see how they could have failed to notice the marks on my arms or realize that my illness was following the typical serum hepatitis pattern. (I knew all about it because I looked it up in a medical textbook.) I guess they had a preconception of what a hype would look like, and I didn't fit the picture, so they were nonplussed. Their minds couldn't maneuver outside of the categories they had set up. Then, when I told them I was using the needle they swung to the other extreme and tried to type me as an addict. I had a hard time convincing them that I wasn't undergoing withdrawal. I don't see how they could have a dumb notion like that either, because kicking causes aching bones, cramping muscles, especially in the legs, and severe pain, and they could see perfectly well that I wasn't in any pain at all.

Anyway, now that they knew what I had they still didn't know how to react. I had the impression that they'd never seen anyone who'd used heroin before. The doctor didn't even know what questions to ask. I didn't want to be asked any questions anyway. I just wanted to lie there so I could get out in a few days. But it wasn't so easy. They called in a psychiatrist, which infuriated me. I talked to her nicely enough though—small talk, because I certainly wasn't going to answer any personal questions so she could get enough on me to work up some construct about some kind of psychological problem. The implications of calling in a psychiatrist were plain and I was outraged. That insult still galls me. I still wish that there was some way I could get those hospital records, especially the record of the shameful fact that there was a psychiatric consultation, and burn them. I've even planned how I might do it, and I still might carry it through. My experiences in the hospital are a good illustration of Goffman's mortification concepts. I had to fight practically every day for my status and dignity as a full person.

To carry on with the story. I was in the hospital almost a month last quarter, but I still carried 12 units and got all A's. I also had an abortion, which is off the subject but may be pertinent. About twenty minutes after I was discharged I got home and found my boyfriend slumped over the sink with the needle still in his arm, O.D.'d. I had already been trying to get rid of him for months, especially because of the black eye and fat lip he'd given me. This time, I decided to make it final. I wasn't going to need any more connections anyway. So, I went and got the neighbors and called the cops. The neighbor man revived him somewhat and he left before the police got there, and I haven't seen him since. His sister called me two weeks ago, all upset because he was kicking and his groans were driving her crazy.

My resolution not to shoot lasted a week or so. I was taking a course in criminology and every time I came across references in my readings to heroin I wished I had some. I had looked up my old friends and met a lot of new ones, all of whom smoked marijuana, so I tried to get to like that. It was all right, but what I really wanted was some smack. Everyone I knew was running me down for even considering it, and always asking: "You're not going to use any more of that stuff, are you?" They were really beginning to make me feel like a deviant. So I pretended I'd never use it again, even though I knew I would if I got a chance. (Looking back, my encounter with an official agency-as represented by those authority figures, the doctors—and the existence of that incriminating record, were making me think of myself as a heroin user, even though objectively I know my use is marginal and insignificant in my identity makeup.)

Six weeks after I got out of the hospital I got a chance. I managed to get a new kit so as to eliminate the risk of hepatitis. I shot reds occasionally. I accidently ran into a local hype I knew and he scored a balloon for me. It was lousy stuff, cut with *brown* sugar, if you can imagine that, and it felt like it was cut with strychnine, too. That's no joke. I've heard of cutting it with strychnine. I've had some of the symptoms too—muscle spasms, vomiting of blood, etc.

A dealer friend of mine said that there wasn't any use in my getting burned, so he introduced me to some reliable people. I think he gets a percentage and that's why he'll score for me now, whereas I knew better than to even ask him a few weeks ago.

My friends know I use occasionally, but they used to think I was crazy to do it, so I don't shoot around anyone and I keep my mouth shut about it when I do. (They must be beginning to accept it nonchalantly because my most vociferous critic got me two new points yesterday.)

A couple of weeks ago I got infected veins. My arm was really a mess. I knew I had to get some penicillin because I was going to start a new job and I couldn't even move my arm. I lucked out and got a doctor who gave me the prescription without writing anything in the file—I'm very uneasy about the written evidence against me that already exists. Incidentally, I also had to tell this doctor what I had because he couldn't guess just by looking at my arms. He gave me an emotional lecture about a patient who had died of an overdose, and the nurse almost cried because she knew the story. It was a terrific scene. I suppose it was humorous because they made such a big deal over it, when I'm such a small-scale user as to hardly count as a user. I also perceive, just as I'm writing this all down, that people's reactions are making me feel more like a deviant now than when I really was using a lot of stuff. And compared to the hypes I knew, I was straight even back then. On the other hand, back then the constant awareness of living a secret life with drugs was a strain. I feel like I'm living a big lie in either of these opposite situations.

My infection has cleared up within this past week. I can see now that the main vein in my right arm is collapsed. That's from shooting reds; I'll never shoot another. However, I fully intend to use a little heroin whenever I feel I need it—every week or two.

Now that I've given a brief rundown on past history, I'll give a prognosis. The obvious question is *why*. I like to think I can give an honest, if not reasonable, answer. I think I need it. It hinges on what heroin does for me, which is something most users seem unable to articulate. Smack is functional for me. It's enabled me to reach a balance, to maintain stability in an upsetting situation. It's enabled me to get along satisfactorily in a state of prolonged, latent crisis. I am consciously unhappy in almost everything I'm doing. I've had the urge to break out for the last two years. (By break out, I mean jump in my car and go to New Mexico or Idaho or someplace.) With the occasional help of drugs, I've been able to keep my nose to the grindstone, act like a study machine instead of a person, and forego all but the most cursory social contacts. I have a very tight schedule and (besides indulging in fattening snacks and candy) drugs are the only gratification I allow myself. When I feel very uptight, instead of winding up until my mental and emotional functions start going haywire, I take a couple of hours to get loaded.

I get loaded preferably with a group of close friends, but I also often use heroin late at night by myself when I lay aside my books an hour or so early. The reason I use heroin, instead of having a drink or using a softer drug like grass, is simple. First, I used to be a heavy drinker, but my liver is shot and I ought to avoid liquor, so that avenue is closed. Second, heroin is by far the most effective drug for the purpose. Pills tear a person's body up. I know from long and unhappy experience. I dread the occasions when I have to take pills, like when I've got to stay up and cram through a paper, or when I've got to go to work after I've already been working all day. I dread the come-down more than from smack. I know when I take pills that I'll feel like hell the next day. Grass is all right, but I don't want a hallucinogen when I'm trying to relax. Somebody asked me not long ago what I wanted to do, expecting me to outline my career plans, but I simply answered, "Split." Symbolically, that's what I did every time I smoked. But my trips were beginning to lose their significance and their efficacy as a stopgap measure. I used to think some of my sessions were shortcut preliminary steps in the self-actualization process, like Jungian analysis or client-centered therapy. But instead of getting valuable introspection, I was getting only trivial thoughts. I smoked frequently for two months and I'm thoroughly sick of it. I'm going to get rid of my stash.

In contrast, the effects of heroin are purely physical, real, sensual, not artifacts of the personality. The most apt description is to draw a comparison to sex. Indeed, smack and sex are very alike. I'll expand on this: both sex and smack are body-centered; they relieve tension equally well; they are equally self-submerging and totally involving—one yields all one's awareness, one's very being, to physical sensations. I once read a quote from a woman addict: "It's like sex. You wouldn't dream that you could get so much pleasure from your own body." I think she hit on a simile that has often been overlooked. At first glance this seems perverted. Since there is only one party, it might seem more closely analogous to masturbation than sex. But it's only by a stretch of the imagination that orgasm can be seen as anything but one-sided, and the health bugs and body-building freaks are just as guilty of over-valuing their bodies. Further support for the notion that smack is an alternative means of gratifying the common physical drives is the fact that sex and smack are mutually exclusive. It is impossible to make love while loaded. There are never exceptions. Non-users arrive at this same idea intuitively with the oft heard comment, "I'll get my highs on sex." In my own case, I am consciously aware that smack serves as a substitute for sex. I say this with some embarrassment because it is so blatantly narcissistic, but I admit it nevertheless. I am necessarily doing without sex because I've learned that casual sex is worse than useless and it takes months to cultivate a good relationship. I don't spend as many hours with all the people I know put together as it would take to get to know someone well enough for good sex. I just don't have that kind of time. I think this lack in my life would disturb me, would actually become disruptive, if I didn't get loaded.

Instead of all this emphasis on the supposed social incompetence of addicts (they can't hold jobs, bear responsibility, stand pressure, and so on), someone ought to hypothesize sexual adequacy as the determining variable—and by extension, the capacity for love (a sociologist would probably make up some ridiculous term like "ability to form strong affective relationships").

Besides physical gratification, immersion in sex or smack is also the greatest and most effective of removal activities (as Goffman uses the concept). For awhile one is completely out of his workaday situation. I'd like to get out of mine altogether, but since I can't, occasional release stretches out my endurance limit a little farther to the future. I don't understand why escape is culturally defined as base and castigated as a sign of weakness and personal failure when *everyone* has a favorite escape activity. People all express a need to "get away from it all for awhile," so they take vacations or go skiing or to the races or something. Drugs are considered an unnatural escape hatch, virtually perverted. I can say one thing in defense of drugs: shooting up is a more positive activity than vegetable-like, impassive abandonment to the TV; at least it's personal instead of vicarious experience, and one is processing the stimuli and reacting instead of surrendering all functioning.

This brings me to the crux of my involvement with heroin, or with drugs in general: any mode of experience is better than none.

I know that drugs are dangerous, and heroin most of all, and I'd rather be living a healthy life. But how can I live a healthy life in Southern California? I work in a shady business and in the other sphere of my life, school, I exist as a computer, methodically incorporating vast quantities of data, relating, reorganizing, or regurgitating it on demand. Considering that I am absolutely trapped in my unhappy situation, it's a wonder I don't undergo some kind of massive rebellious emotional upheaval or personality disintegration.

On these grounds I object to the characterization of drug users as psychic weaklings. I've stood a whole lot in my time. Those who really can't cope use drugs not for the reasons I do, as a temporary alleviating measure, but as a terminal measure—suicide.

It might be fruitful if I described the last time I shot up, which was almost a week ago. I intended to postpone my little ritual until after midterms, but I just couldn't study another page. I was so restless that my muscles were twitching and I looked up after every line. I was sick of sitting in the same chair cramming my tired brain. Something big and important was happening in the world, the Cambodian crisis, and I wanted to join the student community and get out and do something. But I didn't know how to act like a member of the student community—I'm older and have had different kinds of experiences, and we have little in common—and I couldn't spare the study time anyway. But it was just no use studying.

I finally quit fighting it and shot up. Within moments I felt as if I'd been transported to a realm of peace. Surges of relaxation coursed through me and every trace of agitation, mental or physical, dispersed. I felt tremendously relieved. The only idea in my head was "what a blessed feeling." I had been at the explosion point and now I was totally quiescent. I'd been so tense I almost ached and now I felt warm, loose, and tingly. I just sat there and enjoyed the sensation for about twenty minutes or half an hour, and then opened my book and read calmly for the rest of that afternoon and for every afternoon since.

Since writing this paper is having something of a cathartic effect, and since I've allowed myself two dinner dates this week with very nice guys which I expect to enjoy thoroughly, I don't think I'll build up such a level of frustration and tension again for many days.

Losing: An Attempt at Stigma Neutralization

Anonymous

According to medical research, if the parents are both obese, their child will have an 80 percent chance of becoming obese. Further, an obese child has far more fat cells than a "normal" child. These cells are never lost, but merely shrink in size if the child loses weight. Consequently, a tendency toward obesity will be a part of such an individual's physical makeup all of his life. Most medical literature also contends that only 1 percent of obesity is due to some medical problem such as hypothyroidism. Moreover, if an obese person decides to lose weight, he has only a 2 percent chance of reaching and maintaining his correct weight for a year.[1]

The preceding statements all make being obese seem a very remote or abstract thing. I hope in this paper to present some of the more personal elements of being fat. I have defined being fat as a condition in which one is fifteen or more pounds overweight. In giving a description of my "deviant career," I will attempt to show how strong an influence upon one's lifestyle obesity can be. In order to accomplish this task, I will cover, in more or less chronological order, events and feelings from my early childhood, adolescent years, and adult life. Please keep in mind that this "autobiography" covers incidents of a personally rather painful nature. The only reason I am able to explore this area of my personality at all is because I have lost some thirty pounds in the past five months, and am now well on my way to becoming "normal."

THE FAT CHILD

I was born a very normal, healthy, and unstigmatized baby, weighing only a little over six pounds. As I was not born deviant, I began my career at the age of five. At this time my mother resumed a career as a registered nurse, leaving me in the care of my maternal grandmother. I could give some Freudian analysis about childhood trauma due to my mother's absence as a reason for overeating, but it would be quite unfounded, because my grandmother had always lived with us, and being looked after by her was neither new nor threatening. Perhaps she did have a hand in launching me upon a deviant career, for my grandmother had always believed in giving a child bread and butter when hungry, and I was frequently hungry. It is also important to mention at this point that eating was a social activity in my family. Guests were always entertained by sharing meals with them, and dinner was always a family affair. We ate breakfast and dinner together as a family, and I still look forward to meal times as an opportunity to share the day's events with the rest of the family, whenever I am home.

By the time I was six years old, I was well on my way toward being a "fatty," although I am sure that I was completely ignorant of the fact— both of my parents being overweight. Although I am told that I had the bad manners at a birthday party to eat three pieces of cake, I wasn't plagued by any sense of guilt or impropriety. Unfortunately (perhaps), I did not continue in my state of happy gluttony for long, for the public school system, that temple of learning, was the first to teach me who and what I was.

As I entered the first grade, it was painfully pointed out to me—for the first time in my life—that I was different from other children. Other children's taunts of "fatty" and "pig" first brought shock, pain, and tears, and, later, guilt. I remember being afraid of the other children to the point of not wanting to walk home alone, and my mother frequently walked the one block from my home to the school to get me. This fear of young children has always remained, and I still avoid contact with them whenever possible.

The teasing, however, did not cause me to want to stop eating, for I still did not realize the connection between eating and being overweight. Instead, I started to develop two coping or protective devices which became quite elaborate later. For one thing, I started to try very hard to establish my worth in areas not related to physical attributes, while at the same time avoiding activities involving my body. The other mechanism was the creation of an active fantasy world where I was always the center of attention. These techniques were, I suppose, attempts to deny my situation to myself if not to others.

In the area of achieving, I became what might be called a model student. I can remember what a pleasure it was to read the comments on my report cards about what a nice little lady I was. The other side of this coin was avoidance of physical activities, principally physical education. I recall my stomach turning every time I had to line up with all the other children to be chosen for teams. A good day was one in which I was chosen next to last instead of last. The worst time of all, however, was the two-day ordeal called playday— a yearly event in which each classroom competed for prizes in various games and sports. I would usually manage to avoid playday by feigning illness. My mother would allow me to stay home on those days, probably to avoid the fuss I made.

I also learned that by being "sick" I could avoid facing other people. (I doubt that my motives were overt at the time, as my physical illness seemed quite real.) I was in the school nurse's office almost every day while in the third grade with a wide range of ailments, usually centering on nausea or tiredness. A trip to the nurse meant at least an hour away from class, and it was great fun to rest on a cot in a small green room and imagine that the stucco pattern on the wall was a jungle with wild, friendly animals in it. This game came to an abrupt end, however, when two betrayals put a stop to my friendship with the school nurse. At the end of the third or at the beginning of the fourth grade, children in the school I attended were given a general physical by the school nurse. One part of the physical was weighing each child. When the day for my turn arrived, I went to the nurse's office with my best friend (a tall, slender, redhead named Charlotte). Not only was the nurse horrified when the scale read 120 pounds, but my friend laughed, ran back to our classroom, and announced the figure to everyone. I can remember feeling terribly hurt, and somehow punished for a wrong I had done.

The other betrayal was far more subtle. It took the form of the school nurse starting a "fat club" based on the idea that together fat kids could lose weight if they discussed their mutual problems. I was horrified at the thought of joining a group of *them*, probably because I didn't want to admit that I was "that" fat. Anyway, I avoided the nurse, did not join the club, and tried to employ other means to prove that being fat didn't matter.

A pattern of success in other areas—I had the lead in a Christmas play and was becoming an accomplished flutist—was established, yet once successful I would always quit. I figured that once I reached the top there was nowhere to go but down, so I quit while I was ahead, feeling that nothing good ever lasts long.

The other main development of my early childhood years was the creation of a vivid and secret fantasy world. As I frequently played alone, I would try to pretend that I was anything but fat and myself. Instead of being dull, I was a wild horse or a beautiful girl. Later, I even wrote down and named "my family," all of those characters I imagined myself to be. Since discussing this topic upsets me, and makes me feel very deviant, I think that I had better finish the fantasy section now, even though it will upset the chronology of the paper. As I grew older, every night before sleeping I escaped into my imaginary world. I frequently was male, terribly thin, and I had always been dealt a rough deal in life by someone so that others would pity me. I don't know if this is directly related to my being overweight or not, but it became a very major part of my life, especially in high school when other girls dated. At that time I hated being a girl since boys always seemed to have the upper hand in asking girls out. I think I've said as much about this aspect of my life as I can. I feel it was very "un-normal" behavior, and because of that I find it very difficult to write about.

ADOLESCENT YEARS

Along with being overweight, I matured at a very early age. By the time I entered the sixth grade, I had grown as tall as I ever would, and had been menstruating for over a year. I was also fatter than ever. My mind was also maturing, and my feelings about being overweight had begun to change. During the sixth, seventh, and eighth grades I began to be pressured by doctors, family, and friends to lose weight. This pressure brought about some very distinct responses. I began to want to lose weight, but the mechanics were beyond me. I think I expected (emotionally if not intellectually) that someone would do it for me. While I still didn't accept my obesity as *my* problem, I do remember wishing that someone would put me on a diet and make me stay on it.

Around the sixth grade, there was a glimmer of hope for I was found to be lacking in thyroid. At last there was an answer and the weight wasn't my fault. While the medical imbalance was corrected by drugs in about six months, I lost no weight. My parents tried to help me diet, but long-established eating habits interfered. I remember that the after-school stops other kids made at the local drug store for candy were not made by me, but not participating only helped to further my social isolation.

I dressed very carefully and neatly during those three years. I wanted to disguise my figure, and my mother helped by making most of my clothes. Soon, I was one of the best dressed children in school. But eventually, with so many of my clothes homemade (because they "felt better" rather than because store clothes didn't fit), I became envious of girls who had purchased their wardrobes. It seems odd that I should have come to dislike what most girls wanted—dresses made by their mothers. When I did go shopping, it was an ordeal, for nothing fit, except adult clothes, and they were too old. I can remember after one shopping trip my mother said that I just had to lose some weight, even though she loved me just the way I was.

I didn't feel loved the way I was, so I tried to cover up my fat. I also started plaguing my parents with a phrase I have yet to abandon, "Do you love me?" Another thing I started to do was to wear sweaters or a bulky blue carcoat, every day to school. I never exposed myself by wearing anything tight fitting. I felt that people were always looking at me, criticizing me, and laughing at me. I thought that if I could just cover "me" up, nobody would notice. Of course open teasing was a thing of the past, but my covering up was not really successful, as I discovered at various times.

One thing that reminded me of who I was (a fat person and therefore undesirable) was the school dancing class, which every "normal" child attended. I wanted to be just like everyone else, so naturally I went, too. The only problem was that I usually did very little dancing. Believe me, it is no fun having to ask a boy to dance with you (a barbaric turnabout custom used at least once every class), only to be turned down. Even my clothes couldn't protect me. You just can't wear bulky sweaters over a party dress. I can remember one of my friends saying at one dance that her mother had a dress just like mine. Such comments did little to make me feel like a little girl.

Around the seventh or eighth grade, I found another way to hide—lying to my parents. I know this doesn't sound very logical, but I stopped weighing myself so that I would not know how bad the "problem" really was. When my mother would ask me how much I weighed, I would give her a fair estimate based on the last time I stepped on the scale and how much weight I thought I could safely say I had lost. I knew that more than anything else my parents disliked lying, but somehow I could accept myself as a liar more easily than I could as a fat person. I think I was afraid that they wouldn't love me if I didn't lose weight. I don't think I realized that losing my parents' trust was a far surer way to threaten our relationship than being fat. Why I felt I could lose their love in the first place I do not know, for they have never given me any reason that I can remember to feel that way. Perhaps the only person I really wanted to lie to was myself.

Like all good things, my deception came to an end when I was discovered during a visit to the doctor for a physical. Right up to the point of stepping on the scale, something they had a hard time getting me to do, I had my mother convinced that I weighed almost fifteen pounds less. The anxiety the lying had caused was terrible, but it was nothing compared to the way I felt when they found out. I cried hysterically. What was worse, my mother was not angry with me but was upset with herself that I should feel the necessity to lie in the first place. For a fleeting moment I tried to recover a little self esteem by saying that the scale was wrong, but that got me nowhere. My mother stayed and talked to the doctor while I waited outside. I was far too upset to go on with the examination. The doctor suggested that my parents take me to a psychiatrist if I couldn't diet, which they did not do. This recommendation shocked me, and I entered high school with a much different picture of myself. At last I knew I was deviant; I accepted the fact, and I began to act accordingly. I had struggled so hard to remain normal before, that I guess I was the last person to admit I had a problem, one which only I could solve.

HIGH SCHOOL AND ON

By the time I reached my freshman year in high school, I stood five feet four-and-one-fourth inches tall and weighed 167 pounds. I was what might be termed a "lucky fatty," for my weight was well distributed for conceal-ment, the majority being carried in my hips and upper legs. I did, however, look much older than my fourteen years, and my attitudes toward life were that of an older person; partly because I had had more association with adults than with peers, and partly due to the quiet scholastic outlook I had devel-oped. I still employed coping techniques which allowed me to live with myself, but I now faced my deviancy with a sort of resignation, and came to expect very little from other kids, especially boys. How this attitude developed and was maintained I will now try to explain by relating some of my high school experiences.

One of the big pushes in my high school was dating, and I, like my girl friends, wanted to go to dances and parties. In this area, my deviancy was a great handicap, since fat girls were not usually asked out. When I saw an unattractive girl holding hands or dating some boy, I would tell myself that she must be putting out more than a good girl should. I was determined that some boy should get to know me beyond the surface, and come to like me for myself. However, for three years, I had no dates.

One of the most painful date-related events in my freshman year was a girl-ask-boy affair. I was determined to prove that I could get a date just like anyone else, and here at last was an opportunity where I could make the first move. Before going any further, I must explain that although I was no beauty, I still expected to get a prince charming, and the boy I decided to ask was a good looking classmate I had admired from afar for a long time. When I finally called Jim (my victim's name), I thought he would be more likely to accept over the phone than he would if he were looking right at me. This strategy proved effective and I was surprised and delighted when he said yes. The next day Jim called to say that he couldn't go to the dance since it was his little brother's birthday that day, and he had forgotten about it when he accepted. I did not believe his excuse then, and I still don't. I felt let down and ashamed. I dreaded having to face Jim in class, and I avoided him for a long time. This was my one and only attempt at dating for at least two years, but I did find other ways to substitute for a non-existent social life.

One of the first things I did was get a job at the public library. In this way, I occupied my weekend and after-school time. I remember more than once telling someone I would not go to a dance because I *had* to work on that day, and I felt greatly relieved at being able to legitimately excuse myself. As I did with school work, I excelled at my job and was the first high school student to ever be allowed to work as a clerk and wait on patrons instead of just shelving books, the usual position for students. I also received numerous pay increases of which I was very proud, for they were tangible representations of my accomplishment. Once again, though, I was dealing with adults—in this case, middle-aged women, usually unmarried or divorced. I was encouraged to go into library work as a career, but once again I was brought up short, for I wanted marriage and a family, two things most of the women I worked with did not have. It was sort of like moving from one socially stigmatized position into another. By the end of my senior year in high school, it was something of a relief to leave my part-time library job and take a full-time summer job as a typist in Los Angeles. Although I gave a better salary and more work as reasons for leaving, I think it was more a matter of wanting to break loose from what had become an all-too-comfortable position with a bleak future.

My job was not the only excuse I had for not dating in high school. Another outlet, aside from academic achievement, was music. As I mentioned earlier, I play the flute, but for my freshman year in high school I was not a member of the band, since the band was considered to be a refuge for weirdos and outcasts. By my sophomore year, at the request of my high school counselor, I rejoined the band, so as to not let all my talents go to waste. I encountered a problem right away, as a result of my obesity, getting a band uniform—the girls' uniforms were no different from the boys'. I refused to give my measurements out loud in class, and escaped by coming in early the morning of uniform-fitting day and explaining my dilemma to the band teacher. I would probably have had to think of something else had the instructor not been overweight himself, but he understood and let me get my uniform privately. Anyway, band participation allowed me to go to football games as a part of a group, but excused me from going to the dances afterward since the uniform was not proper attire. Once in uniform, I was quite a sight. In pictures of the school band I look something like the team's quarterback, and I was practically indistinguishable from the males in the band.

You may wonder by now why I didn't lose weight, the obvious solution to my problem. I tried many diets, but they didn't work because I really didn't want them to work. I had come to accept my situation and had adjusted. Although I was unhappy at being left out, I came to wonder if it was really my weight problem that was holding me back. In a twisted way, my stigma offered a type of security, for it automatically (at least to my way of thinking) excused me from part of life. I increasingly began to worry that I wouldn't be accepted if I were thin, because it might be me, my personality or something inside me, rather than my body that was repulsive. If I didn't lose weight, I would never have to face that possibility. Also, I had been fat and been treated as an ugly person for so long that I had come to view myself as ugly. I really didn't expect much more than leftovers.

As I have already mentioned, most of my time in high school was dateless, but toward the end of my junior year I was asked out. You might say "great," but the circumstances of my dating and the final outcome only served to reinforce a growing low opinion of myself.

John, my would-be boyfriend, was an extremely homely boy. His face was covered with acne, he had carrot-red hair, and his voice was immature and squeaky. Moreover, he was a twin, and it was his twin brother I met in my third-year Spanish class. Apparently, John's brother (the more forceful of the two) had a date for the junior-senior prom, and he was on the lookout for a girl for John. I will never forget his humiliating (but correct) assumption that I was dateless when he told me that maybe his brother would ask me if he didn't find someone else soon. Even though I didn't know John and didn't like his brother, I hoped all that week that John wouldn't find a date. He didn't, and he asked me to the dance one week before it was to take place, saying something to the effect that since we were both dateless we might as well go together. I accepted, only to find it a great hassle to get a formal dress on such short notice, especially considering my figure and the fact that almost every high school in the area had a prom at that time of the year. Anyway, I got my dress one day before the dance, looked quite good, and had a fairly good time. The prom was not exactly a perfectly wonderful evening, and I felt as if John and I were both accepting second best just to be able to go to a dance. I remember that inside I had to agree when one of my friends, upon learning that I was going with John, told me, "I thought even you could do better than that, Joan." I know that given my attitude toward John, I should never have accepted another date with him, but I did, and I think we both were trying to be a part of something that had been denied us for so long. I found John to be a very persistent suitor; telephone calls, movies, and a string of letters over the summer vacation. One special problem that developed in our romance was that I never wanted John to kiss me because of his acne, and yet, at the same time, I was very hurt that he never tried. I felt as if I had been lied to. Dating came nowhere near being the great thing I had imagined it to be.

By the beginning of my senior year, I was tired of John, and yet I was afraid to lose him. I dieted while I dated him and lost some twenty pounds. We gradually went our own ways, but in the middle of the year, John asked me to go to the graduation night party with him as he didn't want to pay the $20 fee (charged of each student attending) and not have a date. I should have never accepted on that basis, but I did, only to be told two days before graduation that John had changed his mind and was going with another girl. There I was, stuck for the $20 I had paid for my ticket and about $60 invested in a dress, shoes, and a hairdo. More than that, there was the humiliation. I was determined to go, with or without an escort. My brother came to my rescue and took me to the party. In fact, I had a much better time with him than I had ever had with John.

The only other social activity I attempted to become a part of in high school was the service clubs. Membership in such clubs was very prestigious, and during my junior year I applied to three of them. Although everyone was supposed to have an equal chance at membership, I was turned down by all three, while most of my friends were accepted in one or more clubs. The refusal that sticks in my mind was the one that said, "You do not meet our standards."

By the time I entered college, I had gained back about eight pounds. I hated my freshman year, as I was cut off by physical distance from the support of my family. I felt like a reject, kept mostly to myself, and did little outside of going to class and studying. My only male acquaintance that first year was a great disappointment, as he never asked me for a date. His only interest was in whether or not I would go to bed with him. I wouldn't, so our relationship was short-lived. I went home nearly every weekend, and cried most every time I was brought back. My self-image sunk lower and lower, especially when I became our dorm's most exchanged roommate, having gone through three different roommates in only one and one-half quarters. My last roommate was another outcast—an older girl, blind in one eye—who had undergone intensive psychiatric treatment when she had stopped eating entirely about two years earlier because of some emotional hangup. Mary, my roommate, kept a tight grasp on me by telling me all of her problems every day. Her depression became my depression, and by the end of my freshman year, I didn't ever want to go back. I did, though, since dropping out was unthinkable. However, I never roomed with Mary again.

During my sophomore year, I made friends mostly with girls who were also stigmatized—a blind girl and a paraplegic among them. I was a reader for the former and the latter finally succeeded in getting me to be her attendant. Once again I was in the situation of protecting myself by making social contacts only with those who were no threat to me. I still excused myself from social events by working. I went to the counseling center on campus once, but quit when it was suggested that I join an aggressiveness group. I had no desire to confess my problem to a group of other people nor did I want to give in and join something I felt was designed to help sick people.

I think my college depression can best be summarized by the way I felt when both my roommate and my paraplegic friend had dates one Friday night and I didn't. The only outlet I found that night for the anger I felt was the candy vending machine in the basement of the dormitory. How ironic that I should perpetuate the very thing that was helping to keep me home by eating candy.

Well, I suppose you are expecting a happy ending to my story since I have (1) lost weight and (2) been talking in a very reflective way. There is no happy ending, but I can tell you how I feel now and what has happened. I dieted this summer because my brother, who had gained weight upon marriage, succeeded in "losing." This was an incentive for me since I have always competed with my brother. Another factor was that I had come to a point of wanting to know if it was my physical appearance alone that had kept me from being socially accepted. I now weigh 129 pounds and plan to lose at least another 10 pounds. This loss in weight, however, has not been accompanied by any increase in dates or change of mental attitude, and I fear that it really is my internal make-up that is deviant. I still feel fat, and no matter how many times my friends or parents tell me how nice I look, I don't believe them. Perhaps this is in part a result of my parents telling me that I was a nice person, and not unattractive, even when I weighed much more. I think, however, it is more a result of so many years of facing the world as a stigmatized person. I do not know how to get dates, let alone what type of behavior is expected on a date. If I sound bitter, it's because I am tired of having to do all of the changing. I don't like the fact that I have allowed my life to be regulated by the opinions and expectations of other people to the point of feeling that I have very little individuality left. As for the future, I don't know. I used to be sure that I wanted a family and a career in social work, but now I don't really care. All I know is that I have an increasing desire to be loved by someone and to be able to give someone else my love. I don't even think it is love so much as acceptance that I am seeking. If nothing else, I hope I have shown to what extent being obese, and others' reactions to obesity, as well as the various rationalizations one entertains under these circumstances, can influence and even create a lifestyle.

INTERPRETIVE FRAMEWORK

In viewing my obesity as a form of deviancy, I have considered it from the interactionist perspective.[2] Certainly my situation might have been different in another time or place, for example, during the Renaissance, when heavier women were the ideal. Even today in other countries and cultures, normal women are much heavier than in the United States. It is, then, the people with whom I interact in specific settings who give me cues as to my deviancy. As shown previously, such cues caused me to alter my behavior and to define my life from a different standpoint than an un-obese person might have defined hers.

Goffman's discussion of stigma is particularly relevant [his book is cited by page number from this point on] : "Society establishes means of categorizing persons and the complement of attributes felt to be ordinary and natural for members of these categories" (p. 2).[3] In a sense, society defines man through interactions which cause him to have a certain self-concept, in terms of which he will react (p. 132). When a person is recognized as possessing a quality different from others, and that quality is of a less desirable sort, he is viewed in terms of that single difference or stigma instead of being viewed as a whole person (p. 3). A stigma, or negatively different quality, causes certain anticipations on the part of unstigmatized persons as to how the stigmatized person will act, and he is thus stereotyped (p. 4). Although being overweight is a physical attribute, it does not become a stigma until it is pointed out as such. In my case, stereotyping began with being called fatty, and eventually came to entail my exclusion from certain activities simply because I was not "that type," as in the case of social clubs.

My stigma resulted in my becoming a "discredited" rather than a "discreditable" person (p. 4), and I did not have the problem of worrying about whether or not my differentness would be discovered. Yet, in another sense, I was discreditable to myself, as long as I did not accept my deviance. My fantasy world, choice of clothes, and refusal to weigh myself all indicate that my self-perception was different than those of "normals" perceiving me; normal is defined here as one who does not break sharply with what is expected of him (p. 6). I tried to maintain that I was a normal person and was partially successful in this each time I got good grades or won a music contest. But as Goffman points out, the stigmatized person never really feels accepted by others on equal grounds no matter what they say (p. 7). I would certainly agree with this: I asked my parents often if they loved me, because I could not believe myself lovable without continual reassurance.

I find especially relevant the following statement from Goffman: "Shame becomes a central possibility, arising from the individual's perception of his own attributes as being a defiling thing to possess . . . . The immediate presence of normals is likely to reinforce this split between self-demands and self" (p. 7). It is hard for me to explain how this applies except to say that it is accurate. Upon accepting the values of normals, how else could I regard myself except as an ugly person? I did not want to expose my body to others, or even to myself in front of a mirror. It became a sort of paradoxical situation—I wanted to be accepted as I was, while at the same time I was disgusted with myself. I can remember feeling ashamed when I saw my figure reflected in store windows and wishing that no one else could see what I saw.

Naturally, being stigmatized results in certain reactions on the part of the person stigmatized, and I believe that I have covered most of my behavioral adaptions. In contact with normals, I frequently felt as if I were being watched or criticized, a feeling Goffman describes as being "on" (p. 14). If I walked by a group of people and they giggled, I always felt it was I who was being laughed at or discussed. Currently, I find myself walking from classes on a little-frequented path, even though my stigma is not so obvious now. It is as if I expect criticism and therefore avoid contact with possible critics. Some people have said my behavior is stand-offish or frightening at first, but that I am nice once you get to know me. This probably results from my insecurity and a feeling I have that it is better to come on strong—a sort of a get them before they get you approach (p. 15).

Although my stigma caused me to be discredited rather than discreditable, I attempted to "pass," or cover up my problem through such things as my choice of dress (p. 42). I even went so far as to send my fifth-grade pen pal baby pictures of myself when we exchanged letters. I told him I was joking, but in reality I was ashamed to send a current picture of myself, and by this maneuver I could be that beautiful person in my fantasy world since we would never meet each other.

My main association with other overweight people was in my own family, where I found certain supports (p. 28). I can remember my mother telling me that she just had "all the more to love" because I was overweight, but somehow this was always a dubious statement in my mind. My father, who had always been overweight, tried to comfort me when I didn't have dates by saying that his experiences were similar at my age, and look how lucky he had been in finding my mother. Once again, this was not very comforting because while my parents were established and had each other, I didn't, and still don't, have any personal relationship with anyone outside of my immediate family. I don't know if this makes much sense, but it's like someone who has a million dollars telling a penniless man that his future will be rich. Such statements tend to provide small consolation.

Social information about myself (information about the more or less usual or abiding characteristics of a person conveyed in the presence of other persons through certain signs, pp. 43–44) was in part conveyed by the people with whom I interacted (p. 47), and my weight had a good deal to do with my choice of friends. I tended to associate with people who were also stigmatized and not as much of a threat to my security. In high school, almost everybody belonged to a group: the in-group and socialites, the tough group, and so on. My associates were mostly non-group members, and at one point a few of us considered starting a losers club since we were a group no one else wanted. I have already mentioned my college friends who also tended to be losers. In choosing friends, it was as if I were protected, because I was needed for my services while at the same time I was excused from normal activities. I didn't realize how strongly others identified me by my associations until I was called by the university's Special Services office in my sophomore year, and was asked whose attendant I would be the next year. I was shocked that they had assumed that because I had helped my friends I would be a professional attendant.

My being allied with some non-stigmatized individuals eventually caused me to wonder what was wrong with me, a fact that relates to Goffman's point that if a person associates with normals in certain instances he will attempt to view himself through normal eyes (p. 107). I became most self-critical when I was with my most physically normal friends, perhaps because I embraced their views of obesity, which in turn produced in me feelings of ambivalence (p. 106). Although I hated myself for being fat and feared more than anything gaining weight, I also feared losing weight and finding out that my unpopularity was due to my personality. I knew where I stood in life in terms of being a stigmatized individual, but I had no experience in being normal.

The prospect of losing weight also caused anxiety because I was afraid of losing my "in-group or real group" alignment, that is, my family, who were also overweight (p. 112). They accepted me as I was, and in some ways it took a long time to realize that they would also accept me if I were not overweight. The out-group or normal society also defined me in terms of being fat, especially with helpful hints, like what new diets I should try. All of this constructive criticism had to be accepted cheerfully on the basis that everyone, myself included, knew that I would benefit from losing weight. I developed a very sarcastic type of wit which was useful in dealing with such advice, and I even told one person that he had better be nice to me or I would sit on him. Humor became a good way for me to put people off by making them think that I viewed life with a "jolly" attitude. It also served as a good cover-up for my true feelings of resentment and hurt at such remarks. I also found that out-group friends just loved to tempt you to overeat and reinforce your stigma, so that you could again be criticized, which probably affirms their normality. I can think of an instance in which my roommate commented that my weight would hinder my ability to keep up on a hiking trip, should I go with her, and that I would need special help. This type of attitude caused me to eat very lightly in her presence so that she could not criticize me further.

In conclusion, now that I have lost and am still losing weight, I am finding (as I noted earlier) that changing one's body is easier than changing one's lifestyle. Perhaps I shall go back to the counselling center for help, perhaps not. In any case, I hope that this autobiographical sketch has given some insight into the consequences and effects of eating too much. The entire process is rather like a slow social suicide.

NOTES

[1] Gary Alexander, "You Can Lose Weight," *The Plain Truth, a Magazine of Understanding*, XXXVI (November 1971), 27–31.

[2] Earl Rubington and Martin S. Weinburg, *Deviance: The Interactionist Perspective* (New York: Macmillan Co., 1968).

[3] Erving Goffman, *Stigma: Notes on the Management of Spoiled Identity* (Englewood Cliffs, N.J.: Prentice-Hall, Inc., 1963).

Getting Straight: Reflections of a Former Addict

Octavio Rodriquez

I became a drug addict at the age of fourteen. At that time, I used only marijuana. I was kind of a late bloomer in comparison to my old peer group because I had been in Boys' School for about eighteen months for truancy, incorrigibility, and violation of probation. When I was released I came home and discovered that most of my friends, well, all my friends—my group—had become a drug culture. At that time most of them were experimenting with marijuana. I had quite a few reservations about it in the beginning, probably because of the Boys' School. It was a Catholic school and I had absorbed quite a lot of the doctrine, so for the first six months I wasn't involved. I sort of just ignored it, and there was a hassle with it because anywhere I went everybody wanted to turn me on. I was a square, a "lame," in Spanish, "estas tepado."

During this time, I really felt kind of alone; I didn't have anything in com-

mon with the guys I used to hang around with and I sort of found myself
spending more and more time by myself. I was having a hard time adjusting
back to the streets. My family didn't help me at all. My father was an alcoholic, and I found myself trying to avoid him as much as possible. I spent
most of my time running around the streets. Actually, I was a loner because
I wasn't doing what everyone else was doing and, after awhile, I just sort of
said screw it, and I started becoming one of the boys again. I started with
marijuana, and actually the first few times nothing happened. I wasn't really
out for the kick, I was more out for the acceptance. Even after I started knowing what the high was, I wasn't really too enthusiastic about it, but it was the
only way to be one of the boys.

After marijuana, I took reds a couple of times, but I never enjoyed them
because all they did was knock me out. So I went back to weed and that was
all I did—smoke weed—for a couple of years. Well, not a couple of years—
I take that back—for about six months, and during this time most of us were
really experimenting. We were eager to experiment, I should say, but we never
had anything around. Eventually, we came into contact with heroin. I had
never really been afraid to try it. As a matter of fact, I had sort of resigned
myself to it . . . it was inevitable. Everybody else had gone that way so why
not me? I was about fifteen then, and I tried it. It's a weird feeling. I guess
there was really a lot of status in it then for us, and I had the supreme status—
I was a junkie. I adapted to it very well, probably because I was having a hard
time trying to establish relationships with people—I couldn't get to know
people very well. I was very defensive, and I felt at times I didn't know how
to act with people. I kept thinking I was back in Boys' School, but I discovered that if you were a junkie in my neighborhood people really didn't
expect too much from you. That was an easy way out: if I became a heroin
addict, I wouldn't have to try to meet people and people would leave me
alone (which may not have been what I really wanted). Well, anyway, heroin
sort of satisfied my feelings of frustration, and I really became quite involved
in it—as a user mostly. I didn't get involved in hustling at all at that time.
I was just using it. Most of us had little experience with hustling people, or
with doing anything for that matter. We were just interested in getting high.

Eventually, sooner or later, you have to make money as a heroin addict.
My problems really began when I became involved in dealing, but not in
heroin, in marijuana. I was leery of selling heroin because I had known
junkies too well, and the first thing you learn is that a junkie will sell his
soul for a cap; and if that means snitching there's no honor among junkies.
So I knew that if I were to get involved with selling heroin, I would have to
make everybody happy; and if I were to cross just one junkie, one "tecato,"
there'd be no reason for him not to snitch me out. But that's the way it goes

for all of us and for most of the people I hung around with, so I just kept away from heroin, and I concentrated on selling marijuana. A connection I made was introduced to me by a narcotics agent. I guess it was a good case of entrapment. This guy, his name was Jones the Narc, introduced me to a three-time loser. The man, Smith, had the connections and he was game to be a runner, so I, with an investment of about $50, took him up on it, and in no time—within about two weeks—we were selling $1500 worth of marijuana a week.

Things were going very well for me as far as my acceptance problems were concerned. Everybody wanted to be my friend, and I loved it. I had all the friends I needed, all the girlfriends, all the clothing, the car, the money, and I found myself into the little hustling kick. It was fun. I was my own boss—no one bothering me, no one telling me what to do or how to do it—and I gained prestige. So there I was, sitting on top of the world. But like all trips it had to come to an end. The narc who had introduced us had saddled my runner at the border, and he was arrested early in October of 1963. Up to this time, I had been very careful about who I had sold to, and I really wasn't worried about the narc, even though I knew who had tipped them off to Smith. When Smith was arrested in Tijuana, he had all of my money so I was broke except for what little marijuana I had, and I quickly sold that. But I was in the clear. Well, that's what I thought.

On September 11 or October 11 (whatever the state indictment says the date was), I was coming home early one morning, and I was stopped by the Santa Ana Police Department on a routine investigation. The arresting officer asked me a few questions, and that was about it. He was about ready to let me go when his backup officer showed up. That was really bad luck because I knew him. The first thing he did was tell me to get out of my car, and then he began searching it. He found on the back seat—and this was how mickey mouse it was—thirteen seeds and a couple of roaches. He told me then that I was going to go to Chino, and he said, "Well, we finally got you, and it was just a matter of time." And I thought he was kidding, because I figured it would be more trouble than was worth it to them to take me to court for thirteen seeds and fragments, but he was serious. They took me in, and they booked me for possession of marijuana. I got out on bail the next morning, but there went all my money. I was broke, and I didn't know what to do. I tried to see a lawyer, but he wanted a large retainer. I went out and got a job, but the money I was going to make on that job wasn't enough to pay for the retainer before my trial date, so I was in a pinch. Like a fool, I went around and borrowed some money. I had decided to go down south by myself, with a friend, to score just enough to get the retainer fee. We went down south and scored, but we got kind of wiped out and a little reckless and did a poor job of stashing the weed. We came across the border at six o'clock in the morning, which is probably one of the worse times to cross, and we were arrested—that's what the second state indictment for illegal importation and concealment was about.

I was tired. I hadn't really realized how tired I was of narcotics. I had spent the last three years every day blowing weed, shooting stuff, running around, never taking care of myself—living in a fantasy world really. From the moment I was up, I was loaded until the moment I knocked out in the evenings. I was really exhausted physically as well as mentally, and when I was caught for that possession in Santa Ana it made me aware of how tired I really was. But I didn't want to go to jail. I wanted to give it all up, but I just didn't want to go to jail, and I couldn't find a solution. I knew if I stayed in Santa Ana I'd be around the group all the time, and probably to this day I'd be a junkie, fixing every day with no other goal in life except fixing. Most of my friends are like that. They're thirty-year old junkies. All they think about is sticking a needle in their arm. But I was confused, and I was trying to find a solution to my problem, and when I got busted down south, that was it—that was my ticket away from home, and I really wasn't too shocked or too scared. I accepted it, and I really looked forward to some kind of rest.

My partner and I were put in jail, and we both pleaded not guilty. I went to trial, and I was found guilty, and because I was under 21, I was sentenced under the youth act, and given something like six months to six years with eligibility for parole instead of a straight five years which the law demands for adult offenders.

I spent four months in a San Diego county jail, and during this time I was very seriously giving some kind of thought to what I wanted to do with myself. I was trying to find some kind of direction. I knew there must be something more to it than sticking a needle in my arm every day, so I thought that once I got to prison, I would try to find an answer to my questions about identity, acceptance, what was important to me and what wasn't.

The first thing I think I did when I got to prison was to get rid of much of my own identity. I began by cutting all my hair off. I got a butch—something I had never done before—just shaved my head bald. I next cut my partner loose. We were in the same prison together, but during the year I was there I talked to him about twenty times. I really wanted nothing to do with him and I avoided him as much as possible. I also cut my Chicano reference group loose. I didn't want to be a part of any group—nothing. And I became a recluse, really. I wasn't interested in becoming one of the stereotypes, as I had been in the streets. When you go to prison, there are all these roles you can fall into: you can become a jailhouse pimp, a jailhouse lawyer, a jailhouse psychiatrist, a jailhouse sociologist, a jailhouse punk, a jailhouse intellectual, and so forth. Well, I didn't want to become anything. So I guess I became a jailhouse hermit. I made very few friends while I was there. All the time I was there I think I ran with about eight guys—a Jew, a Cuban, two Greeks, two Anglos, and two Chicanos. I wasn't involved in any kind of sports activity—I really stuck to myself.

Another thing I didn't do was to get close to anyone in authority. I avoided the guards, and my probation officer or caseworker. He called himself a parole officer—let me correct that—but I guess he was a caseworker. I avoided my probation officer because the only thing I wanted to know from him was when I was getting out, and he would never tell me. Every time I asked him he would always say, "I don't know; it depends on you." And after I went to the board hearings, and I was shot down, I'd ask him why didn't I get out, "Didn't you recommend that I be released?" He would answer by saying, "Yeah, I did, but Washington shot you down." They would always say that Washington made the final decisions. It was just passing the buck, so why spend my time trying to get an answer that he wasn't going to give me.

I didn't go to church, which most people do in jail—they figure that if they go to church the priest will give them a good letter of recommendation. Well, the priest they had there didn't know whether he was coming or going. I mean he had 600 Catholics asking for letters of recommendation, and he would write out the same letter for every guy that asked him. That was just a standard procedure. I didn't want to hassle for it. It wasn't worth anything to me.

Most of the guards I met I think to this day were perverted. I can recall only two that could pass for human. The rest delighted in the position of authority they had over you. They abused it and they took advantage of it. If they didn't like the way you looked, they'd needle you. I've determined that in a state joint the trouble is usually between inmates. In a federal joint, it's the opposite. There wasn't much friction between inmates, but a lot of friction between inmates and guards. So I avoided them because I knew that was the best policy. I could really never take prison very seriously, that is, the prison officials. I'll give you an example: When you first go to prison you spend thirty days in ANO. It's what's called admissions and orientation. The purpose of this is primarily to socialize you to the prison system—to indoctrinate you really—to tell you what to do and what not to do. Besides that, they have thirty days to check you out, to find out if you're homosexual or if you're going to be a troublemaker or what. And they give you a psychological test—an I.Q. test I think—and a physical and everything. And after thirty days of this evaluation you go before a placement committee consisting of your caseworker, your social ward and custodian, your social ward and treatment, and a few other people; besides those, you have quite a few visitors from the streets that sit in—I guess they are acting P.O.'s (probation officers) and judges and what not. You go into this room and they're all seated at this long table and they put you in the middle in front of them, and they begin discussing you, but not one of them ever looks at you. They're all looking at each other and discussing: "Wow, this is the score on this, this is the score on that, and this is what we found out about that." Finally, one of them looks at you and says, "Well, what do you think of the place?" or something stupid like that. And you usually say, "I like it. It's a nice place; it's wonderful." And they tell you, anyway they told me, "We have the results of your I.Q. test and it shows that you have above average intelligence. You know what that means?" I said no. And he says, "That means we're not going to have any trouble with you, are we?" I said, "No, sir." He said, "We'll try to find a job for you—find a unit, a cellblock where they will place you." So I figured with an above average I.Q. I'd land a pretty good job, maybe a clerk or something. That night when my job was posted, I found out where they could use me most. They assigned me to vegetable preparation—peeling potatoes. So after that I just sort of gave up on them all, completely. I wanted nothing to do with them, and the whole year I was there I had very little contact with them. I saw my P.O. after release from my ANO and twice before the parole hearings. And all he did was sit me down, pull out his little file box, look in there to see if I had any writeups—and both times there were none—and said, "Fine, see you in a week," and that was it. I think that just by avoiding the officials I became a model prisoner.

Well, anyway, after about ten months, I went to the second parole hearing, and I was cut loose about two months later in January. I was released through the pre-release guide program—the halfway house in Los Angeles. I had to spend at least three months there, and it was really to my advantage, because in the old days when you got out of prison, they gave you an old suit, five dollars, and a pat on the butt, and said don't come back. What was a guy going to do with five dollars? So this program was a gradual release. I went to live there on January 6, I believe, and I was released in March. I had been there two weeks when I landed a job in Los Angeles in a shipping dock for an importing company. That was a good start.

But the first time I went home for a day and the weekend, the weekend passed and I was loaded again. I was blowing weed. I wasn't even out of prison yet. I mean all that time in jail hadn't straightened me out. There I was. I wasn't even out and I was already blowing up. So that really disgusted me, because I didn't want to ever go back to prison. I just didn't know what to do. I knew one thing though, that I couldn't go back to Santa Ana because I'd be caught again in no time and I'd be in jail without parole. So I decided to stay in Los Angeles for awhile, at least until my parole was over. On my parole plan which I put in at the halfway house, I stated that I would stay in L.A. and work in L.A., and they decided it was a good idea. I was released from the halfway house, and everything went fine for me. I had a good job. It didn't pay much but it was good in the sense that it gave me pride. I felt good working and I was independent—I had my own apartment and a little spending money, and I was kind of happy with that. But every time I went down to Santa Ana I ended up being loaded again, and guys would come look me up in L.A. and before I knew it I would be getting stoned; and in about six months, I was shooting heroin on the weekends.

Things went on like this for three months until one night when I went to a motel with a couple of friends for a fix. I was just a little dreamy that night, and I kept asking for a little more and a little more. I overdosed and they left me. All I can remember is that I ran out of the motel room into the streets, and that was it. The next thing I knew, I was lying in someone's back yard in the mud—it was raining. I woke up in the rain and I was scared. I thought I was dead. I was in shock, I guess, for a week, because I had come so close to dying. I couldn't believe that my so-called friends would leave me to die, and that I was so stupid that I would put myself in that situation. That was the last time I used heroin—and that was four years ago.

It's sad but it's true, I have yet to meet a reformed junkie. *I think the only reason I reformed was because it scared the hell out of me—no other reason at all. To this day, the first thing I say in the morning is I'm not going to shoot stuff, and that's my only rehabilitation program—take it day by day.* [Emphasis added.] I think sometimes it's kind of foolish to say I'll never use heroin again because it's such a long-range goal. And it hurts when you fail. When I say I'm not going to fix today, that's a small thing to do, and after awhile, it just builds up. For me, it's been four years.

For me, I think, drugs—heroin—replaced people. I wanted to make contact, but I just couldn't, and when I did, the relationships usually had no meaning. I had a friend with whom I was very close when I was younger—about sixteen or seventeen. He was probably the only person that I could be honest with and frank, and not have to worry about being put down. He was killed when we were seniors in high school, and that sort of set me back a little. When I think about that, I think it might have been the cause of a lot of my problems with drugs. I always resorted to drugs when I couldn't interact with people. It was easier to go home and turn on a radio or a TV or a record player than go out and try to establish some kind of meaningful relationship. I think the reason that when I got out of prison I went back to drugs right away was because there wasn't anybody there that I could talk to, someone I could relate to. It was much easier to go get high again and hide from everyone.

3. THE SOCIO-LEGAL MANAGEMENT OF DEVIANCE

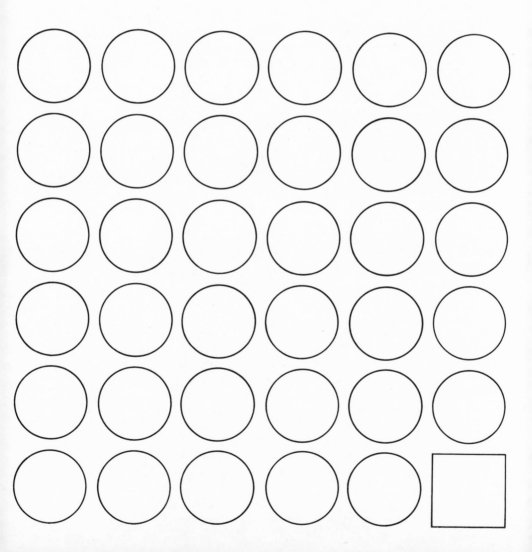

THE SOCIO-LEGAL MANAGEMENT OF DEVIANCE

3. It is generally held that the bureaucratization of "people-processing" agencies has led to greater rationality.[1] By this it is meant that the objective, dispassionate conduct of business according to a consistent set of abstract rules by a hierarchy (based on expertise) of personnel pursuing a career within the agency, provides an organizational arrangement best able to serve the greatest number of persons per unit time.[2] When, as is more and more the case, people-processing agencies are in the business of processing deviants, then it is further assumed that one of the key goals of the agency is the reduction or elimination of deviance. In the following readings, agency personnel come to believe that persons seeking their services have, in one form or another, exceeded the bounds of normative behavior.

Positivistic sociologists have formulated such deviant behavior as the unproblematic transgression by individuals of some formal set of rules, such as passing a red light, getting less than an acceptable score (objectively determined) on a driving test, or attempting to defraud a welfare agency. However, the transgressions that bureaucrats have in mind when they label their clients deviant, and the way in which they arrive at this definition of the situation, are very different. The criteria workers use to establish the respectable or deviant nature of persons coming before them frequently have little or nothing to do with the individual's actual violation of some formal rule or set of rules.[3] Rather the definition is based upon the worker's ad hoc interpretation and evaluation of the client's good character, responsible nature, moral worth, good intentions, or future behavior.

It is important in studying the labeling process to appreciate the definition of the situation held by the victim (the one being labeled) and the labeler.[4] (The former will be referred to here as the *service seeker*, the latter as the *service worker*.) The form and content of the interactions that result from these encounters will, to a large extent, be determined by the meanings that the service seeker and service worker confer upon each other's behavior.

What must the service seeker do or say, how must he look, or what must he indicate to the service worker in order to acquire a deviant or respectable identity? Generally, the service seeker's successful presentation of self to the service worker will hinge not upon the worker's objective determination of the seeker's innocence or guilt with respect to the alleged violation of some formal rule, but rather upon the worker's "subjective" assessment of the seeker's past behavior and future potential for making trouble for the agency by interfering with the agency's otherwise routine people-processing procedures.[5] The three readings that follow present some specific examples of the general case noted above by discussing in some detail the interactions between traffic court judges and defendants, Department of Motor Vehicles licensing personnel and persons seeking renewal of driver's licenses, and case workers and their clients. The essays will deal with the ways in which service workers define and deal with service seekers and how the latter come to be considered "trouble makers" as a result of their inept efforts at "impression management."[6] One result is that people-processing agencies organized to serve deviants and reduce deviance, frequently create the very problem they seek to eliminate.

Much turns upon the formal constraints placed upon the worker by the bureaucratic agency to process all comers, a number far exceeding his capacity. As a result, service workers are obliged to "accommodate." The way in which they adapt to troubles they routinely encounter on the job, while at the same time convincing themselves and the service seeker (as well as the general public) that they are trusted, competent, and respectable persons, working within the agency rules in pursuit of agency goals will be considered below.

In brief, the following chapter deals with the way in which the bureaucratic organization of deviance is accomplished and comes to be taken for granted by service workers, service seekers, and the public at large.

NOTES

[1] John Kitsuse, "People Processing Institutions," *American Behavioral Scientist,* XIV (Nov.–Dec. 1970).

[2] *From Max Weber: Essays in Sociology,* translated by H. H. Gerth and C. Wright Mills (New York: Oxford University Press, 1946), p. 215.

[3] Egon Bittner, "The Police on Skid-Row: A Study of Peace Keeping," *American Sociological Review,* XXXII (October 1967), 699–715.

[4] Howard S. Becker, *Outsiders* (New York: Free Press, 1963), p. 9.

[5] *op. cit.,* Bittner.

[6] Erving Goffman, *The Presentation of Self In Everyday Life* (New York: Anchor Books, 1959), pp. 208–237.

One, Two, Three, Red Light: Judicial Review in a Traffic Court

Grante Ute

● ● ● Cicourel's analysis of the "Social Organization of Juvenile Justice"
● ● ● (1968) views the relationship between juvenile offender and police
● ● ■ or probation officers in terms of the authorities' attempt to change
the juvenile's conception of himself and to have him accept their blueprint
for how his previously "unsuccessful self" may be made over into a more
adaptive person.[1] Cicourel describes the rhetoric within which this exchange
takes place between the "reforming" agency and the deviant, and shows, in
addition, that this interaction occurs within a certain social organization
which, in itself, has great effects on the temper of the ritual.

According to Cicourel, the authorities' optimal course of action is to have
the juvenile voluntarily admit and express his remorse and describe his plan
to reform. But the juvenile comes to the meeting hoping to gain only a brief
sermon and, if necessary, a short sentence. Sermons are given to show the

evils of criminal acts and to point out a general flaw in the boy's "attitude" toward life. Cicourel goes on to explain the nature of the probation officer-juvenile relationship as one of "trust"—that any actions committed by the juvenile in the time questioned were not really seen as criminal manifestations but as due to "personal" problems or circumstances. Thus, the frequently encountered "neutralizing" statement, "You didn't think, did you?" is offered.

The juvenile is faced with having to accept the authorities' definition of the situation and to play along with his structuring of the events in order to protect himself. Thus, accepting the invitation to show remorse is the most rational means to his ends—termination of the interview and the threat of the authority. "Arguing" from a very weak position (his status of delinquent), the juvenile does not have the right to question the social organization of this relationship. Given no power and the threat of further troubles in court or in the Youth Authority, the juvenile takes the probation officer up on his offer of non-placement in Juvenile Hall as a reward for a quick admission of involvement. Whether he is guilty or not, the juvenile can avoid the bad consequences of fighting the system by admitting whatever it was the officer claimed he was involved in and by accepting the officer's offer that it wasn't really purposively irresponsible (that is, criminal), but excusable on the grounds of personal problems.[2]

It can be seen that by admitting the public definition of himself and the imputed motive, the juvenile gets what he wants—the least trouble from the all-powerful authorities. The probation officer gets what he wants—a "solved" case which can be reported within a paradigm which protects him. By accepting the official view of himself and showing appropriate remorse, the juvenile, in effect, barters away part of his self for a reduced sentence.

In order to examine the social organization of other situations within which people labeled "deviant" try to handle their identities, we sat in on several sessions of the Riverside Municipal Traffic Court. What follows is an analysis of the social organization of traffic court within which defendants (people put in the hapless position of having to protect their selves from the effects of a deviant label) are faced with a social organization which they do not understand. A description of the setting will follow along with the examples of interaction between judge and defendant which will reveal several aspects of the organization of traffic court.

In most cases, when given a citation for a moving violation one may post the bail necessary for the ticket and not appear in court. One's failure to appear is then interpreted as an admission of guilt and a fine is set at the amount of bail. The case is ended. The violator (here a "deviant") loses generally from $10 to $30 and gets a "point" on his driving record in the Department of Motor Vehicles. Other (more frequent or more serious) violators will have to appear. Thus, those who appear in traffic court tend to be those who cannot afford another citation on their record and also those who feel themselves to be innocent of the claims made against them.

What follows in court is a negotiation between the judge and the defend-ant which has less to do with justice and the determination of guilt than it does with neutralizing the "wrath" of the authorities (shown by the amount of the fine) and expediting justice (or enabling the judge to handle perhaps 100 cases in the two sessions of the day set aside for traffic court).

But before proceeding in our description, let us introduce the people in-volved. There are three people composing the court—leaving out the police officer making the citation (who is not present). They include the judge who hears the cases, a court clerk who records their dispositions, and a county marshal or bailiff who explains the deposition to the defendant and generally by his presence adds to the authority of the court. On the other side of the railing sit the defendants, accused of the commission, in Ross's term, of a folk crime—traffic law violations.[3] Ross states that the "criminal behavior in folk crime is rooted, not necessarily in lower-class culture, but in the cul-ture of groups most affected by the social or technological changes that the legislation attempts to control." Looking about *this* courtroom, we would say that the lower class is that class most affected by the automobile.

It is into this situation that the judge walks. He proceeds to address the courtroom with a speech that is well thought-out, and well-worn. The ad-dress reveals several elements of the arraignment process which will become more evident later, during the actual proceedings. The substance of his speech is as follows:

> Nobody likes to get a ticket. But look at it as a safety reminder. Don't look at this one and say how "unlucky" you were; remember the lucky ones where you haven't been picked up. See the other side of the coin.
>
> It should be made clear that I get no commission on the fines collected here. The money goes to a traffic safety fund—to improve highways. There is no appeal to my own self-interest. Look at this as a United Fund contribution to reduce deaths and injuries on the highways.
>
> The average person receives one citation every five years. Depend-ing on how many you have, you may be way above or under the average. This court is empowered to suspend licenses for up until six months. No one here will have his license suspended. Most fines here will fall in the $120–$600 range. You will find that the fines that this court assesses will be substantially below the possible max-imum fines. As a general rule, if you are financially embarrassed, this court will allow you one month in which to pay. If you do not

pay in full by this date, you may work off the fine at the rate of
one day in jail for every $5 of fine.

Within this speech one can clearly see an attempt to "cool out the marks"—
to pacify the unlucky and unhappy defendants. The defendants are told to
restructure their view of the situation they are in—to see the citation not as
an unlucky event, but as a safety reminder. As for the fine (which may be
substantial), they are to view it as a contribution which works toward some
positive good—highway safety. Defendants are also given evidence of how
they stand when compared with other drivers (it is implied that they compare poorly).

Following this assault on a defendant's view of his own driving ability (that
is, on his "self") he is given a taste of what the prescribed "wrath" of the law
is for the offenses which are to be handled. For a first offense, fines up to
$62 may be imposed. But the judge has said that most here will fall in the
$120–$600 range. Thus, the defendant realizes the serious situation he is in.
He is quickly reassured that fines will be assessed far below these amounts,
but the important point is that one *could be* assessed far more. The court also
offers quite liberal payment plans (up to one month), with the option of paying the fine in "kind" (time at the rate of $5 per day in the county jail).
Finally, any suspicion that the judge profits from your trouble is dispelled.

Viewed in this way, one's day in traffic court may be seen as embodying
elements of a "degradation ceremony": both the event and the perpetrator
are seen in an out-of-the-ordinary character (statistically at least); the judge
is seen as a public figure with no private gain to be made from the proceedings; and the denunciation is delivered in the name of super-personal values—
consideration of others and safety. (We do not believe that traffic court is a
successful "degradation ceremony," however. The "wrath" generally is less
moral than financial, and the courtroom's aura of fearsome majesty soon dis-
solves into an atmosphere of a well-meaning bureaucracy at work. Traffic
court does not try to transform the social identity of the defendant. Strong
elements of the "collective conscience"—perhaps the most conspicuously
missing element—are not really aroused. There is no real ritual denunciation
of the offender, and there is no increase in group solidarity as a result of the
"trial.")[4]

In discussing the social organization of the court, we will look at it from
the point of view of the court—the judge, the clerk, and the bailiff. Faced
with the need to handle a great many cases quickly, the judge's primary goal
is to expedite justice—with the emphasis on the expedition. Like the probation officer cited by Cicourel, he makes no attempt to affix guilt or innocence; his primary concern is to clear the court calendar by the easiest means

available. And the easiest means available is for the defendant to plead No Contest so the judge can affix a penalty fine on the spot. But the No Contest plea is similar to the mechanism of pleading guilty to a lesser offense, except that here one is not advised to do so by a public defender or lawyer, but subtly by the judge of the case.[5]

It should be pointed out that it appears that defendants do not realize that they may continue their Not Guilty plea and demand a trial, either by judge or jury—in the morning session, twenty-one of the fifty-three cases pleaded Not Guilty. These excerpts from notes taken in the courtroom will show the plight of the defendant before the court—especially the unsophisticated, or the first defendant before the court in each session. One of the very first persons to face the court was a woman who pleaded Not Guilty to a violation incurred as a result of an accident she had. When asked by the judge if she wanted to plead No Contest and "end the matter here," she replied, "I only want to do what's right." Although the judge didn't say so explicitly, as the morning wore on it became obvious that for the judge "what was right" was to plead Guilty or at least No Contest. (By sitting through twenty or thirty cases before theirs was called, defendants gained some idea of what this No Contest plea meant, one could assume.)

The court's operating definition of what the No Contest pleas meant came from the bailiff, who stepped in on the case of an older man who said he didn't know what No Contest meant. The bailiff's translation ran as follows:

"You may say that you don't want to fight about it any more."

To this the defendant replied, expressing the opinion of most of the other defendants:

"I just want to get it over with."

The No Contest plea may be seen as a "surrender," in one sense, which is brought about under some of the conditions of duress. Take these examples:

J: I could settle the whole matter here if you would enter a plea of No Contest. I could determine the penalty right now.

D: Well . . .

J: Do you plead No Contest?

D: [dejectedly] I guess so.

As the morning wears on, what one gains in knowledge about the operation of the court and one's rights from watching other cases is purchased at the cost of increased inconvenience and time off from work. Take, for example, this man who felt that he was innocent:

D: I don't feel I'm guilty but I'm losing work. I've spent three hours here, and I've already been penalized. I don't want a trial.

J: Do whatever you wish, sir.

D: No Contest.

Later in the morning more and more defendants change their pleas to No Contest in order to save time and get out of court.

One well-dressed man insisted on maintaining his Not Guilty plea. With him, the judge became more explicit about the reasons why one should avoid a trial:

D: I don't want my record sullied if I'm not guilty.

J: This citation is of such a nature that it will be removed from your record after 36 months. It would take a lot longer to try [the case] if you used this type of procedure [a trial].

D: I'm interested in justice.

J: I just want to tell you.

In the morning session of approximately fifty cases, perhaps no more than three people insisted on a trial (insisted on maintaining their innocence). But the court left them the option of still avoiding trial by setting bail in the amount of the fine that would have been assessed if they had pleaded No Contest, and by informing them that the whole matter could still be closed if they would call the court the day before the trial and say that they would not appear.

Thus the No Contest plea may be seen as an instrument of speeding up court output by having the defendant surrender, either out of ignorance or boredom. If guilt were the main concern in traffic court, surely more than three or four of the twenty-one who originally pleaded Not Guilty actually should have stood by their pleas, even if it meant going to court. If one interprets the No Contest plea as a guilty plea (which one has every right to do, since a judgment is made against the defendant), it can be seen to be a means by which rates of deviancy are inflated—by getting innocent persons to accept the effects of a guilty judgment in order to avoid more trouble or inconvenience.

A second aspect of the social organization of traffic court is seen in the method of discrediting witnesses. This process has two functions: first, to make tnose who objectively might have a good case feel that their chances of convincing a jury would not be very good if they took the case to trial; second, to discourage those whose appearance in court is motivated solely by considerations of reducing the fine.

Discrediting in the form of the question "How many citations have you had in the last 36 months?" usually came after defendants questioned the very basis of the whole court organization—the judgment of the police officer. For example:

D: How could the police have known I was the one passing the bus, if they were 100 feet up a side street when it happened and couldn't see my license number?

J: How many citations have you had in the last 36 months?

Or, for another example:

D: This guy passed me on the right; I was maneuvering to avoid him and wasn't able to signal for my right turn. I thought the cop would go after the guy passing me.

J: How many citations have you had in the last 36 months, say?

D [mumbles] Four.

J: Regarding the $120 which could be imposed, I'll reduce it to $19.

Here we can see the process of intimidating the defendant so he will not pursue a case that he might be able to win if it were taken to a jury trial. The defendant's story seems to have no impact on the judge. Tacitly, the defendant is told that no matter how good his story, his previously blemished record will work against him in a trial.

Others (twenty-nine of the fifty-three in the morning session) pleaded Guilty with Explanation, clearly in order to talk the judge down on the fine. Here the judge used the discrediting process (especially the question concerning a previous driving record) to counter their arguments for a lenient fine. Take these cases for examples of the bargaining:

D: I just think that a fine of $33 is too high [cut off by the judge]

J: How many citations have you had in, say, the last 36 months?

Or:

D: I don't think that the fine should be $105.

J: What do you think it should be, $500 [as prescribed by law]?

D: I just paid a fine of $38.

J: How many citations have you had in the last 36 months?

D: [mumbles.]

J: How would it be if you got a $600 fine every time you drove without a license?

The whole matter of discrediting the defendant to himself is an interesting process to watch—especially since defendants consistently guess that they have about one-half the citations that appear on their record. The judge has a copy of each driving record stapled onto the citation so he can always make a comeback—usually to the detriment of the defendant.

D: [to the judge's question of how many citations] I can't remember.

J: Had so many you can't remember. [Proceeds to read them out.]

The law provides for increased penalties for frequent offenders; it further stipulates that the question of the number of previous citations should be asked only after the determination of guilt. But in the Guilty with Explanation plea, the guilt is already admitted, so it is only a matter of bargaining over the penalty. Here, however, the question of a previous record can be used subtly to impress the defendant with the futility of insisting on pleading extenuating circumstances. It could be considered that the judge and the defendant are here sparring in a shadowy area near infringement on the defendant's constitutional rights. One defendant interpreted it this way after an especially vigorous effort by the judge to intimidate him:

J: How many citations have you had in the last 36 months?

D: 10 to 12.

J: [with a smile] : How about violations which you weren't caught on?

D: I'm here on this one; I shouldn't be judged on the others.

J: $24.

Finally, some defendants plead Guilty with Explanation *solely* to get a reduced fine. Discrediting and other mechanisms are also used by the judge in these negotiations. These people are obviously guilty and offer no extenuating circumstances, just a sad story or a cynical appeal. For example:

D: I don't want this citation on my record. That's why I'm here explaining it. I want to keep my record clean.

J: Clean record? I count four citations here on speeding in the last 12 months alone. [Sarcastically.] That's a good record to really try and keep clean! It takes some people a lifetime to build up that.

A final example, an old woman trying to avoid a ticket for parking in a red zone while she was unloading her car, shows how the judge can appeal to the gallery for laughter to get rid of the defendant.

J: How long were you "unloading?"

D: I was just inside for about an hour.

J: If you're going to park in red zones you have to dash in and dash out and not get caught. [Snickers in the gallery.]

J: [looking to gallery] I'll fine you . . . $1 on this. [Applause.]

Discrediting may be seen, then, as a mechanism for cooling out the defendant (in its extremes, it may appeal to violations the defendant was not cited for, or to direct appeals to the audience for laughter, to convince the defendant of the futility of a plea). It is a means of furthering the ends of the court—the expedition of bureaucratic justice.

As in the social organization of juvenile justice, the social organization of justice in a traffic court derives from the authorities view that the "deviant" must change his conception of his *act* in order to bring it more into line with the court's conception of it. The process of changing the defendant's plea (that is, his view of the act) is "negotiated" in the ritual of traffic court, within which both parties try to maximize their own goals (either "expedition of justice" or less "hassle" in court). Bargaining from a position of greater power, the court has the advantage of being able to manipulate the defendant into accepting its optimal disposition of the case—the fastest and most immediate resolution of the matter. It is to achieve a No Contest plea that the mechanism of discrediting is used; the defendant is further pressured by the offer of a reduced penalty for a Guilty plea.

From this exchange—a No Contest plea for a reduced fine—one can see that both parties get what they want. The court gets to handle the maximum number of cases in the alloted time, and the "offender" gets a reduced fine and the satisfaction of having the matter settled quickly. In bureaucratic justice, then, the concern is less with determining guilt or seeing justice done than with arranging the most efficient handling of the matter. To reach this goal, each side must compromise a little.

NOTES

[1] Aaron Cicourel, *The Social Organization of Juvenile Justice* (New York: John Wiley and Sons, Inc., 1968).

[2] See Robert Emerson, *Judging Delinquents; Context and Process in Juvenile Court* (Chicago: Aldine Publishing Co., 1969).

[3] H. Laurence Ross, "Traffic Law Violation: A Folk Crime," *Social Problems,* VIII (Winter 1960-1961), 236-237. (Reprinted in Rubington and Weinberg, *Deviance: The Interactionist Perspective,* pp. 170-172.)

[4] See Harold Garfinkel, "Conditions for Successful Degradation Ceremonies," *American Journal of Sociology,* LXI (March 1956), 420–424.

[5] David Sudnow, "Normal Crimes: Sociological Features of the Penal Code," *Social Problems,* XII (Winter 1965), 255–270.

Driving Is a Privilege: License Among Licensers

Meredith R. Ponte

● ● ● Theoretical developments of George Herbert Mead's symbolic inter-
● ● ● actionist conception of the relation between self and society,
● ● ■ notably in the work of Anselm Strauss and Barney Glasser, and
works drawing upon the phenomenological social theory of Alfred Schutz
and the ethno-methodological investigations of Harold Garfinkel, have in
common a focus on the organization of and the process of social interaction.
Both perspectives have been used extensively in the study of people-processing institutions.

"People-processing institutions" refers to a type of social institution in
which human beings constitute the raw materials and the products of organizational work. The term is restricted to those whose primary goal is the
reshaping, removing, overhauling, retooling, and recording of the physical,
psychological, social, legal, or moral aspects of human objects.[1] The intent

of this study was to apply, through the techniques of ethno-methods, the theoretical, methodological, and empirical materials for the examination of various aspects of one people-processing institution, a substation of the California Department of Motor Vehicles (DMV) in a large urban area.

The literature on people-processing institutions[2] is characterized by several dominant concerns. First, there is the conception of people as products of organizational work, which has directed attention to the processes by which members are socially differentiated and officially or unofficially categorized. Second, the question is asked what criteria are applied to differentiate one class or object from another and how the criteria are applied. That is to say, what is the problematic social construction of reality? Status outcomes, whether they be suicide, "mental illness," alcoholism, or whatever, are contingent on the perception of facts by agency personnel, the interpretative framework within which they are given meaning, and the treatment which is organized by that meaning. Third, the concern over the ways in which people-processing institutions, in the interaction between staff and clients, shape and develop identities. The people-processing perspective has come to be associated characteristically with research on deviant-processing institutions. Yet Goffman has included monasteries, boarding schools, and army barracks in his study, and has thus expanded the notion to include institutions dealing with the general society. The DMV is another institution that processes members of the general public rather than an isolated population of "deviants."

AWARENESS CONTEXT PARADIGM

Ethno-methods require, ideally, that the investigator enter field research without preconceived ideas about what his specific findings should be. In this regard, the participant observer differs from the "traditional empiricist." The writings of the participant observer apply the phenomenological rule of initial openness, so that theories or hypotheses arrived at prior to the investigation are less likely to interfere with the accuracy of the findings. Bruyn finds that "the traditional empiricist sets up many preconceptions of his subject through his study of background materials, his definition of variables, his hypotheses, and the causal order he expects to find among his variables. The . . . participant observer, on the other hand, tends to let the variables define themselves in the context of the research. And they examine causal relations between these variables on the basis of the social perception of the subjects themselves."[3]

Bruyn also finds that an integral part of ethno-methods is the "watching of modes of appearing." Ethno-methods are applied by keeping dated field notes which document the developmental sequence that takes place in the interactional sequence. What was needed, I felt, was a paradigm to guide my field findings that would allow me to take into consideration for study both the effects of the social structure, having to do with the particular nature of the DMV as it is set up to process people, and the social-psychological or interactional aspects of people being processed. This paradigm or set of directives was for my guidance only, and was also to help me organize my observations so as to take account of the developmental aspects of the inter-actional process. The paradigm, then, allowed me to explore and extend the limits of my data in the field notes and helped me in stating clearly what was done and why. To these ends, I drew upon the paradigm of awareness contexts developed by Strauss and Glasser in their study of another people-processing institution, the hospital.[4]

The developmental focus of the paradigm derives from its sequential analysis, instead of the usual simultaneous factoral analysis. The contrasting models follow the discussion by Howard Becker.[5] The factor approach is legitimized by the notion that one can only consider so much at one time with precision and clarity, and therefore boundaries must be chosen, usually according to one's interest, provided they are theoretically relevant. A se-quential model takes into account the fact that patterns of behavior develop in an orderly series of steps—changes in the individuals' behaviors and per-spectives—and that each step therefore requires explanation. What may operate as a cause at one step may be of negligible importance at another step.

By the term "awareness context" I mean the total combination of what each interactant in a situation knows about the identity of the other and his own identity in the eyes of the other. The concept of awareness is a struc-tural unit, not a property of one of the standard structural units such as group, organization, community, role, or position. The "context" means that the structural unit "awareness" is of an encompassing order larger than the other unit under focus: interaction.

The least complex situation of the total awareness context—guided, suc-cessive interactions between two interactants over periods of time—occurs when two interactants (whether persons or groups) face the dual problem of being certain about both their identity in the other's eyes and the other's identity. Three types of interactional situations can obtain in this context:

1. An *open awareness context* obtains when each interactant is aware of the other's true identity, and of his own identity in the eyes of the other. This is the phenomenological situation formulated in the works of George Herbert Mead.

2. A *closed awareness context* obtains when one interactant does not know the other's identity or the other's view of his identity. Erving Goffman's work usually is concerned with this situation.

3. A modification of the closed context is the *suspicion awareness context:* one interactant suspects the true identity of the other, or the other's view of his own identity.

These types illustrate how the sociologists' total picture may differ from that held by each interactant. The sociologist must ascertain independently the awareness of each interactant. The method used is to observe behavior and statements directed toward the participant observer which indicate each interactant's awareness of his own state.

The successive interactions occurring within each type of context tend to transform the context. A closed context can be shattered by arousing suspicion; but if suspicions are quelled, the closed context is reinstated. If suspicions are validated, the context may change to an open awareness.

The component parts of the paradigm are as follows: (1) a description of the given type of awareness context; (2) the structural conditions under which the awareness context exists; (3) the consequent interaction; (4) changes of interaction that provide the occasion for a transformation of context, along with structural conditions for the transformation; (5) the tactics of various interactants as they attempt to manage changes of awareness context; and (6) some consequences of the context for interactants and for the organization.

Questions addressed specifically to the data collected in my field notes, and observations of the daily operations of the DMV, included the following: What were the recurrent kinds of interaction between applicants and DMV personnel? What were the kinds of tactics used by DMV personnel in dealing with the applicants? What were the conditions of DMV organization under which interaction and use of these tactics occurred? And in what ways did they affect the identity of the applicant?

COLLECTION AND ANALYSIS OF DATA

Field work seemed to coerce its own analysis. The field work situation allows the researcher to plunge into social settings where the important events, from which hypotheses are developed, are going on in a natural laboratory: I watched these events as they occurred; I followed them in their developmental and sequential features; I could observe the actors in their relevant social dramas. Being there, I could informally converse with or formally question the actors about their observed actions. My field work experiences, therefore, did not differ significantly from those described in the readings in ethno-methods.[6]

The literature on ethno-methods puts stress on the fact that in field work the formulation and testing of hypotheses begins early in research. There is a continuous and cumulative interweaving of observation and inference. The inference becomes expressed in my field notes, in both analytic comments written directly into the field notes and in research notes, or memos to myself addressed specifically to concerns I want to focus on in the future. The coding process began to be used and to show up in the notes at about the third series, as I began to think systematically about the data in terms of the awareness-context paradigm. As in all qualitative analysis, there tended to be a blurring and intertwining of coding, data collection, and data analysis from the beginning of the investigation.[7]

As a personal matter, the emergent analysis continued in reflective thought during my coffee break periods, when I would leave the DMV office and muse over what I had seen. These periodic withdrawals, like other aspects of the field research, usually were forced by a lull in the clientele's demand for services, making it strategically advisable for me to withdraw because of the attempt on my part to be unobtrusive, as well as because fewer applicants meant less opportunity for relevant observations. The respite and concomitant musings provided on-the-spot-generated directives, which allowed me to avoid collecting huge masses of data. Events I observed and reported initially were dropped later (even on the first day), and I did not report occurrences that seemed incidental to the direct concerns of the DMV's people-processing activities. For example, on the first day while sitting in my car observing the road test, I chanced to observe a transaction between high school "heads" and a dope dealer of "whites," or "bennies" (stimulants like benzedrine or the amphetamines).

Another major reflective period which had influence on the emergent collection and coding was during the weekly reports and discussions in the graduate seminar on ethno-methods. Hearing what others were doing and what problems they had and how they were dealing with them, I found that my own research was greatly influenced. The discussions in that seminar of my notes with the other graduate students, as well as the considerable help and many insights obtained from the instructor, also affected the direction of the research.

Coding seemed at first to be on a cognitive level below that of an explicit linguistic formulation.[8] The incident with the old fellow that I witnessed on the first day remained fixed in my mind's eye and seemed to generate a focus of attention on events that confirmed or provided negative evidence for the generality of his situation. Long before I had explicitly formulated a category of "incompetence," I was looking for persons who did or did not fit the category and observing what happened to them in the interactional process of getting a license. The coding became refined in this process.

At first I had tended to look for broad categories of persons who might be subject to negative stereotyping effects, such as the aged, hippies, and low-status ethnic group members. But at some point, after many hours of observation, I was able to take the role of the examiner and appreciate that these categories were too gross. I became sensitive to a more fundamental categorization procedure on the part of the DMV staff:[9] Of all the persons in minority status, only certain ones were held for a road test.[10] All the while, I was still early in the research and working on an explicit institutional category of licensing renewals. That is to say, the implicit coding preceded the explicit formulation of how persons were categorized. While I was still concerned with all the persons getting a renewed license (as differentiated from a universe that contained all applicants as well as persons there for vehicle registration), I began to focus on the fact that certain broad categories of applicants for renewals were, in greater numbers than others, being required to remain for special testing. I explicitly developed a category of minority group status to account for this, while at the same time my notes show that implicitly a more refined understanding again took place in that my attention to certain behaviors showed a further refinement of coding. Finally, only toward the end did I begin to code persons explicitly in terms of whether or not they fit the sensitizing concept of "incompetence."

Although my field notes reflected this firming up process, they always lagged behind my subjective awareness. I often remembered events that I had failed to note in the first instance. Yet these events remained stored in my memory and were accessible. The field notes also became more cryptic toward the latter part of the study, as a kind of shorthand reporting reflected my more refined and narrowed focus of attention. These last notes also began to serve another purpose in the data collection.

Initially many hours had been spent in only one of the DMV field offices. The data collected, therefore, was restricted in its import to one office. But by then turning to participant observation of several such microsocial settings, I could utilize a strategy of maximizing credibility through comparison groups. When the significant categories and hypotheses had been reasonably well formulated and articulated via the awareness-context paradigm as applied to an intensive study of the first office, I began in the later phase to observe different offices located in different human ecological settings to check out and refine my initial observations. Glasser notes that multiple comparison groups function to improve the research in several ways: (1) replication is built into the research; (2) credibility is maximized because researchers are helped to calculate where a given order of events or incidents is most likely to occur or not to occur; (3) constant comparison quickly draws attention to many similarities and differences between groups that are important for the refining of hypotheses; (4) this analytic strategy then is more powerful and precise than comparing positive and negative cases within a single structure.[11] In the latter case one can only compare the internal structure of the negative to the positive incidents, whereas comparisons of groups allow for the pointing to different sets of external structural conditions. Bringing this strategy to bear on the subject at hand, I found that in a study of a DMV office in a high status area, negative cases were provided that required me to re-think my data so as to consider the effects of readily-perceived high status on the licensing procedures.

Besides being a dry collection of "facts," the field notes used certain devices in an attempt to describe vividly the subculture of a DMV office: notes on pertinent phrases dropped by the informants, brief descriptions of scenes in the first days, subjective impressions gained through introspection while on the scene, and direct quotes of the actor's conversations. Such descriptive diversity in the qualitative field notes also allows the reader to judge the range of events I saw, the persons whom I interviewed and who talked to me, and under what conditions, and perhaps how I might have appeared to other people on the scene. As we learned in the seminar readings and discussions, these all are important for making an independent determination of the credibility of the qualitative research completed.

THE DMV: INFORMATION CONTROL

To the extent that the DMV is involved in information restriction or control concerning the "actual or real" versus the publicized procedures of examination, its staff members operate in interaction with certain categories of persons in a closed awareness context. Those persons in suspect categories do not know that their behavior is under special scrutiny. Of course, the DMV does. As the applicants go through the various processes, their focus of attention is on "passing" a seemingly objective set of criteria, the written examination and the visual test. Other processes such as the use and correct filling out of bureaucratic forms, the taking of a thumb print, the photographing process, and so forth, are seen as secondary to getting their licenses renewed. This closed awareness is supported by the *Drivers' Handbook*, which defines the tests as the critical areas. "Your examination for a driver's license includes the following: An eye test, a road sign test, a traffic law test." Under "renewal" the applicant is told only that "a road test *may* [emphasis mine] be required as part of any driver's license examination." No clue is available that the applicant, as he traverses the various processing stations, is under examination by the staff to determine if he is to be placed in the possibly incompetent category, that is, to be singled from the whole population of license renewal applicants and held for a road test.

A major structural condition that determines this closed awareness context includes the requirement that a public bureaucracy avoid any suspicion of utilizing non-objective criteria in dealing with the general public. The rationale of all governmental agencies is that they will treat everyone by the same well-defined rules of law.[12] Because the applicant only visits an office once every four years, he is unfamiliar with its general procedures. Should he question being held for a road test (and hence increase the probabilities of not passing), he will be told that it is "just routine" or that he "missed too many on the written test." The extra procedure would be justified to him in terms of objective criteria. Through many hours of observation, I was able to strip away the facade of objectivity. People who missed eight or nine questions on the driving law examinations were routinely not held for road tests, while others who had missed the same or fewer questions were held. Several persons commented on the fact that they passed the eye examinations without glasses when in fact they could not make out street signs while driving without glasses. The objective tests functioned as structural screens to maintain the legitimacy of the DMV as operating on universal criteria.

Another structural feature was the great number of persons requiring the services of the staff. Long lines and hours of waiting were routine, yet the public also demanded of the staff that they receive expeditious treatment. Often there were loud complaints voiced about the waiting. Because those waiting were members of the enfranchised general public (unlike, for example, disenfranchised persons in total institutions), the DMV would be judicious in showing some concern that the public be processed as rapidly as possible. Large numbers and the need for relatively expeditious processing required the examiners to deal with persons in a highly abstract or "shorthand" manner. They had no time for a careful consideration of the applicants' potential as drivers, and yet apparently part of the duties of the examiners was the "screening" of these hordes to get at the few whose licenses should not be renewed. Some coding procedure, then, was needed to do the job. Possible incompetence had to be singled out under circumstances not allowing for the detailed inspection of the applicant as an individual. The examiner had only sufficient time or data to make a quick categorization, to "fit" human beings into some reified mold. The "product" had to be processed through or else held for detailed examination with the possibility of rejection held in reserve.

The closed awareness context depended upon the examiner's ready apprehension of clues[13] that allowed him to determine the identity of the applicant. Obviously "products" which differed in some way from the majority became subject to being placed in a suspicion awareness context on the part of the examiner. Deviations such as minority group status (ethnicity, age, or counter-culture membership) separated persons from the masses of middle Americans. Their minority group status often was linked with middle-class judgments of incompetence in driving. "Old people" and "dumb greasers" (or Orientals, or farm laborers, whatever the local minority) are accessible folk images of the poor driver. "Hippies" use drugs and are "hopped up" when driving, and therefore, the reasoning goes, are unsafe on the highways. The structural conditions provided the grounds for these groups to be placed in a suspicion awareness context in interaction with the staff.

Other interactive factors resolved the suspicion awareness context into either an open or a closed form. Social control factors operated by the staff functioned to maintain the closed awareness on the part of applicants. Staff members used facework techniques and specialized jargon or coded communication. Open conversation only took place in non-public areas or toward the rear of them. The staff always acted collusively in a "professional" manner with the applicants. For example, when conversing with each other in front of an applicant, staff members talked as if the applicant were a non-person, a thing to be worked on. Routinely, the applicant who attempted to break into these conversations would be ignored. Similarly, the applicant who attempted to deviate from the ordered processing sequence would be ignored, that is, he would be given collusive non-person status by the staff. Teamwork also kept all staff-applicant interaction on a formal basis. Any applicant who attempted to break down the formal barriers (and hence threaten the closed awareness status quo) would be treated in a polite but firm manner.

Props included many signs limiting the choices of action available to the applicant. Each processing step was marked by formal instructions about procedure and legal warnings, commands, and so forth. Other staging props included police-like badges prominently worn by staff members and other external signs of authority such as clipboards, coat-and-tie dress, legalistic forms, and physical barriers separating the public from the staff.

However, I did observe certain spontaneous structural arrangements between the applicants themselves. Occasionally, strangers would begin talking about their problems in getting a license. Informal groups would arise and

draw upon their mutual fund of knowledge on how to "beat the system."
Following Harvey Sachs, I termed these bond-formation activities "adequacy
of social environments." They gave each other support in finding ways to
overcome the difficulties in filling out forms, passing the various tests and
performing competently and efficiently the various rituals of fingerprinting,
photography, and so on. Besides providing members with information which
at times transcended the institutionalized closed awareness contexts and
transformed them into suspicion awareness, these groupings also were a
source of encouragement and emotional support. But given the overwhelming
collusion of the permanent staff, these efforts were usually only slightly
successful.

The consequent interaction that goes on under the various structural conditions has been suggested above. The applicant's attention is concentrated
upon the objective test criteria. He is concerned with "passing" the written
test and "getting through" as quickly as possible. This attitude is fostered by
stage-management procedures that emphasize the importance of correctly
"doing" the expected thing. The staff acts as if these criteria are important
while giving no hint of their subjective on-going evaluation of those persons
who are in a suspicion context. The "situation as normal" techniques include
the overt ignoring of applicant behavior which functions as cues to perceived
"competency." All the rituals of test correction, eye testing, and so forth, are
gone through, and only at the end of these, something such as, "Now, Sir, the
last step is a road test," is said to the applicant. No sign is given that this is
anything but routine for all applicants. In fact, if the applicant challenges this
he will be told, "Just routine procedure, Sir." What is in fact the interactional
situation, according to my observations (backed by focused interviews), is a
continuing, subjective evaluation of the applicant's behavior by the examiner
as the applicant gets through the various processing stations. As the applicant
proceeds through, if he shows signs of behavior "abnormality" such as
extreme confusion, disorientation signified by the need to have the processing
instructions repeated or doing the required acts incorrectly (filling out forms
improperly, not performing as per verbal instructions at the various stations),
engaging in disruptive behavior such as loudness, inappropriate laughter, anger
or other emotions, stumbling, fumbling, dropping things, or showing jerky
and erratic body movements or some evidence of physical deformity such as a
hobbling gait—all of these are signs or cues taken by the examiner to change,
in the course of the interactional sequence, the awareness context from a
suspicion one (itself, as noted above, usually arrived at via signs of minority
group status), to a closed one of judgmental conceptualization of the applicant as an incompetent. In sum, while the applicant's attention is focused on
passing the objective test because of his closed awareness vis-a-vis his identity

in the eyes of the examiner, the examiner is changing from a suspicion to a closed awareness context in which the identity of the applicant is resolved into a category of incompetent.

However, the interactional sequence may also be one of going from a suspicion to an open awareness context. I have observed two general interactional situations in which this sequence can take place: (1) where an applicant performs the rituals competently, in an orderly, routine manner, or (2) where an applicant has such high status that the deviance is ignored. The latter occurred in a substation in a high status area when the applicant was identified as a physician. This was a clear case of incompetence, because the doctor was so confused and disoriented in undergoing the licensing process that he needed the continual direction of his wife to get him through. I observed further that he made several errors on the test and filled out the forms incorrectly. Yet all this was glossed over, and the only factor I can isolate beyond that of chance is that the doctor's high status functioned to change his identity in the eyes of the examiner.

Closed awareness on the part of the applicant may change to suspicion awareness when he has quite obviously performed adequately on the objective tests. For example, an elderly applicant who had behaved erratically made high scores on the written test and easily passed the eye test. Yet the gentleman was requested to wait for a road test. He demonstrated his suspicion by protesting vigorously to the examiner. Later, I heard him voice the suspicion that the examiner thought "he was a jerk." Because of team collusiveness, the suspicion awareness on the part of the unsuccessful applicant is seldom resolved. The subtle judgment of his behavior is not revealed. Rejection of the license is falsely rationalized to his "failure" on some objective criteria.[14] The applicant has no means by which to penetrate the closed awareness context and achieve an open one. Occasionally, a staff member may let slip clues about the applicant's true identity such as in a too-loud backstage comment by one examiner to another, "Here's another rough one." But the structural conditions are set up so that the applicant in fact has little chance to verify his suspicions.

The consequences of the closed awareness context for the staff is that they are able to do a subjective screening job under the pretext of using only objective criteria. The examiners, therefore, do not come under personal attack for the applicant's failure. The transition into the extra testing is made easier because the applicant himself is made to seem responsible for the failure because his performance was not up to some well-defined standard. For the DMV, the closed awareness context allows it to maintain the public fiction of doing its job of processing all persons through equally applied and well-known testing standards. Without a closed awareness context being maintained, the DMV would doubtless have to process all renewal applicants through a road test—a time consuming and expensive procedure requiring many more extra man hours—or not be able to screen out those they felt were incompetenct to handle a car on the highway. Through maintenance of a closed awareness, the staff can process people while giving the appearance of conformity to universalistic ideology.

THE DMV: CODING PROCEDURES

One aspect of the interactional sequence has yet to be developed. I have mentioned several times the subjective coding procedures that are going on within the suspicion awareness context during the giving of the objective renewal tests. These coding procedures undertaken by the staff have the effect of resolving the suspicion awareness context with the interactional consequence of either holding or not holding the renewal applicant for "outside," or a road test. A discussion of these coding procedures requires a different social-psychological perspective.

As mentioned at the beginning of this paper, the second of the two social-psychological approaches to the study of people-processing institutions is ethno-methodology. One topic of ethno-methodological interest is the conception of and concern with the documentary method of interpretation. "A person undertaking an inquiry about social structures in the interests of managing his practical everyday affairs . . . can assign witnessed actual appearances to the status of an event of conduct only by imputing biography and prospects to the appearances, which he does by embedding the appearances in presupposed knowledge of social structures."[15]

A study of how coders treated coding rules in dealing with the contexts of records of a psychiatric clinic illustrates the interest. Garfinkel found that no matter how elaborately a set of instructions was developed for coders, coders nevertheless found that they had no choice but to employ ad hoc practices for deciding the definite sense of the instructions when they encountered actual notations in the clinic files.[16] In the course of coding, they discovered and employed qualifying conditions for the proper use of the rules. They found that on many matters no clear decision could be made, although in order to get the work done, they nevertheless had to opt for categorizing the noted event one way or the other.

Three features of this documentary method of coding process were:

> (1) The coders found that they could not proceed in the work of coding and still recognize that they were coding actual events in the round of clinic affairs if they suppressed the use of these practices.

(2) But the use of these practices means that in no clear sense do the coding rules that the coders use describe what they are doing and what they were looking for when they coded.

(3) The coders could argue that they had coded the contents of the clinic folders in accordance with the rules, but in so doing they would have to appeal to the same ad hoc grounds that they employed in doing the coding in the first place.

The same coding and ad hoc elaboration of rules have been studied in other institutions. Zimmerman studied the work of receptionists in a public welfare agency:

> It would seem that the notion of action in accord with a rule is a matter not of compliance or noncompliance per se but of the various ways in which persons *satisfy* themselves and others concerning what is or is not "reasonable" compliance in particular situations. Reference to rules might then be seen as a common sense method of accounting for or making available for talk the orderly features of everyday activities, thereby making out these activities as orderly in some fashion. Receptionists, in accomplishing a for all practical purposes ordering of their task activities by undertaking the "reasonable" reconciliation of particular actions with "governing rules" may thus sustain their sense of "doing good work" and warrant their further actions on such grounds.[17]

In an ethnographic study of halfway house residents, Wieder found that they perceived diverse behavioral events as "documents of" or "pointing to" the same underlying motivational source and thereby see-able and describable as parts of the same pattern.[18]

After several days of observation, I questioned the DMV staff concerning their coding procedures. Generally, their answers confirmed my observations and inferences. That is, first, that they could not proceed with their duties as screening examiners if they proceeded in accordance with the objective criteria. Some applicants were subjectively perceived as in some way incompetent to handle a motor vehicle on urban freeways, and yet these persons were able to meet minimum objective test standards. Second, in no sense did the objective rules the examiners used describe what they were doing and what they were looking for when they coded some applicant as incompetent and scheduled him for extra testing. To this point, examiners would describe their procedures as "looking for someone who is all beat up," or who "doesn't seem to know what he is doing," or who "fumbles around and isn't too alert." These ad hoc elaborations of the objective criteria were justified in accordance with the overall purposes of the DMV examinations: to screen out those persons who are incompetent to drive.

Very diverse behaviors on the part of the applicants in the suspicion awareness contexts were seen as "pointing to" or documenting the underlying notion of incompetence as a motor vehicle operator. Some persons were erratic, acted inappropriately, couldn't follow instructions, were crippled, were too nervous, were not alert, and so forth. All of which may be summarized under what Garfinkel refers to as the *et cetera* clause. Persons placed in the suspicion context based on master status categories, and showing or *being perceived as showing* the above or similar varied behaviors, were coded as incompetents and relayed in the people-processing belt to "special handling."

SUMMARY AND CONCLUSIONS: ETHNO–METHODS AND AWARENESS CONTEXT

The unique perspective of social phenomena which is apprehended through ethnographic methodology is interior, in contrast to the external view yielded by a more objective perspective. The social system is seen from the inside. Consequently, many of the categories having their origin in evaluations made from the outside become difficult to maintain, since they achieve little prominence in the interpretations and definitions of persons in daily life. And it is the subject's definition of the situation, the illumination and comprehension of his view and the interpretations of the world as it appears to him, that is the aim of the researcher using ethno-methods.

The problem of validity and reliability in ethno-methods rests on the ability to take this inner perspective. "It is crucial for validity—and, consequently, for reliability—to try to picture the empirical social world as it actually exists to those under investigation, rather than as the researcher imagines it to be."[19] The ethno-methodologist is committed to the principle of rendering the world of the phenomena with fidelity and without violating its integrity.

Also basic to this analysis is the location or assertion of an essential feature of the phenomena. For the qualitative methodologist, the location of essential features is crucial because he must attempt to cogently assert what the phenomena is. In conventional sociology, the parallel situation is the researcher posing the relationship between variables. This analytic summary is necessary to escape the tendency toward sheer descriptive detail which is an inherent problem in ethno-methods.[20]

The problem in ethno-methods quickly becomes one of maintaining the integrity of the subject's world while also escaping from merely detailing a mass of unsorted facts. A tension exists between the analytic summary of the phenomena without unnecessary reductionism, on the one hand, and undifferentiated description on the other.

Awareness contexts as a framework for the presentation and analysis of the data helps avoid both pitfalls of ethno-methods. The data is organized meaningfully for the reader, and there is also a natural "fit" of the data, because it falls easily, almost naturally, into such a framework. This fit grows out of the fact that using awareness contexts to look at the subjects in their relevant social dramas in the DMV offices, we look at them in much the same ways as they look at themselves. Listening to conversations, I immediately had the feeling that concern for information would be one way in which the subjects would organize their own experiences. The licensee is trying to get information that will get him through the bureaucratic maze. The examiner is trying to do his job, namely, get information about the applicant's potential as an operator of a motor vehicle. The awareness context is in fact only a formal method of dealing with that heuristic concept "member's definition of the situation." And it is finding the subject's definition of his situation, or how he "sees his world," that ethno-methods is all about.

FIELD NOTES

DMV Office, City A

In conformity with the seminar assignment, I have gone into this study without any specific or clearly formulated theories. My interest or reason for study of the DMV, however, stems from personal knowledge of how, among my acquaintances, there seems to be a feeling of "being hassled." Persons will say something like "Oh, I hate to go down there." With this vague sense of research orientation, I then begin this study. I am initially looking for social processes or reasons why people feel hassled (or indeed if they really do, since I may know only neurotics!).

I am located at the visitor-designated seating section next to rest rooms and drinking fountain. In front of me are lines of persons having to do with the registration of their vehicles. There seems to be little interaction between the clerks and customers. The clerk simply takes the proferred documents, forms, and so on and stamps them or whatever else is necessary to process them. Not much in the way of greetings by either clerk or clients. Clerk moves the line along with "next please." People simply shuffle along, not talking, staring abstractly but with no visible uneasiness, except that of boredom. The line moves swiftly. Not much of interest here.

Lunch Time. DMV office is crowded. I have changed location to the opposite side of the building. In this area is the driver's licensing sections. Somewhat worried as to my own role. Signs on the walls say Loitering Forbidden, near the area where the written test is being taken Visitors Prohibited. I will attempt to lurk in the crowd at the back of the lines. Immediately noticeable is the uneasiness in this area. Application forms and instructions alongside are being read with concentrated and almost grim expressions. Much puzzled glancing around by new arrivals. Jerky movements, false starts, turning back to this line and that indicating indecision, hesitation. Man standing at window, hunched over a counter with elbows resting one foot on top of another. Others are wringing hands or rubbing themselves, hitching up clothes, giggling inappropriately with clerk when mistakes are made. (Clerks are all women sitting behind typewriters. Examiners are all males dressed in white shirt and tie with a badge on their pockets.) Mistakes for which the applicants are called down by the clerks and examiners include:

(1) Incorrect filling out of forms, such as placing of information on wrong lines. (2) Erroneous moving from one line to another in processing sequence. (3) Test errors. (4) Failure to stand in a manner satisfactory to the examiner so that photo can be taken. (5) Failure to attend properly to various contingency verbal instructions in the processing sequence (such as handing the left thumb rather than the right thumb as instructed for fingerprinting).

1:00 P.M. Out in the parking lot. Overheard conversation: "Well, maybe it's a good thing they marked me down for it. I don't want to drive . . . until I'm ready." So (subject) male with a foreign accent talking with a companion, gesturing wildly. (Note: Next time park in area where the inspector and applicant's interaction can be observed while out in the car for the road test.) Another conversation: "Phew,—Oh Boy sure is crowded, Phew sure is crowded." Shake of the head, squinting up of eyes. Parking Lot behavior: everybody wants to park near the entrance. Lots of delays in movement of cars due to waiting for those leaving. Loss of face seems to be present. Have watched several persons who have been told they must retake the test come and stand and go into long explanations to sympathetic wife, companion, mother, and father.

1:30 P.M. Returned inside building near the Inspector's line. S's in line are pulling wallets in and out of pockets, rechecking forms, staring into space. Some relieve anomie by talking to one another. Bond formation attempts among apparent strangers. Proximity leads to discussions based on readily apprehended symbols of commonality. Gripes about waiting, "Well, another 30 minutes." Clerk at head of line puts up a Closed Line sign. People who have been waiting must shift to another line and begin again at the end. Seem to react with no visible anger. Resignation. Now holding conversation concerning puzzling out forms.

(Note on role: best time seems to be during lunch. Afternoon is busy and my lurking doesn't seem to be noticeable to anyone.)

Principally, I am located near the three lines that are the initial process. Subject turns too quickly, looking for next line, bumps into metal trash can, loud noise, everybody stares then looks away. S blushes, focuses eye on next line designated by clerk and walks there. Might tentatively divide process into two phases. The initial one is simply having forms typed and paying fees and getting directions to the next phase. Some status testing, however, with the paying of fees, for example, identity cards are needed and telephone number and address required on the check. Activity involves simply waiting on the part of S's. Little contact between clerk and S's and a terminal "thank you and go to window, please." Some questioning concerning proper address, name, expiration date of license, and other bureaucratic red tape minutiae.

Conversations overheard. Husband to young wife standing in first line. "This is nothing here honey, just relax dear." Middle-aged woman going to next line says "Well, here goes" to companion. Some S's seem to perceive difference in the processes.

2:00 P.M. Location near the written test area. Can hear conversation between S's and Inspector (I). "How are you" to each of three S's by (I) standing with visible symbol of authority pinned to his shirt. Non-person status. S enters building and approaches open window. But no clerks or (I) will approach. All walk by to desks or other windows while "doing business." S finally gets the message and moves to a line. Mechanical picture-taking, "smile" demanded, much shuffling as S attempts to stand "with the left foot behind the red line." Eye testing, S's must call to (I) proper letters. One confused S doesn't understand. Discussion with other S's staring but no laughter at his confusion. (I) to (I) conversation. "We've got a pretty big load today." Second (I): "Hold the load, Irma," to clerk in first line.

The "how are you today" may be a mechanism of social control. Have watched five S's and I's interact. One S didn't respond and another did so only with a nod. (I) became equally brusque. Three S's all middle-aged women, ducked chins nicely, grinned shyly "fine." (I) will be friendly "glad hand" style. (I) will imitate approach with good "O.K., fine." S's have showed proper deference and (I) can be cast accordingly into patronizing attitude. Interesting note on the processing of people. Each particular aspect of the process has clear indicators as to ending and what to do for next phase except for the picture taking phase. Here the applicant waits for, "O.K. that's it," while the examiner waits for the polaroid picture to develop. Many S's however do not pick up on the offered routinized guides to behavior and have to be told exactly what to do. Eye contact of I's. After initial glance sizing up S's, during the "How are you today," seldom looks at S unless S causes "trouble" in the non-cue perception just mentioned. Evidence of differential treatment. Warning read to "sullen" appearing working class youth. "Fine and imprisonment for perjury" read loudly for "misstatement on application." Did not do this for other S. Calls this S by first name. S held for driver's test although passed written test. (I) turns to (I) "looks like another rough one here." Second (I) administers driver's road test to some S's. Note how S's are selected for road test. Meaning of this? Is it perceived as some sort of threat by S's? Is it utilized as a threat by I's or is it routinized?

DMV Office, City B

10:00 A.M. It is a weekday morning and the office is not too crowded, about twenty-five applicants waiting. Differing ages of the morning population immediately apparent. At least three-fourths are elderly. Most of the males are dressed in coat and tie though the quality of dress ranges from threadbare and mismatched to newer and more expensive cuts. The women similarly vary. Sequined glasses with pointed tips connected to chains are adjusted with nervous frequency. There is a sense of extreme anxiety in the social atmosphere. Last observations noted that all of the applicants seemed to express some sort of uneasiness during the examination process. Yet these betray a sense of greater importance. Taking the role of these people in the Meadian sense and viewing the social situation through their eyes, I suspect that this is one of those social defining agencies that has the latent function of telling them "You're old and incompetent." Failure to pass the driver's test and not having a license renewed is something of greater importance to these people than the inconvenience it would mean in obtaining transportation. The whole process has to do with society's judgment of their worth.

Eye test line. An elderly applicant has protested that he can't follow the eye instructions while using the "eye test" machine. The inspector then has him look at the wall chart. Holding a paper over one or the other eye, the inspector asks him to read off the letters. The applicant does so while a line of about ten people are waiting behind and looking on.

Another elderly applicant goes up to the clerk with a hand full of forms. She hesitantly hands them to the clerk. The clerk hands them back and repeats instructions to "please step to the next window." Abashed, the applicant attempts to explain her mistake. "Oh, I'm so confused. I bet you sure do get tired of people like me." The clerk nods courteously but cuts off further conversation by turning to the next applicant. Jerking her head around, the woman finds her way, shuffling, to the next line. There, when the applicant fails to understand the fingerprinting instructions, the clerk tries to ease her by saying "that's embarassing isn't it," but her tone is patronizing.

I am becoming aware of a definite difference in the manner in which people enter the DMV office. I can roughly sort them into two categories. The more self-assured walk toward the vehicle registration section to pay their license fees. This is a routine matter, as noted previously. Those that betray nervousness in gesture and varying degrees of hesitation upon entrance invariably are here to be examined.

A disruption of the orderly routine is occurring. An elderly applicant, thin, with wild, long grey hair, is answering the inspector's questions at the eye station in a bull-horn voice. Heads are turning even on the far side of the building. The inspector has a displeased expression. The other waiting applicants are looking embarassed except for a long-haired couple who are giggling and enjoying the whole disruption of middle class order. There is an apparent rupture in social control. The next process, photographing, being completed in the same boisterous manner, the inspector turns to another and says, "Hold for a driver's test." The applicant starts to protest that he didn't miss any on the written test (informal norm?) but the inspector assures him that the "road test is routine." My observations are that it is not. At the eye test station the inspector seems to be making a joke about it to the next applicant. This seems to repair the rupture in order and business as usual. The elderly client has been directed to sit on a bench and await the "road test" inspector.

Long-haired couple are going around reading all the instructions and warnings posted on the wall. They are quietly giggling to one another. A woman clerk glances at them and frowns. The girl then goes through the processing procedure, getting some cold stares from the employees. She is also held for a road test. The elderly applicant with the loud voice has left with an inspector armed with clipboard. The couple look around and occasionally mumble "far out." They see me lurking nearby and flash an "in" smile.

Hypothesis: Holding for a driver's test is some sort of labeling process. Those that disrupt the routine by abnormal behavior are held for a road test. Old people, Chicanos, long-hairs seem to be held most frequently on a non-routine basis. Routinely, all those who miss more than the five allotted questions or are getting a California license for the first time are held for a road test. But beyond this, the decision to hold for a road test seems to be up to the discretion of the inspector.

People are being kept waiting while the examiner has a lengthy conversation over the phone. Sheep-like anxiety.

I've been here since 10:00 A.M. and it is now almost 1:00 P.M. I'm getting questioning glances from the various employees, so I'd better leave. Next time I'll move to [City C] DMV station. These are bureaucratically organized offices run by a centralized administration statewide, so it seems justifiable to treat the data obtained at the different branches as identical. However, I will try to be alert for any evidence contrary to this. An examiner has just walked by openly looking at my notes and giving me a "hard" stare. I think of the "No Loitering" signs and leave.

In the parking lot I am behind the elderly loud-voiced man, who has just completed his road test. He is talking to a woman, presumably his wife, and his voice is considerably subdued.

Man: "Well, I couldn't hear him, besides I ain't—I don't know the area. How could I just turn right when he said so?"

Wife: "Well, I was waiting . . . and he was running around failing everybody and giving them all a hard time."

Man: "Right off, I could tell he thought I was crazy or somethin'. Kept calling me Ralph. I should a told him Mr. Jones to you; and my hair all long, I shoulda got a haircut, he probably thought I was just some jerk."

DMV Office, City C

Upon entering the building, I find myself standing beside two others who appear to be some sort of officials. They are intently observing everything that is happening. I suspect that they are some sort of state functionaries because they are equipped with clipboards and other bureaucratic paraphernalia which have "State of California" written on them. Their manner is that of an inspecting team. Their conversation seems to be spiced with bureaucratic jargonese. Reinforcing my suspicion is the exceptionally polite behavior of the clerks and inspectors. This in spite of the 80-degree heat, swirled around by a single fan, the stench of smog and cigarette smoke which is already burning my nostrils, and the very crowded conditions. I count 35 S's at this time awaiting processing by four employees. The vehicles registration section is also crowded, with lines of persons filling the building and forming long lines outside into the parking lot and into the street. Conversation overheard between the two presumed inspectors. "Sure is packed. I think they should deputize some people to handle the overflow there (pointing to processing station)." "It's no use—it's this way statewide, all the time, no money." They leave, the first speaker shaking his head.

A young girl comes up to a middle-aged man standing next to me. She says, "It must have been only fifteen minutes but it seemed like two hours. I was standing in the wrong line and then I got to the window and he said 'get in the next line' and all over again." Waiting woman and daughter are talking to another woman. "Oh, I don't care myself but my daughter is worried."

Orderly flow disrupted by a discussion between a couple and an inspector about some court case involving one of their driving licenses. "Well, driving is a privilege, not a right," the examiner states. Various comments: "We'd better get to another line; they're going to take a long time, I bet." "How come dealers get special treatment?" (referring to special office and marked Dealers Only). "Why don't they help get these lines moving?"

An examiner is repeating a set of instructions over to a befuddled applicant who is nodding his head in time with the examiner's words. I have heard the examiner repeat these same instructions many times. The examiner is interrupted by a child who has "to go to the potty." He takes the child to the restroom. His actions are noted with approval by several applicants. "That man must be a father." Returning, the examiner tells the applicant again: "You don't have to answer that question, but you must answer this and you didn't–also there and there." Two middle-aged workmen tell one another: "That must be these questions on this form about tickets and suspensions." "Make sure you bring it with you when you return" is yelled by the examiner after a hastily departing applicant. "Sign again on that line and that line," his neighboring clerk is simultaneously intoning.

In the parking lot. "Hey you? Where are you going?!" I look up and see a young man with DMV forms and test sheet turning toward a red-faced, beefy DMV examiner who has done the shouting. "What do you think you're doing. You can't pull out that test and all that stuff." "Huh," the boy replies, "I've got to take my driver's test." "He can't sign that out here anyway," says the examiner. Boy answers, something I couldn't hear. "No, go inside and wait in line."

Standing inside again. I notice that where spontaneous conversation develops, there is an initial sizing up by visual glances exchanged (Strauss' awareness contexts) and then conversation begins, apparently between persons of similar statuses and groupings. "Heads" to "heads," young mothers to young mothers; matrons to matrons; working class males to working class males; and so on. Proximity alone doesn't seem to allow for conversation. Many, simply sheep-like, clump through the process. Others, however, bring their own friends or family, who act as advisors and commentators. A middle-aged woman has marched up to an open but unattended window. Ignored, she attempts to commandeer a clerk but is told to "wait in the first line please and someone will help you." Abashed and red faced she meekly complies and then seems to ease her embarrassment by striking up a conversation with another person in front of her. Another applicant with a foreign accent has strayed near a sign reading "Test Area Please Visitors Not Allowed." He is now challenged by a roving examiner. "Please don't bother the young lady while she is taking her test."

An applicant asks an inspector: "Where should my daughter go when she is finished?" He replies testily: "There's only two lines . . . see (pointing), either one."

The woman clerk is opening up the "overflow" window again. "Next in line." The indicated applicant doesn't hear and is directed by others. Clerk says: "That's right," as he hesitates and then haltingly hands her the forms, "if you're next?"

An examiner passes by and asks an applicant to "step aside please." The applicant jerks himself out of the way differentially, then looks around, frowns, looks down, and fingers his tie. He then stammers as the examiner, with a glance at the clock which shows that it's nearing closing time, poses a set of rapid-fire questions. The applicant doesn't comprehend and the examiner repeats. He stands meekly while the examiner completes his inspection of the forms, clasping and unclasping his hands. In the next line, the woman clerk is saying to a young teenager, "Your parents sign this?"

The overflow clerk again selects a waiting applicant. Another in a torn T-shirt also starts to change lines. "No, don't get out of line. Just one person at a time, please." T-shirt returns, exchanges laughter with males dressed in work clothes standing behind him. They have not talked previously. Now they are comparing each other's forms and shaking their heads disgustedly. Another male dressed in white-collar, "junior executive" attire is complaining to a well-dressed woman in twenties. (Shakes his head) "Whatever happened to the civil servant?" "Uh, what do you mean?" "Well, look these little clerks ordering you to do this do that, and with personalities like mooses." "Yes," she agrees, "back east they sure handled it better."

Sign: "Please No Food Or Drink In the Building."

My befuddled applicant is now undergoing the "eye ritual." Loudly the examiner observes, "Can't see too well, eh?" "Now see the square in the lower right-hand corner?" No apparent response. "O.K., now put your forehead against there. O.K., that's better." T-shirt to friend, "Better clean our glasses before we get up there (laughter)." Executive to chic woman: "You've got to take one of these things here and then go right to that door over by window 19." Clerks and examiners are shutting doors and turning away latecomers. As I leave, an irritated parent is complaining to daughter, "See, now that you've got it, it doesn't mean a thing."

DMV Office, City A

An environmental note: this office is large and crowded. Social controls by the examiners are more difficult for examiners to exercise because of more people and less space. It is much easier for me to circulate unobtrusively. I can stand within good visual and hearing distance of the processing clerks. I shall take this opportunity to extend my observations about what persons get held for road tests.

California Driver's Handbook, Revised April 1970. Section entitled

"Renewing Your License," p. 37: "A road test may be required as a part of any driver's license examination. Road tests are not required simply because of age." Immediately before this statement are the procedures for applying for renewal. "When applying for renewal you will need to (a) fill out the information form; (b) pay the required application fee; (c) pass the test; (d) pass the traffic law test; and (e) have your picture taken." (End of paragraph)

Contrast this with the following, taken from the section about obtaining a first California license. "Your examination for a driver's license includes the following: An eye test . . . A road sign test . . . A traffic law test . . . A driving test" (*Ibid.*, p. 34). The procedure as spelled out in the above sections thus *requires* a road test for those obtaining a first license. For those persons who are renewing their California license, the procedures indicate that a road test *may* be given. The section provides no information as to who will and who will not be given a road test when renewing their license. This ambiguity required a clearing up of official procedures, and this could only be obtained by a direct interview.

I have stood in line and directly confronted the examiner on duty with the question: "How is it determined who will be given a road test when applying for a license renewal?" Answer: "It depends upon how well you do on the written test." Question: "How well do you have to do?" Answer: "Oh, if you miss around five questions we'll give you a road test and see how well you can do actually driving." Question: "If a person is renewing his license and misses only one question will he be given a road test?" Answer: "Usually not." I was then told that there were a "lot of people waiting." The problem for observation: determine how the decision to require a road test is made in the case of those persons renewing their license. Based on previous observations, I am speculating that the decision is based more on the examiner's predisposition toward the applicant, than on the applicant's performance on the written test. The [City A] DMV office is located in a ghetto area with both Mexican-American and black people. There are several "Latin"-appearing persons in the driver's section of the office. One is now being processed by the clerk. There is an involved discussion about the initial application information sheet. It seems the applicant had received his first license under a nickname and now wants to have his new license issued under his full and proper name. The clerk tells him to maintain the same name as the old license because otherwise the "records will get all fouled up." The applicant complies by scratching off the name and writing in the other.

A note on the subjective effects on me as I respond to the physical surroundings. All contrasts in the building are blurred. There is a low ceiling which seems to stretch endlessly in all directions. It is lined with long rows of harsh fluorescent white lights. Pastels are the colors of the walls and floor.

Architecturally, the subjective impression to me is one of barrenness. Everything seems ordered and sterile. Uniformity seems to be characteristic of the DMV examiners as well. Most are slightly overweight, middle-aged with salt and pepper gray hair clipped in a flat top. They are invariably dressed in reserved gray suits. A large sign on an office door reads "Do Not Enter."

My applicant has been processed and is now at the examiner station. The examiner inspects the application form asking, "and how are you today, senor?" "What happened here? Didn't understand it?" The applicant is given no chance to answer. The examiner turns to another examiner who is waiting outside, where he has been giving road tests, and tells him, "We've got another rough one here." Applicant looks down with a frown. Applicant gets through the eye processing and fingerprinting procedure without any trouble and is given the written test. He leaves for the examination area.

The usual slow-moving lines of anxious people. Three persons have been held for driver's tests—all are new licensees. A matronly woman has missed four questions, but she is not held for a test. Three persons are rushing up to an examiner asking questions. The two are dressed in suit and tie; he deals with them first and shows reasonable deference, addressing them as "Sir." To the third he says, "For heaven's sakes, young man, one at a time." However, each is told substantially the same thing, "Wait and we'll get to you."

Now my Chicano applicant had returned to the test station. The examiner grades his paper. One answer wrong. The examiner hesitates and then says severely, "All right, but next time be prepared for a driver's test." Another Chicano comes in and misses three. He is held for a road test. A Caucasian misses three and is not held for a road test. A Caucasian following him, however, misses two and is held for a road test. The difference that seems apparent to me is that the first responded quickly to verbal instructions about eye ritual, and the rest, while the second was nervous and fumbled during the routines. A long-haired youth who misses two is held for a road test. He seems very competent, but is wild in appearance, barefooted and with a "natural" hair style á la Jimi Hendrix. An examiner comments to examiner as they stand in the back drinking coffee, "Sure do get some weirdos here."

Two elderly males are held for a road test while a third is not; none missed any questions on the written test. All were nervous and fumbled at the stations, but I think the third was not held because there are now over twenty persons waiting to be tested. I suspect that another problematic element is the number of persons waiting for the road test. If there are too many, "borderline" cases will be let go. Substantiating this is a comment by one examiner to another to "ease up" on the road testing. All "borderline" cases (the examiner's word) are warned to be prepared for a road test next time. Others are not warned.

The overflow awaiting the road test also includes many long-haired youths and three blacks who have had licenses suspended by the traffic courts. All of the respectable looking Caucasians awaiting road testing—except one—are out-of-state applicants—that is, they are defined as getting a license for the first time and thus not placed in the category required to take the road test. The DMV does not seem to be a racist institution in the direct sense. Black people are in the majority among renewals awaiting road testing, but all of them who are here today have had so many traffic citations that they have had their licenses suspended and do not therefore fall into the "renewal" category. The DMV seems in their case to be simply an extension of the racist judicial legal and law enforcement system reported on by others. I have seen several black persons go through the renewal program without being held for a road test. One elderly black man was held, but then he had fumbled through the eye test and other rituals. The situation is more complex than simple racism in the case of minority group members. The same holds for "long-hairs." Although no evidence can be obtained on the point here, I suspect that "hippie types" are, like their minority-group fellows, more subject to citation and hence license suspension than are the more respectable appearing and behaving "middle Americans."

But my observations today indicate that there is some subjective testing going on as the applicant goes through the objective test rituals. Some definitions are made as to whether the applicant is competent or not, and this judgment then makes the difference in "borderline" cases. Mr. and Mrs Respectable American—those closest in dress and demeanor to the examiners themselves—have the best chance of escaping being held for a road test. Disruptive persons, such as black persons with natural haircuts and dark glasses, wild-looking hippie types, Chicanos speaking broken English, and elderly persons who fail to perform competently during the various rituals, will have the greatest probability of being held for a road test. The whole process is highly subjective, however, and it is only after several days and many hours of observation that I am beginning to grasp the covert construction of reality.

A young woman, a blond suburban housewife, is now bringing her test to the station. She has missed six. The examiner laughs and tells her to study harder next time. She is not held for a road test even though the number of those waiting has decreased.

A note on the use of ritual to describe the test procedures. This is because I can see little correspondence between performance on the written test and actual driving behavior. Further, one person had told me that he had passed the eye test without his glasses and yet would be afraid to drive on the highway without them. This informant told me that he could barely make out road signs without his glasses.

A further interesting note. An applicant who identified himself to the examiner as an attorney has refused to have his fingerprint taken. When asked, the examiner told the attorney, "Yes, it's true you don't have to have your fingerprint taken, but we just don't say anything unless people ask."

I asked an applicant (Mexican-American male) why he had to take the road test. I had previously observed that the applicant had missed only five questions and was renewing his license. He answered, "I missed too many" (on the written test). This is what the examiner had told him. I had been observing him because he had to be given repeated instructions about taking the eye test and other rituals. He was a farm laborer and seemed unsure of himself in this middle-class bureaucratic setting.

I haven't observed the road test procedures yet. I moved out to the parking lot, and observed where the examiners leave and arrive in cars with applicants taking the road test. A woman's car has broken down and I have been drafted into helping get it started. She complains that her son has just spent two hours taking the test and now, when he has to take the road test, the car won't start.

Generally I haven't noticed much of interest in the road test section. Most of the conversation is in the car and can't be overheard. I have overheard some of the leave-taking conversations. After the test the examiner apparently tells the drivers where they were in error. Reactions vary as they get out of the car. Some taking their cues from the examiner, nod their heads sagely. Others, rattled by success or failure will gush with non sequiturs or rationalizations. "Yeah, I know, but my foot was behind it and it slipped." These the examiner treats with rapid disengagement by slipping out of the car and closing the door as a signal that the interview is finished. This is a good area, however, for overhearing conversation about examiners themselves, since they often meet each other and talk briefly. This is a back region of the lot where the staff cars are parked. So far, I haven't noticed anything of relevance for the study. Simply "joking relationships" and personal matters.

Back inside now. It is closing time, and there are still about fifty people waiting to be processed. The doors are all locked except for an exit guarded by a uniformed officer. Cop standing at exit and saying "good evening" to all the well-dressed high-status persons. As I go out the door, he looks me over carefully and then glances away saying nothing. I guess I am not high status.

DMV Office, City A

Note: Afternoon is the wrong time for old people. Generally they seem to come in the morning hours. Rural carryover? The DMV office is crowded with off-duty sailors and marines with wives and kids. All up for renewals are being processed through and not held for road test. Interesting difference in deferential behavior shown by clerks. Poorly dressed working status people are herded through the processing stations indifferently, while an occasional suit and tie applicant is treated with "Yes, sir." Long-hairs and minorities are treated coldly—the long-hairs and Chicanos especially getting curt handling from the DMV staff. One portly, red-faced examiner "chews out" a Chicano for not putting the proper information on a form. A long-hair has just been rebuffed by a clerk in the "information line" and told brusquely to "get in line." Immediately after him, a coat-and-tie does the same thing and is given attention. The long-hair turns to me and complains about "Jerks who have to feel important." "Some people enjoy coming to the DMV" is the remark in return by a man behind us. The long-hair turns and they begin to talk of the irritation of "coming to this place."

I move to a better vantage of the renewal road-test processing station. An elderly woman is going through the ritual. She is hunched over and walks with a limp. Her movements are slow and disjointed. She converses with another younger woman and seems mentally alert. At the eye ritual she seems to perform competently, although, presumably because of the infirmity of her legs, she acts slowly in response to the examiner's instructions. I suspect that she will be held for a road test. I am correct. She has been held. Sitting on the waiting bench, she complains to her companion, "I thought you weren't held because of age if you have good eyes and everything." I learn that she missed only two questions on the written test.

The black applicant has had his test corrected and is at the processing station. The examiner is a young woman and is new to the job—at least I have not seen her before. She takes the applicant's records over to the head examiner (who is correcting tests) and he instructs here, "hold for outside."

I am sitting on the "waiting bench" where I can get a good view of the various processes as well as hear most of what is going on. Research Note: will spend the remainder of the time making a shorthand tally of the population of renewals; then, if there is a break before closing, I will interview an examiner.

One incompetent, I suspect he will be held. Aged male, with palsy. Renewal. Passed written test, three missed, eyes O.K., held for exam. No protest.

Long hair in natural. Hip, calm, cool, not held.

Long hair, "dancing around," keeps saying "far out, man" to the examiner, looks around distractedly as if he can't believe 1984 is here. Eyes glazed; I think he is stoned. Dressed in T-shirt and ragged jeans and bare feet. Rings in ears. Beads on chest and belt made of peace medallions. Not appreciated by some of the off-duty servicemen applicants. Has attempted to buck into line, ignoring the non-person treatment. Examiners are openly looking at him. He yells, "Hey, I want my license *renewed, someone!*" Some people laugh; others look irritated. No response, and he gets in line. He misses five on the law test. Held for a road test.

Renewal, young housewife, Caucasian, nervous, confused. Examiner laughs with her. Tells her, "take it easy and you'll do all right." She misses eight questions. Not held. "You'll do better next time," the examiner tells her.

No renewals at present. Break.

Fifteen renewals have been processed in the last hour. None held for road test. All middle-aged Caucasians.

Ten renewals processed this hour, all young or middle-aged Caucasians, none held.

Heavy, poorly dressed Caucasian mother with five young children in tow passes through. She missed seven questions on the written exam but is not held for a road test. Her daughter kids her about missing so many questions and she replies, "don't rub it in" as she leaves. Southern accent.

Elderly couple, well dressed, both up for renewal. Seem alert and competent. Man gives age as 75. They are both passed through.

Elderly man on a cane. Mismatched clothes, work shoes and suit pants, no tie, hat and suit-coat different from pants. Seems disoriented at first. Gives appearance of deteriorated physical condition. Age 52. He passes the written test with only three missed questions and seemingly passes the eye test. He is held for a road test. Makes no complaint. I am sitting on the waiting bench near him. We express mutual complaints over the wait, and I ask him why he is here. He replies that he is getting his license renewed. I say something like, "I didn't know you had to take a road test for a renewal." He says that "they didn't used to, but things are changed, I guess, with all the traffic and so forth. I guess they check everyone now." "Does everyone have to take the test now?" "I think so, that's what the examiner said." In fact, the examiner had said something like "We'll have to give you a road test now," with no hint of special treatment.

I considered asking the examiner directly why this applicant was held, but I rejected the idea. The role of the participant observer is that of non-interference, and raising a question about a particular applicant would be seen as advocacy on his behalf. Such action might adversely prejudice the man's treatment while taking the road test. Hostility might be directed at him. Non-interference seemed the best course, even with the possible loss of significant data.

Since there is a lull and it is near closing time, I catch an examiner at the window and put several questions to him. First, I went through the usual routine of showing him the ambiguous phrase in the booklet and asking him to interpret it. He answers, "If some people are screwed up then we hold them for a road test. By screwed up I mean if they look like they might have trouble driving in the city, you know."

Question: "Is this only a matter of physical condition, I mean unable to hear, etc.?"

Answer: "Not necessarily—some Mexicans might not be—uh, coming from rural areas might not be good drivers on Southern California freeways so we want to make sure and handle—see how they handle themselves in a car."

Question: "What other conditions do you look for in holding people for a road test?"

Answer: "Oh, we get some people who look like they might be habitual dopers, that is, persons who are driving a vehicle under the influence of dangerous drugs, and we want to screen them out carefully." He continues: "Ha, ha, you should see some of the people who come in here. The other day some guy came in stumbling around and laughing. He had a hair, long hair like some Negroes wear it, but it was about three feet on all sides, you know. We held him for a road test but he didn't have a car."

Question: "How about blacks?"

Answer: "Oh, some of the—we're not prejudiced; we're just looking for those incompetents to get them off the road, that's our job and that's why you pay us. The DMV staff is just a group of conscientious persons attempting to do a job of keeping *you* from getting hit by someone making a left hand turn from the right lane or driving twenty miles an hour in the left lane of the freeway."

NOTES

[1] John Kitsuse, "People Processing Institutions," *American Behavioral Scientist,* XIV (Nov.-Dec. 1970).

[2] Literature on people-processing institutions with a micro-sociological focus on participant observation studies includes: M. Baum and S. Wheeler, *Controlling Delinquents* (New York: John Wiley, 1968); E. Bittner, "Police discretion in apprehending the mentally ill," *Social Problems,* XIV (Winter 1967), 278-292; A. V. Cicourel and J. I. Kitsuse, *The Education Decision Makers* (Indianapolis: Bobbs-Merrill, 1963); R. Emerson, *Judging Delinquents* (Chicago: Aldine, 1969); E. Freidson, "Disability as social deviance," in M. Sussman (ed.), *Sociology and Rehabilitation* (Wash., D.C.: Amer. Soc. Assoc., 1966); E. Goffman, *Asylums* (Garden City: Doubleday Anchor, 1961).

[3] Severyn T. Bruyn, "The New Empiricists," *Soc. and Soc. Reshs.,* 51, 317-322.

[4] Barney G. Glasser and Anselm L. Strauss, "Awareness Contexts," *Amer. Soc. Rev.,* XXIX (Oct. 1964), 669-679.

[5] Howard S. Becker, *Outsiders* (New York: The Free Press, 1963).

[6] Howard S. Becker, "Problems of Inference and Proof in Participant Observation," *Amer. Soc. Rev.,* 23, 652-660.

[7] Barney G. Glasser and Anselm L. Strauss, "Discovery of Substantive Theory," *Amer. Behav. Sci.,* VIII (Feb. 1965), 5-12.

[8] Gideon Sjoberg and Roger Nett, "Impact of the Observer's Conceptual System," *A Methodology for Social Research* (New York: Harper, 1968), pp. 169-173.

[9] Herbert Blumer, "What is Wrong with Social Theory," *Amer. Soc. Rev.,* 19:3-10. Emphasizes the need for the use of "sensitizing concepts" in participant observer research as contrasted with operationally defined concepts.

[10] "Occasionally," "often," "few," "certain ones" and so forth, are used in the explicit sense of Becker's notion of "quasi statistics" in participant observation studies. H. Becker, "Problems of Inference."

[11] Glasser and Strauss, "Discovery of Substantive Theory."

[12] Jerry Jacobs, "Symbolic Bureaucracy," *Social Forces,* 47:4 (June 1969).

[13] William H. Form and Gregory Stone, "Status Symbols and Urban Anonymity," in A. Rose (ed.), *Human Behavior and Social Processes* (Glencoe, Ill.: The Free Press, 1966).

[14] Buchner calls the police behavior of bringing their subjective reality, their "knowing" that a suspect is guilty, in line with legally required objective reality the practice of "overwriting." I suspect the same process in in practice here. See Buchner, H. Taylor, "Transformations of Reality in the Legal Process," *Soc. Resh.,* XXXVII (Spring 1970).

[15] Harold Garfinkel, "Common Sense Knowledge of Social Structures," in Scher (ed.), *Theories of Mind* (Glencoe, Ill.: The Free Press, 1962), p. 190.

[16] Harold Garfinkel, *Studies in Ethnomethodology* (Englewood Cliffs, N.J.: Prentice-Hall, 1967).

[17] Don H. Zimmerman, *Paperwork for Peoplework,* unpublished doctoral dissertation, UCLA, 1966.

[18] D. Lawrence Wieder, *A Study of Moral Order as a Persuasive Activity,* unpublished doctoral dissertation, UCLA, 1969.

[19] William J. Filstead, *Qualitative Methodology* (Chicago: Markham, 1970), p. 4.

[20] David Matza, *Becoming Deviant* (Englewood Cliffs, N.J.: Prentice-Hall, 1969), pp. 26-27.

Symbolic Bureaucracy: A Case Study of a Social Welfare Agency

Jerry Jacobs

This paper is concerned with certain ideas about bureaucracy presented by Weber and qualified and expanded by Blau. Based upon information gathered in a year-long participant observation study of "the Single Men's Unit" of a public welfare department during which time he was employed as a "social caseworker," the author has introduced the notion of "symbolic bureaucracy." The discussion, which is centered around this concept, seriously questions whether Blau's "unofficial change" and "adjustive development" will suffice to save Weber. It seems more likely to the author that the introduction of the concept of unofficial change, if it serves to rescue Weber's "ideal type," succeeds in doing so only at the serious risk of losing bureaucracy.

"Bureaucratization offers above all the optimum possibility for carrying

From *Social Forces*, XLVII (June 1969), 413-422. Reprinted by permission.

through the principle of specializing administrative functions according to purely objective considerations. Individual performances are allocated to functionaries who have specialized training and who by constant practice learn more and more. The 'objective' discharge of business primarily means a discharge of business according to Calculable Rules and 'without regard for persons.' "[1]

INTRODUCTION

Weber's classic analysis of bureaucracy is largely responsible for sociology's general orientation toward the subject.[2] His presentation rests primarily upon the construction of an "ideal type" where it is assumed that the organization best approximating the central conditions of an ideal bureaucracy will function with the greatest efficiency. It is assumed that any increase in deviation from the ideal type is accompanied by a decrease in efficiency. The basic conditions of Weber's model as given by Blau are as follows:

1. "The regular activities required for the purpose of the organization are distributed in a fixed way as official duties." The clear-cut division of labor makes it possible to employ only specialized experts in each particular position.
2. "The organization of offices follows the principle of hierarchy; that is, each lower office is under the control and supervision of a higher one."
3. Operations are governed "by a consistent system of abstract rules . . . (and) consist of the application of these rules to particular cases." This system of standards is designed to assure uniformity in performance of every task, regardless of the number of persons engaged in it.
4. "The ideal official conducts his office . . . [in] a spirit of formalistic impersonality, 'Sine ira et studio,' without hatred or passion, and hence without affection or enthusiasm."
5. Employment in a bureaucracy is based on technical qualifications and is protected from arbitrary dismissal. "It constitutes a career. There is a system of promotions according to seniority or achievement, or both."[3]

Blau sees the above model faced with several dilemmas, for example: maintaining a hierarchy of command without submitting subordinates to a feeling of inequality and anxiety, coping with anomie while retaining standardization, maintaining hierarchy and close supervision without causing resentment in a democratic culture, and providing for social cohesion while maintaining impersonality.[4] His findings in *Bureaucracy in Modern Society,* and the findings of others, led Blau to take issue with Weber on the point that unofficial change is inherently detrimental.[5]

Blau contends that unofficial change may increase or decrease administrative efficiency.[6] Unofficial change which expedites administrative functions, reduces the dilemma inherent in the "ideal type," and does not prove detrimental to the attainment of the organization's objectives is referred to by Blau as "adjustive development." This process is one of gratification through self-imposed rules, unofficially created and mutually subscribed to by the subordinate group. So long as this fully internalized system provides a rigorous standard of workmanship, increases efficiency, and does not violate the organization's intent, its effects will be beneficial. What must be guarded against is the acceptance of a policy which is detrimental to efficiency or the achievement of organizational ends, since this too may develop through unofficial change. Blau recognized this danger and in several instances enjoins the administrator to be ever watchful. However, what remains conspicuously absent is a description of what to watch for or how to watch for it. Blau deals with the problem in these terms:

> To establish such a pattern of self-adjustment in a bureaucracy, conditions must prevail that encourage its members to cope with emergent problems and to find the best method for producing specified results on their own initiative, and that obviate the need for unofficial practices which thwart the objectives of the organization, such as restriction of output. What are these conditions? We do not have sufficient empirical evidence to give a conclusive answer to this question. But some tentative hypotheses can be advanced, although these must be qualified by the recognition that the same conditions may not be required for adjustive development in other cultures or in other historical periods.[7]

As I see it, the problem is not so much what conditions are necessary for the achievement of adjustive development as how one would recognize them if they existed. I find this question especially troublesome, since my own observations and experiences with "bureaucracy" have led me to realize that it is possible for an organization to conform little or not at all to the conditions of bureaucracy, while maintaining an image of complete adherence to bureaucratic ideals. The existence of such a situation will hereafter be referred to as "symbolic bureaucracy." Under such conditions, the relative success of the organization in realizing its ends in a more efficient fashion would not easily be subject to an accurate assessment, either by the agency's administrative personnel or the outside observer. It was just such a situation that I witnessed as a participant-observer in a year-long study of a unit of a public welfare department.

The following discussion is, in one sense at least, not intended as a critique. I would agree with Blau that a strict adherence to Weber's ideal type would render "bureaucracy" inoperative and that unofficial change is a necessary addition, at least to save Weber. Whether or not bureaucracy is saved as well, by this addition, remains to be seen. It is this aspect of Blau's thesis that I feel warrants our attention. It is my contention that implicit in Blau's hopeful position of unofficial change in the furtherance of administrative efficiency, is the possibility of destroying the necessary conditions of bureaucracy (if they ever existed) while retaining an image of complete adherence to bureaucratic ideals. If such a state is achieved, the basic elements of a functioning bureaucracy cease to exist, while at the same time the organization is unaware of any apparent deviation from the bureaucratic principles which seem to govern operating procedures. There would exist no objective criteria to discern the positive or negative effects of unofficial change since no significant change would be apparent. Since the organizational arrangement was defined at the start as a bureaucracy, everyone concerned would remain convinced that it was continuing as one. The possibility of such an organization fulfilling its goals would actually be more random than "rational."

An example of an organization closely approximating an instance of "symbolic bureaucracy" was the department studied by the author. The following discussion will concern itself with whether or not this department functioned within what Blau considered to be the four most essential conditions for bureaucracy, i.e., specialization, hierarchy of authority, system of rules and impersonality.[8] Each of these aspects will be evaluated with respect to the degree of their functional adherence against the degree of their apparent adherence within the department.

SPECIALIZATION

Consider the first of these conditions. Did specialization exist within the department? The only prerequisite for taking the Civil Service examination for the position of "Social Caseworker" was a college degree, and even this had not always been the case. Professionality was not a requisite. It is true that anyone passing the exam and "placed" was by definition a "caseworker." However, this did not presuppose any professional schooling, training or experience in the methods of casework. Very few caseworkers, i.e. persons holding a Master of Social Welfare degree, were employed by the agency. Most "caseworkers" employed by the agency were historians, artists, sociologists, etc. Commendable as this liberal hiring policy may have been, it did not constitute specialization.

A better grasp of this lack of specialization at the agency and/or the need

for it can be had by briefly describing the duties of the caseworker. These can
be divided into essentially two specific tasks, i.e., determining eligibility and
dispensing services to the eligible client according to the dictates of agency
policy. The determination of eligibility rested primarily upon a consideration
of "residency" and the availability of other resources. If one had not lived in
the state for a period of at least one year, one could not establish a residency
and was by definition ineligible for aid, notwithstanding his needs or his
inability to otherwise meet them. (The consitutionality of state residence
requirements is currently being considered by the United States Supreme
Court.)[9] Then, too, if one had available from other resources, e.g., relatives,
outside income, real property, etc., income sufficient to maintain oneself
according to the minimum set forth by the country, one was again ineligible
for service. If one could prove residency and show that he was temporarily
unable to support himself through no fault of his own, he was eligible for aid.
The options available to the eligible client under these circumstances will be
outlined below and discussed more thoroughly later in the paper. The point
to keep in mind here is that since it was primarily the client's problem to
prove to the worker's satisfaction his eligibility according to the above criteria, it required little skill or insight on the part of the worker to decide
whether or not the client met these criteria. It was not surprising to find that
many other persons in the agency holding offices lower in the hierarchy than
the rank of "caseworker" could have easily fulfilled this function, given its demands. This aspect will be dealt with in greater detail on the following pages.

The second duty of the caseworker, i.e., dispensing to the eligible client
the various services prescribed by the agency, was not a task requiring any
special skill or insight either. Assistance took one of several forms. Which of
these options was offered to the client and for how long was often left to the
discretion of the worker. Aiding the client according to the discretion of the
worker was not a matter of agency policy. It was, however, a matter of
worker policy. Clients were eligible for assistance in the form of bus tokens
for transportation, rent payments on an apartment ($30 to $45 per month)
plus a food allowance of $30 per month, or $1 per day payment in scrip for
"hotel accommodations" and $1 a day in scrip for food, or in place of any
of the above, "camp." "Camps" were located in outlying districts and constituted a kind of ghetto. One found at "camp" food, lodging, medical assistance, and the company of persons in similar circumstances, i.e., indigent
single males. One found there little else that is generally associated with a
"normal" outside environment. "Camp" was then a "total institution," subject to all the ramifications of that form of society.[10] It was considered by
the client the least desirable option in a series of services offered by the agency. Very few clients intended or desired to go to "camp." The option of

"camp" will be discussed in greater detail under the section dealing with "rules" and "expediting cases."

Fulfilling the duties of a caseworker in the department required little expertise that could not have been mustered by many, if not most, of the agency's non-caseworkers. For example, going down the scale from case-worker, there was the position of mailboy, many of whom could have administered the duties of a caseworker, while any of the caseworkers could have doubled as mailboys. Clerk-typists had no special training beyond being semi--proficient typists. Many caseworkers in my office, the mailboy notwithstanding, were better typists than the "clerk-typists," and I have small doubt that some of these women could have doubled as caseworkers. In fact, one who received her B. A. degree from a local state college several months after my arrival (having attended night school for several years) did receive a position as caseworker in the agency. The transition was noteworthy. On Friday she was the "clerk-typist." The following week she returned to work a "social caseworker."

Going up the scale, there was the supervisor who also had no professional schooling and came up "through the ranks." She knew more of company policy than the subordinates, but functionally this was inconsequential since it was not on company policy that the organization ran, unless it was particularly expedient for the worker. When the supervisor left on vacation, a subordinate assumed the position of supervisor for two or three weeks at a time, and no change in the unit in particular, or in the organization in general, was evident beyond a marked increase in morale. So long as persons occupying positions in the hierarchy upscale and down were, to a large extent, functionally interchangeable, there was little real evidence of specialization or expertise. There was only a division of labor, conveniently mistaken for specialization in the name of expediency.

HIERARCHY OF AUTHORITY

Consider now a hierarchy of authority, the second condition of bureaucracy. Was this condition operative at the welfare department? Obvious at the outset is a chain of command ranging from subordinate to superordinate. However, what did these rankings actually mean? For example, our immediate superior, the supervisor, every week or so, as the fancy took her, held a unit meeting where a long list of new policies, directives, and form changes were aired. This was followed by a question and answer period, in which all seemed to participate in earnest. An outside observer might suppose the existence of a keen interest on the part of the workers, and that a great effort was being made by them to remember these changes and institute them as company policy. To best summarize the need for such meetings and the positive contribution of the supervisor in the above regard, it should be noted that no change in working procedures (from the worker's perspective) occurred as a result of these meetings and discussions during my year on the job.

There were, of course, the indispensable duties of the higher echelon members, who could be seen at any time of the day staring out the window of an outer office or, in not so desperate moments, conversing in the cafeteria over tea.

The inactivity of higher ranking agency personnel was not necessarily a function of lack of interest or industry, but was rather a byproduct of the lack of essential duties. Parkinson's Law was rife. The greatest single function of this group, in terms of the daily routine operations of the organization, was to affix its signature to the one above the many quadruplicate copies of official paper that filed through their offices. Once this operation was set in motion, the process was automatic. The paper work continued along through an increasing chain of command, each level presumably giving their consideration and approval, when, in reality, they contributed little more than their signature. It was true that the supervisor's signature was required on all cases to insure proper adherence to company policy. The supervisor actually did review the cases and, as a matter of fact, was very conscientious in pursuing her duties. However, we have already noted some instances in which the supervisor's considered opinion seems to have had little influence upon whether or not worker practices conformed to the agency policies. Other examples of this will be presented below under a discussion of "Rules."

Since the heads of command contributed little to any actual change in the organization's working procedures in spite of their good intentions and many directives, their position as policy makers held little import for the worker or client. As persons responsible for checking on and improving the decisions of the lower echelons, they were to a large extent operationally superfluous. In conclusion, the organization gave every appearance of maintaining a vital and necessary formalized hierarchy, but in reality it is difficult to imagine how this hierarchy of command could have justified its existence in the name of increased organizational efficiency.

RULES

Did the agency have a set of standardized rules to which its members referred in making decisions, a code that would insure a standardization of administration and provide for impartial and unbiased service? A cursory search revealed the "welfare and institutions code," which, having presumably anticipated every contingency, had set down in an orderly and precise manner the way in which the worker was to expedite company business as it arose: which forms, for which case, how many copies, and with or without notary. What function did these tomes play? Were they taken as gospel, or was every man seeking his own salvation? A few examples that extend themselves many times in this agency's setting will give some indication.

It is only possible for the worker to handle a certain number of cases at a given time, and when this "case load" was exceeded, as it often was, it became the sole intent of the caseworker to dispose of the excess, however possible. The organization actually encouraged this activity since the "best" worker was the one who "expedited" the greatest number of cases per unit time. Since the supervisor had to read and approve all cases to insure adherence to company policy, the solution to the problem of disposing of excess cases had to come within the limits of action provided by the rules. This would seem to insure impartiality to the client and the standardization of agency procedures. The fact is, it did not. As an example, in interviewing the client, the worker was asked to list on a form provided for the purpose all persons who might be of some assistance to the client. Such persons were then contacted by letter or phone. The case remained open until answers to such inquiries had been obtained. If none were forthcoming, a second letter was sent. This process might have been expected to extend itself for weeks, during which time the worker was to aid the client and as a consequence was unable to "expedite" the case. As a result of this situation, an interview might take the following form:

Worker: Have you any persons who might contribute to your support, Mr. Jones?

Client: Yes, twelve: four cousins, my mother, father and six brothers, all out of town. But I doubt that they will help me.

Worker: (Records answer: None. Mother and father deceased. No friends or relatives to contribute to support.)

When reviewed by the supervisor, this case would give no indication of a breach of the rules. The supervisor had never met the client, the questions were asked, the answers given, and the spaces on the form were appropriately filled. Everything would seem to be in order. With this obstacle out of the way, the worker was now in a position to "expedite" the case as best he could, within the limits of the "rules." He was no longer subject to that particular constraint. Another example of the way in which workers succeeded in "expediting" cases is given below.

Persons with hospital appointments were to be aided until such appointments had been completed. This presented the worker with another type of case that was impossible to "turn over." On interviewing a new client, the worker would ask: "Are you in good health and have you any hospital appointments, Mr. Jones?" The answer might be: "I have an ear infection and my first appointment is in two weeks." The worker experiences a temporary setback, but there are still the impartial and equitable rules to refer to which require the client to show an appointment slip as proof of the appointment.

Worker: Have you your appointment slip, Mr. Jones?

Client: No, it was stolen with my wallet last night.

Worker: (Answer recorded: Mr. Jones has no hospital appointments and is apparently in fair health.)

This is yet another instance of overcoming the constraints of the rules and manueuvering a case into position for a quick turnover. The appearance is of meeting the rules and the reality is of beating them. Space permitting, I could extend this list to include violations of a great many routine "casework" procedures at the agency. The fact was that the rules were essentially meaningless with respect to their ability to standardize operating procedures and insure that company policy would be adhered to.

The illustrations given above were of the consistent lie variety. They were one means of "working" the rules and were part of the process by which the fiction, "symbolic bureaucracy," was created and perpetuated. Another method was that of using acceptable exceptions to the rules. For example, the rules stated that caseworkers were to come to work professionally attired. This excluded such apparel and styles as: no tie, festive sport shirts, open collars, or sandals. As a result, a typical exchange might have taken the following form:

Supervisor: Mr. B., why are you wearing sandals? Are you going to the beach?

(As a matter of fact, this is precisely what he and a co-worker had in mind for the afternoon, but it would never do to explain the sandals.)

Worker: (Chuckle) No, Mrs. L., I have a toe infection and my podiatrist requires me to wear this ridiculous footwear lest I lose my toe.

Supervisor: Oh, I'm sorry to hear of your illness, Mr. B. It isn't contagious is it?

To indulge in such a system of lies and acceptable exceptions was to provide for individual subjectivity regarding personal action toward co-workers and especially clients, while indulging all outsiders in the illusion of abiding by the impartiality insured by the rules. If one persisted in the above process over time, one became convinced that this state of affairs (whatever it was), and not bureaucracy, was the "given," and proceeded accordingly. Since the new worker soon reevaluated the nature of his task from that of learning and doing bureaucracy to that of learning to do in bureaucracy, and since he succeeded in doing this in such a way that those who had defined their task as establishing and perpetuating bureaucracy would not recognize the difference, everyone was happy. Both sets of persons were convinced that they were achieving their desired goals. The result is that whether we take Weber's conception of bureaucracy or Blau's, it may well be the case that neither exists, when either and/or both seem to.

IMPERSONALITY

The last condition, that of impersonality between ranks, was perhaps the one phase of bureaucracy best adhered to. This did not exclude favoritism. But such cases were not overt and, because of the potential embarrassment in having them pointed out, were few in number. However, this generalization did not hold so well in the relationship between worker and client. Since it was actually within the worker's discretion to aid the client or not, independent of rules, those clients exhibiting belligerent attitudes were soon "straightened out," while those leaving an impression of the "nice guy" stood a better chance.

One method of "straightening out" the client was to offer him "camp." This was, after all, one of the agency's legitimate services, and it was left to the option of the worker to offer "camp" sooner instead of later in the event it became expedient. "Camp," because of its unpopularity among the clients, was a very popular option for the overburdened worker looking for ways to "expedite cases." If the client, having been assisted with "outside" help for a week or so, was unsuccessful in securing employment (as most were), he could be offered "camp" as a way of either "straightening him out," in the case of a particularly troublesome client, or, in a more neutral vein, to simply dispose of the case. If the client refused the agency's services, i.e., "camp," he was free to seek service elsewhere and the case was closed. This was one way for the worker to "work" the client.

On the other hand, there was something of a dilemma for the worker trying to "expedite cases" by initiating this procedure. Because of the popularity of this form of assistance among the workers, and the limited number of spaces at camp facilities, there was often a long waiting list. The worker was obliged to assist the client "outside," if he accepted "camp" as a form of aid, until a "camp" opening became available. The clients came to know this. Indeed, many knew agency policy better than the "caseworkers" and recited it chapter and verse. This, of course, provided the client with a way of "working" the worker. The client had only to accept "camp," be assisted outside until his turn on the "camp" list appeared, and then not show up for placement. The case was then closed with one of the two epitaphs: "whereabouts unknown," or "refusal to accept assistance." The client was temporarily without assistance, but might show up at the agency in a week or two, and, having been assigned to a new worker, report how he "fell ill" on the day of the "camp" appointment. It was now for the new worker to turn over the case, as best his experience or lack of it allowed, within the guidelines provided by the agency.

There were many such transactions between worker and client that were characterized by the reciprocal act of "conning," followed by a period of "cooling out the mark."[11] In fact, so subtle had these unofficial transactions become, and so skillful the participants, that it was often very difficult to establish who had been the "mark." For example, in the above instance, the complexities of the situation were often compounded. After all, it was the client who sought out the worker, and the subordinate standing of the client in this relationship placed him at a distinct disadvantage in trying to "work" the worker. In the situation of offering "camp," there was interposed between the worker and client another member of the agency referred to as the "camp man." This "caseworker" was in charge of administering "camp" placements. The "camp man" was very popular among the workers, since it was left to his discretion (again not according to agency policy but according to worker policy) to assign "camp" dates to clients. In the case of a particularly difficult client, the worker had only to enlist the aid of the "camp man" who could be relied upon to "unexpectedly" uncover an available placement at "camp" for the client by moving him forward on the list.

There were, in short, available to the worker greater resources within the agency than there were resources available to the client. This handicap did not prevent the client from trying to manage his affairs as best he could under the circumstances. Indeed, it is more than an idle proverb that "necessity is the mother of invention." While the client was in fact in a distinctly disadvantaged position with respect to the worker, this very disadvantage and the necessity of overcoming it provided a strong and constant source of motivation toward invention. For example, bus tokens were another source of assistance to enable the client to get to and from the agency and to investigate possible employment opportunities. The client's task became one of talking the worker out of as many tokens as possible. There were many approaches to this problem. Perhaps the most common was to draw up a long list of appointments with prospective employers, and, in one way or another, try to convince the worker of their legitimacy. Having secured as many tokens as possible, the client had only to walk to the nearest bus stop and sell them at a cut rate to persons waiting for a bus. He could thereby unofficially enlist the agency's help in raising his subsidy. The worker, in time, became aware of this procedure and, depending upon his predilections toward the client that day, would dispense bus tokens (via a requisition form) accordingly.

Another unofficial transaction took place between the client and his local merchant. The task here was to negotiate the exchange of scrip for wine, a commodity that the scrip was specifically designed to exclude the client from purchasing. The transaction generally required little effort on the part of the client. It simply meant that the merchant, in exchange for this service, would charge the client more than the usual retail price for wine. In short, the client found that food scrip and tokens were negotiable, but only at a disadvantaged rate of exchange. While the merchant and the public at large had managed to negotiate a "good deal" at the expense of the client, the client was at least partially consoled by the knowledge that he had once again "worked" the worker. The public's resourcefulness in negotiating favorable rates of exchange in "tokens" has recently taken on the aspect of big business. An article in the Wall Street Journal notes:

> If you can stand a guilt-edged investment, go long on subway tokens.
>
> Subway riders—and many non-riders—are doing that here, hoarding the 20-cent tokens as a hedge against a fare increase. Speculation has become so rampant that many of the 840 token-short change booths are limiting sales to one or two at a time . . .
>
> Its shortage is so acute that 5 million new tokens have been ordered. A transit man estimates that 29 million tokens are in circulation—but that 7 million are held by hoarders. Normally the agency has a stockpile of 6 million tokens; now it has practically none.
>
> One Wall Street broker, for example, began buying tokens two years ago when they cost 15 cents: he made a handsome profit when the fare was increased by a nickel . . . The farsighted broker who says he's no longer hoarding concedes that he never was in it for the money. "Token hoarding is peanuts," he says, "but it's a matter of principle to try to stay ahead of the game."[12]

I need hardly point out that such dealings were unlikely to instill basic trust into the worker-client relationship. In fact, there were in these agency transactions what can generally be described as mutual suspension of trust. This is not to say that all clients and workers spent all their efforts at conning each other. Some clients, after all, used their bus tokens to reach prospective employers in search of work. Some clients may have even been teetotalers. Caseworkers, within the constraints of the "caseload," sometimes assisted the clients according to the intent of agency policy. However, because of the characteristics of the general population of persons seeking assistance from this particular department of the agency, the above practices on the part of the client and worker were "common practices." Most of the clients seen at the agency were unskilled, unemployed single men, generally in poor health, non-teetotalers, isolated residents of "skid row," and generally unemployable. In my year on the job I can only recall three clients who were sent for "rehabilitation" by the workers of my unit. Some clients did find work. Others spent time in and out of "camp," while many moved to other locales. However, there was a hard core of clients whose case records went back many years. These were on what could be described as a "revolving account." No one at the agency, least of all the clients, believed that agency services would suffice to extricate them from this situation. For these clients, the practices and procedures, some of which are described above, had become a way of life.

Although it was often the case, workers were not always at odds with the needs and sympathies of the clients. An example of caseworker sympathy for the lot of the client, even when the latter had officially placed himself outside the pale, is as follows: Clients at "camp" were allowed to accept farm employment outside of "camp." They were not required to do so and might refuse such work when it was offered. Many took this course. This was not surprising when one realized that the client, once he had accepted a farm job, had to pay his own transportation to and from "camp," his meals on the job, and any other operating expenses for the day. Because of this, and the low wages paid, coupled with the fact that clients were not steadily employed at farm work and were not in the best physical condition, such employment often amounted to clients working a long hard day for a net gain of a dollar or two. One might better stay at "camp" and recuperate. Not everyone, however, thought this way, and some welcomed the opportunity to get away from "camp" and make some "spending money." If an individual elected to accept farm work, he had to show up on the job at the appointed time and work the day. If he did not, it was considered a case of "refusal to accept assistance" or "whereabouts unknown," and he became temporarily ineligible for all aid, "camp" included. In one instance, a group of men at "camp" contracted to work at a farm picking vegetables. When the trucks transporting the clients arrived, they found they were asked to pick a vegetable other than that for which they had contracted. "Picking" is a specialized task. Picking one kind of fruit or vegetable can be very different from picking another variety. As a result, those familiar with one kind of work cannot even "cover expenses" if required to do another. Because of this, the men refused to work. The agency took the position that the men had refused services and were ineligible for aid in or out of "camp." A list of these clients was circulated to the agencies in the surrounding districts so as to alert the caseworkers who might otherwise have unwittingly assisted them. The opinion of the workers studied by the author upon hearing of this was a general indignation at what they felt constituted an arbitrary and unjust act on the part of the agency. Some threatened to take it up with the union, while others threatened to write an expose. To the best of my knowledge, nothing was ever done. However, it was an example of the caseworkers as a group expressing sympathy for the clients as a group, even when the latter had acted contrary to agency policy.

CONCLUSIONS

The above are only a few examples of the many discrepancies between the real and the apparent workings of one "bureaucratic" organization. If a list of actual worker practices at the agency were compared to a list of supposed worker practices, and the discrepancies evaluated for how they affected the workings of bureaucracy, I believe that little more than an image of bureaucracy would remain. Since the actual operation of the agency seems not to have been according to bureaucratic principles, it would be an area of interest for future research to determine in what manner it is operating. I say "is" because I doubt that worker practices have changed very much, notwithstanding possible changes in agency policy that may have occurred with time. It was the opinion of some of the long-established workers at the time (there were not many because of the considerable turnover in agency personnel at the "caseworker" level) that things have been the way they were for many years, in terms of workers' policy being designed to meet workers' needs as opposed to client or agency needs

I would agree with Blau that deviation from the "ideal type" is necessary in order to contend with the dilemmas outlined at the beginning and, more specifically, to meet the obvious objection that in the agency studied by the author the conditions described by the "ideal type" are nowhere to be found, ideally or otherwise. However, in introducing "adjustive development," it becomes crucial to be able to discern which unofficial changes are beneficial and which are detrimental, if we are to be able to save Blau's dynamic bureaucracy. This necessity presents one with a dilemma that seems to have thus far received little attention. I would suggest that unofficial positive change cannot easily be distinguished from unofficial negative change, and, in providing for the one, we must contend with the other. The real problem lies in the fact that it is possible to institute unofficial change while maintaining the appearance of no change at all. If the change is not discernible, it is impossible to subject it to criteria which will allow for the recognition and retention of beneficial change while guarding against the unknowing acceptance of detrimental change. It seems unlikely that bureaucracy will be saved by introducing the notion of "unofficial change," as long as persons within the organization (or those outsiders looking in) find it as difficult as they must to assess whether or not they are operating in a bureaucracy (or ever were), or whether they have lapsed into a state of "symbolic bureaucracy."

NOTES

[1] From Max Weber, *Essays in Sociology,* translated by H. H. Gerth and C. Wright Mills (New York: Oxford University Press, 1946), p. 215.

[2] *Ibid.,* pp. 196-244.

[3] Peter M. Blau, *Bureaucracy in Modern Society* (New York: Random House, 1956), pp. 28-30.

[4] *Ibid.,* pp. 59-60.

[5] *Ibid.,* pp. 36.

[6] *Ibid.,* p. 57.

[7] *Ibid.,* p. 61.

[8] *Ibid.,* p. 19.

[9] *Montgomery vs. Burns* declared state residence requirements unconstitutional in the state of California (April 19, 1968). This case in now on appeal from the U. S. Ninth District Court, Northern California, to the U. S. Supreme Court.

[10] Erving Goffman, *Asylums* (New York: Doubleday & Co., 1961), pp. 1-124.

[11] Erving Goffman, "On Cooling the Mark Out: Some Aspects of Adaptation to Failure," *Psychiatry,* XV (1952), 451-463.

[12] *Wall Street Journal,* January 16, 1968, p. 1.

4. THE MEDICAL MANAGEMENT OF DEVIANCE

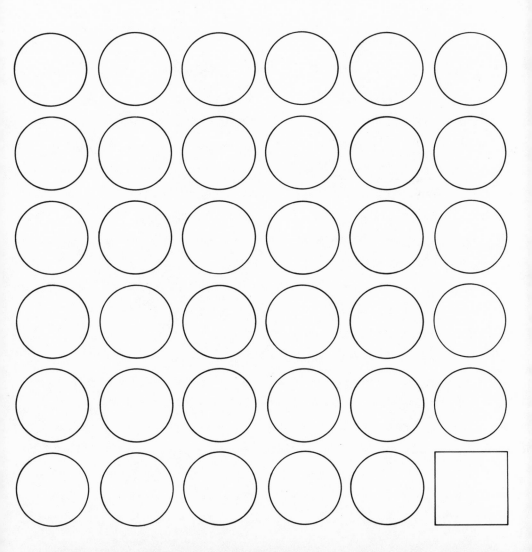

THE MEDICAL MANAGEMENT OF DEVIANCE

4. Part Four will be concerned with deviance within medical settings. In keeping with the leitmotif of the book, we will see how practitioners intentionally or inadvertently label others, how these labelling processes have untoward consequences, and how the interactants work to neutralize negative labels and their effects.

"The Clinical Organization of Sub-Normality" discusses the way in which medical experts resolve the apparent dilemma of cases of "miraculous recovery" within the constraints of medical science by referring to another practitioner's misdiagnosis. In such cases, "science" is invariably saved while the patient is lost, in terms of providing him with the most rational course of treatment. The clinician's inability to transcend the constraints of the medical model with respect to the form of "severe mental retardation" considered in the essay, and the "ad-hocing" procedures they evoke to resolve the discrepancy between the original diagnosis and the patient's later performance, will be discussed in an analysis of case history material. The untoward consequences for the patients in such cases, and why the "taken-for-granted" assumptions discussed in the study warrant a reevaluation, also come under consideration.

In the second reading, "The 'Quack' as Healer," we will see how persons frequenting a marginal practitioner at a "quack" clinic for the treatment of rheumatism and arthritis did so only after a sampling of more traditional treatment plans proved ineffective. For most patients, the clinic was seen as a last resort in their search for help (or at least hope) with what they regarded as an "incurable" disease and a release from the chronic pain that accompanies rheumatism and arthritis. In this they were not disappointed. The doctors got results. The pain was lessened and the patient was in most cases better able to function. Grateful for the relief of symptoms, patients were not overly worried about the negative short-range or long-range side effects. Many brought news clippings about these potential side effects to the doctor's attention. They received for their trouble a knowing laugh, an indulgent smile, or an open refutation by the miracle worker of the claims of legitimate medicine.

The patients had little or no knowledge of what "miracle medicine" the doctor had prescribed or why it seemed to "work." At least a partial reason for its efficacy is given in the essay—the drug was cortizone. This drug, while helpful in giving relief from the pain of rheumatism and arthritis, may also produce hazardous side effects such as bleeding ulcers. However, when they were told that they were *not* being treated with cortizone, the patients were so relieved to hear it that they did not pursue the question of the "miracle drug" any further. Why patients were satisfied with their own interpretations of the miraculous doctor and his miraculous cure becomes clearer upon consideration of the nature of the doctor-patient interactions described in the study. In the final analysis, a good deal turned upon the doctor's presentation of self, the confidence he exuded, his offering grounds for hope, his charming manner, and, finally, "the results." All of this established in the patient a blind acceptance of the doctor and his treatment plan, and, with few exceptions, an unswerving confidence in his medical competence and moral character.

In this essay both the patients and the clinic doctors are cast in deviant roles. Persons with medical problems seeking solutions to them outside of accepted and legitimate medical channels are viewed by others as "odd-balls," "health-food nuts," "mystics," or unfortunate and misinformed persons. In brief, the general public and the legitimate medical community attempt to stigmatize persons who go outside the establishment in search of help. The clinic patients, while they do not see themselves in this light, are nevertheless viewed in this way by others. The clinic doctor, who prescribes drugs whose contents remain unknown, who says that his prescriptions do not contain harmful drugs when they do, who falsely claims to have been associated with the Mayo Clinic, and who implicitly claims to be able to diagnose one's ailment with little or no examination of the patient, must also be viewed within the constraints of acceptable medical practice as deviant.

Both essays deal with doctor-patient interactions in a social setting connected with what Goffman calls "the service model." The service model exhibits some peculiar tensions when applied to the social situations connected with medical practice. Many of these trade on the fact that the thing the doctor is to "fix," and the person he fixes it for, are one and the same. Once a patient comes to the medical practitioner with some trouble, the service model dictates a strict separation of roles, as between the "repair man" and "the object to be repaired." Therefore, from the doctor's perspective the salient characteristic of the patient role is passivity. The nature of the trouble, what is to be done, how it is to be done, the definition of recovery—all are matters to be properly decided by the doctor. In short, the practitioner expects complete control over the definition of the situation. However, the patient's personal involvement insures that he is more than a passive recipient of treatment. He tends to get actively involved in defining his own condition, and its treatment. The resulting tensions in such settings are well known to doctors. They engage in special efforts to assure the passivity of the patient and his acceptance of their definition of the situation. These efforts on the part of the doctor are standard operating procedures.

In both of the essays we can see the practitioner's concern with convincing the patients, and their significant others, that the doctor's definition of the situation is the authoritative one. In the case of retarded children, this takes the form of preserving the status of medical practitioners, as well as medical knowledge and procedure, as the legitimate and authoritative agencies for correctly labeling the nature and extent of subnormality. In the essay on the Mexican "clinic," one of the key functions of the quack is his ability to define the situation of patients in a positive light. The doctor is able to succeed in getting the patient to accept his definition of the situation by convincing him that he is a competent "repairman."

The Clinical Organization of "Sub-Normality": A Case of Mistaken Identity

Jerry Jacobs

In his essay "Tacit Knowledge of Everyday Activities," Cicourel states that sociologists "seldom concern themselves with the properties of everyday social life" but take them for granted. Furthermore, both the "natural" and "laboratory" events studied "are not established by asking first what a 'natural order' is like, and then what it would take to generate activities members . . . would label 'unnatural' or 'natural.' Instead, the problems taken as points of departure are assumed to be 'obvious' instances of *the* 'real world.' " Any sociologist insisting that such a study should begin with an examination of the properties of routine practical activities in everyday life "is not likely to meet with the approval of colleagues who have already decided what the 'real world' is all about, and they have already been studying 'it' for a long time."[1]

This description of certain key assumptions routinely made by sociologists applies equally well to psychiatrists. Psychiatrists also take as a point of departure the "obvious" instances of the "real world," without being overly concerned about what it would take to generate activities that members of society would label "unnatural." I will be concerned in this paper with psychiatrists who evaluate the possibility of mental retardation in children, and with the ways in which these evaluations generate and preserve certain categories of mental retardation. I will also consider the reasons why these categories do not seem "unnatural" to those who accept and perpetuate them. I will begin by considering one class of "severely retarded" children—non-verbal, non-testable children with no discernible organ pathology—and the general belief among physicians that all children so diagnosed relatively late in childhood have no prospect of ever achieving a normal or above-normal level of intellectual performance. When such children have miraculous recoveries later in life, it is invariably held, in retrospect, that they were wrongly diagnosed to begin with; that is, it is usually assumed that the retardation must have been a case of childhood schizophrenia all along. On the other hand, when children who had been diagnosed as childhood schizophrenics miraculously recover, it is *not* assumed that they might have recovered from severe retardation, or from a combination of schizophrenia and retardation. The evidence seems not to warrant such assumptions, especially when it is so difficult to establish the existence or influence of either schizophrenia or retardation at the time of the diagnosis,[2] let alone several years later. The issue is further complicated by the fact that so many of these cases seem to carry a mixed diagnosis of severe retardation and childhood schizophrenia, with an emphasis on one or the other.[3]

A question then arises. Why, in cases of miraculous recovery (the recovery of children initially diagnosed as severely retarded and later found to possess a normal or above-normal level of intelligence), is it invariably assumed in retrospect that the inconsistency found between the physician's initial prognosis and the child's later performance is best explained by presuming against the original diagnosis? A more convincing hypothesis in many of these cases seems to be that severe mental retardation, at least in the class of children noted above, is sometimes reversible. The reason why this latter position is never entertained, let alone accepted, must be sought in the fact that it is a psychiatrist who is later called upon to rationalize any apparent contradiction found between the anticipated "before" and the resulting "after." This they do by entertaining the possibility of an original faulty diagnosis and then accepting this possibility as "given." The reason for this is to a large extent based upon the psychiatrists' prior "background expectancies,"[4] which in turn rest upon certain assumptions given in the medical model of mental retardation and assimilated by physicians in the course of their professional training. These have been succinctly presented by a popular and influential spokesman as follows: "In the light of present knowledge, mental retardation is essentially irreversible. This does not deny the possibility of prevention or amelioration; but though many therapies and other maneuvers have been hailed, few have survived the test of time. Preventive measures . . . have had some limited success; but *adequately diagnosed mental retardation probably never is reversed to normal* [Emphasis added.] ."[5]

Psychiatrists are subject to other constraints in their attempt to rationalize "contradictory" findings. This depends upon their acceptance of some generally held position on mental retardation, which in turn is determined to a large extent by the assumptions and practices of the particular institution or agency they work for. Garfinkel has formulated the general case of this influence as follows: "In short, *recognizable* sense, or fact, or methodic character, or impersonality, or objectivity of accounts are not independent of the socially organized occasions of their use. Their rational features *consist* of what members do with, what they 'make of' the accounts in the socially organized actual occasions of their use. Members' accounts are reflexively and essentially tied for their rational features to the socially organized occasions of their use, for they are *features* of the socially organized occasions of their use."[6]

For example, a psychiatrist—a consultant at several children's services— recently told me of a case where he had occasion to see the same child in five different clinical settings, and in each instance the child received a different diagnosis. In a psychiatrically oriented evaluation center, "non-verbal" "non-testable" children without discernible organic pathologies are likely to be diagnosed as cases of "childhood schizophrenia," whereas in an "organically" oriented center they are likely to be diagnosed as "brain-damaged." One authority has referred to "The diagnostic schizophrenia that exists in many states—in this commonwealth, for example, where certified psychiatrists in one institution claim a patient is primarily retarded, whereas in another they say, with the same conviction, that the person is primarily psychotic or mentally ill, making an individual patient a virtual football between two teams of experts. The commissioner in the state house usually referees these games."[7]

This practice is so routinely accepted that an authority on mental retardation lecturing to an audience of doctors I was attending, got a big laugh by opening with this gambit: "Let's see, I must get oriented. Am I lecturing at X clinic or Y clinic? Oh, yes, this is X clinic; they're all schizophrenic here, aren't they?"

Apart from the inconsistencies in orientation and practice, the confusion of terminology within any one camp can be overwhelming. The use of the terms "functional mental retardation" and "mental deficiency" is a case in point. Functional retardation means that the child is functioning at a subnormal level of intelligence; in addition, it is inferred that the child may possess the potential to operate at a much higher level of intelligence than his current performance would indicate. Autistic children are often given this diagnosis. Whereas those who are "functionally retarded" may improve even to the point of achieving a normal level of intellectual performance, those who are "mentally deficient" are given no hope of recovery. Mental deficiency usually assumes organic pathology for which no known remedy exists. Where it is impossible to isolate the particular organic pathology that a diagnosis of "mental deficiency" implies, such pathologies are not infrequently inferred on the basis of "clinical insight." Then, too, there is considerable disagreement among practitioners regarding the concept of childhood schizophrenia. For example, some consider the terms autism and childhood schizophrenia to be synonymous, while others believe they are distinct entities.[8]

Quite apart from whether or not they are the same, there arises the prior question of what they are: "In planning such corrective remediation, the therapist inevitably assumes a theory of etiology though it is most often more implicit than explicit . . . Indeed, one must not lose sight of the additional fact that the descriptive entity childhood schizophrenia is grossly defined and differences among the children within any schizophrenic sample are as striking as are the similarities. Certainly the notion of a disease in the sense of a single definable pathologic agent remote in time, an inevitable course of development, and a predetermined course of treatment is still a mythical one."[9]

Arbitrary distinctions such as those we have noted need not cause undue confusion here if we keep in mind that among the class of children being discussed, the position of the medical community is that those whose intellectual performance reaches or exceeds the normal level at some later date are by definition not "really" retarded (for example, in the case of childhood schizophrenia), whereas those whose I.Q.'s do not reach a normal level at some later time are considered retarded or retarded and schizophrenic.

The popularity of this medical position notwithstanding, an alternative hypothesis can be drawn: severe mental retardation, at least in some instances and for whatever reasons, is reversible. Furthermore, since it is extremely difficult to determine in the above instance whether a child is autistic or retarded or both (or what these terms mean), one cannot help but wonder if some cases of miraculous recovery by "autistic" or "schizophrenic" children were not instances of recovery by retarded children.

I will present in the remainder of this paper well-documented case history material and verbatim accounts which will indicate the difficulty often encountered in establishing the etiology of retardation in cases of non-verbal, non-testable children. This will be followed by a discussion of a case of miraculous recovery diagnosed as childhood schizophrenia, where there was good reason to suppose that retardation was also a factor. Finally, two cases will be cited to show how, when a diagnosis of severe retardation proved "erroneous" because of the individual's complete recovery, it was accepted as given that the error lay in the diagnosis, and not with the commonly held view that the intellectual functioning of *all* "severely retarded" children of the class noted above is somehow permanently impaired.

I will begin by pointing out how difficult it is to establish the "etiology" of mental retardation. Edgerton has noted over one-hundred "causes" of retardation in the literature.[10] Another authoritative source gives twice this number.[11] As things currently stand, it is the exceptional case that allows for a causal relationship to be shown. "With present knowledge regarding the causal factors in mental retardation, it is possible to identify precise causes in approximately 15 to 25 percent of cases. In such cases, organic pathology as a result of disease or injuries is often demonstrable, most readily in instances where the degree of retardation is severe and there has been gross brain damage."[12]

The problem of isolating the causal factor or factors in retardation for the group of children being considered here is graphically illustrated by the following case history. What is to be presented below is not an entire case history but only a series of relevant excerpts taken from the case history accounts.[13]

Case No. 1

Paul is a seven and a half year-old Caucasian boy. Both parents are professionals, well-educated, and occupy a high socioeconomic status. Paul is non-verbal, non-testable, and not toilet trained. He seemed to develop normally until about the age of nine months. It first came to the mother's attention at that point that Paul was "slow," and they began to be concerned about his rate of development. In 1961, at the request of their pediatrician, Paul's parents took him for a psychological examination. In March of that year, his I.Q. on the Kuhmann and Cottel scales was 74 and 61 respectively. By August, his I.Q. on the same scales was 55 and 46. In August of 1962 he was tested a third time by the same doctor (one of some eminence in the field of retardation) and his performance had regressed to I.Q. 31 and 28. The diagnosis and prognosis was stated as follows: "There can be no question of this child's retardation, and the failure to make any progress on the tests during a year, all of which were given by me, indicates lack of ability to develop beyond the infantile stage." Paul's parents went to great lengths to establish the reasons for his retardation. Every effort was made to isolate the causal factors. He has undergone psychological testing, observations, chromosome analysis, pneumoencephalogram, EEG, neurological exams, skull films, and more. All findings were either negative or sufficiently ambiguous to exclude the possibility of any definite conclusions being drawn. The case records note: "Paul's current status is an enigma. No medical person has been able to give a diagnosis of his condition. The Joneses have been to a series of professionals, all apparently quite eminent people."

The professionals' inability to offer a reason for Paul's retardation presented the parents with a series of dilemmas. For example, should they have another child? The case record notes that when Paul's parents put this question to the geneticist, "he could not predict what the chances were of their having another retarded child and made no recommendation as to whether they should have other children." On the other hand, their pediatrician recommended that the Joneses have more children and have Paul put in an institution. Another question was what could they realistically expect of Paul. Whereas the doctor who tested Paul felt he would not progress beyond the infantile level, others were more cautious in their prognosis, since the cause of his retardation could not be established.

The contrary inferences drawn by different professionals regarding the same piece of information has led to much frustration and anxiety for Paul's parents. This account is not intended to reflect upon the competence of practitioners (although this is sometimes an important factor); it is intended only to give some indication of how difficult it can be to establish the cause or causes of retardation, even among the "severely retarded," where it is supposed to be most easily established.

Problems of diagnosis, as previously noted, result from more than the imperfect state of the medical sciences. They are also a function of the orientation of the particular agency for which the clinician works. In this regard, we find that Paul has recently undergone another medical and psychological evaluation at still another agency. There he was diagnosed as both "severely retarded" and "psychotic." The prognosis for his future development is poor. An optimistic prediction at this point would be that he is "trainable." The current evaluation, like the past ones, has left the question of the cause or causes of Paul's retardation unanswered. Furthermore, it has added for the first time to the long-standing diagnosis of "severe retardation" the diagnosis of "psychosis."

The next case presents an example of a diagnosis of childhood schizophrenia being made where the question of mental retardation cannot easily be ruled out. Retardation in this case was deemphasized in much the same manner that childhood schizophrenia was in the preceding case.

Case No. 2

Joanne is a thirteen-year-old Caucasian girl who lives with her mother. The father and mother are divorced. When first seen in 1959 Joanne was five years old and characterized as isolated, "bordering on mutism," and non-testable. All physical, neurological, and laboratory findings were within normal limits. Her diagnosis at the time was "schizophrenic reaction, childhood type." By 1961 the psychologist stated: "In summary, Joanne's functioning is on such a higher, more integrated level than at the previous evaluation that an I.Q. test can be administered to her." Upon testing she was found to be *"in the upper range of borderline defective level."* [Emphasis added].

In 1964 the psychologist's report stated: "Joanne readily understands highly abstract concepts . . . her test responses as well as her behavior indicate many changes during the last one and a half years. Her performance on the Information and Similarities Subtests and Sequin Form Board were adequate, and her spontaneous use of language suggest above average verbal ability."

Currently, Joanne is thirteen and has just completed the sixth grade of normal classes in public school. The case record notes: "She is very verbal and demonstrates an above average intellectual endowment. The reader will, no doubt, be struck by the marked difference in the case summary of 1959 of an autistic child 'bordering on mutism.' "

The first two cases were both instances of mixed diagnosis, the first with an emphasis on retardation, the second with an emphasis on childhood schizophrenia.

The third case, to be presented next, was also one of a mixed diagnosis, in which the diagnosis of retardation in childhood was replaced ex post facto with a diagnosis of childhood schizophrenia; currently neither the retardation nor the schizophrenia is in evidence. In none of these three cases were the clinicians involved able to offer a more or less conclusive statement regarding the etiology of either the retardation or the childhood schizophrenia.

Case No. 3

Johnny is a fifteen year-old Caucasian boy who lives with his mother and two siblings. The father died in 1956. The case record notes: "John's development was slow from the beginning. He sat at nine months and did not start to walk until age two. He had no speech until age 6. He could not yet distinguish colors at the age of six. At age five, mother attempted to enroll him in kindergarten. He sat in the middle of the classroom screaming, soiled and smeared himself and all he could reach. Mother was asked not to bring him back. He

was seen by a psychiatrist at that time and diagnosed as mentally retarded . . . . and needing special education, to be started at age eight."

For the next three years, Johnny did not attend school and was kept at
home. Most of his early years were spent in England. There were a number of
moves during this time, and when he was ten his mother enrolled him in a
special school in Germany. "He was there evaluated by a German psychiatrist
in a residential setting. The conclusion was that John was not retarded, but
rather, severely neurotic. John did very well in the special school. In six
weeks he learned German and caught up with the class."

Johnny remained in the special school until he was fourteen. By then he
had learned to read and write. At the age of fourteen he was no longer eligible
to remain at the school because of an age limitation. His mother emigrated to
the United States and Johnny, because of his past history of "retardation,"
was initially enrolled in an "educable" class for the mentally retarded within
the public school system. It was soon apparent that he was capable of normal
work and he was placed in regular classes. He is now enrolled in junior high
school in regular classes and getting A's and B's.

An explanation of John's recovery with respect to the diagnosis of mental
retardation is noted in the case records as follows: "In childhood, John was
severely retarded and was apparently suffering from a psychosis which is not
apparent at all at present."

"Severely retarded" as used here referred to severe "functional retardation," a distinction previously noted. I believe that there is good reason to
question this diagnosis imposed by hindsight. John's slow development indicated retardation, his past social and intellectual performance indicated retardation, and he was diagnosed professionally by a psychiatrist at age five as
being retarded. To suddenly state in retrospect, in the light of his recovery,
that the retardation was in fact a case of childhood schizophrenia (he was
diagnosed as "severely neurotic" at age ten) is a position that is not easily
tenable. It seems to me more reasonable to suppose that he was in fact severely retarded and for some reason recovered. Such a position was not even
entertained by a group of psychiatrists who heard this case. Indeed, they all
spontaneously enjoyed a good laugh at the "obvious error" of the original
diagnosis. Nor was this case unique. Several others of this kind have been
brought to the author's attention within a single clinical setting. A final one is
offered for the reader's consideration.

Case No. 4

Joan is a four-year-old Caucasian girl who resides with her foster mother.
She was first seen at the age of two and a half, when she was functioning at
the six-month level. The case record states: "Diagnostic impression was mental

deficiency, severe idiopathic, with severe stress being extreme emotional deprivation and lack of care by parents." Joan was unable to walk or talk and was totally unresponsive to her environment. Her behavior was characterized as "essentially placid and unresponsive." Prior to this, she had received an in-patient medical evaluation elsewhere and was found to be "physically and mentally retarded without specific detectable cause."

A few months after she was first seen, she was taken from the care of her natural mother and placed in the care of a foster mother. Within the period of about a year, Joan had shown striking progress. "She now feeds herself well, is completely toilet-trained, well-groomed, verbal, affectionate and responsive to adults, and engaging in play with obvious pleasure with other children."

It is true that Joan still shows some residual symptoms in terms of her prior emotional disturbance. However, the case record states: "It was clear a striking change in this girl had occurred in response to a change in her mothering relationship. In a few months' time, a girl who had originally been considered to be severely mentally defective at the late age of two and a half years demonstrated capacity for rapid growth and development, physical, mental, and emotional . . . The diagnosis of severe mental deficiency is of course not appropriate at this point and further evaluation is indicated to clarify the nature and extent of her emotional disturbance as well as more definite evaluation of the degree of any remaining functional retardation as indicated perhaps in her play and speech."

There is no way to know for certain whether Joan will eventually reach a normal level of intellectual performance. However, based upon her miraculous rate of development in the past year or so, there are at the very least promising indications. It seems almost certain that she will reach at least a level of "mild retardation" and may well go on to become a normally intelligent child.

How many other cases of this kind can be brought to light is a question that warrants our attention. An attempt at a systematic collection of recorded cases of miraculous recovery among "severely retarded" or "autistic" children and a reevaluation of these and new cases in the light of the above analysis might prove very rewarding, given the serious implications for diagnosis and treatment of accepting per se the widely held set of assumptions described above.

The key question is really whether or not in the case of miraculous recovery of non-verbal, non-testable children (when no organic pathological cause can be established) from a state of severe retardation to one of normal or above-normal intellectual functioning, it needs to be assumed that the potential to realize this new intellectual level had always existed in the individual and that it remained only to liberate it. Case history accounts indicate that the potential necessary to perform at a normal or above-normal level of intelligence may be lost at one point and recovered at some later period. Should this prove to be true, the prognosis for the class of severely retarded children discussed in this paper may not be so hopeless as is now supposed. The author believes that in light of the evidence, this possibility has been too quickly and easily disposed of—or perhaps more accurately, has not yet been entertained.

NOTES

[1] Aaron V. Cicourel, *The Social Organization of Juvenile Justice* (New York: John Wiley and Sons, Inc., 1968), pp. 3-4.

[2] S. A. Szurek and I. Philips, "Mental Retardation and Psychotherapy," in *Prevention and Treatment of Mental Retardation,* Ed. I. Philips (New York: Basic Books, 1966), p.221

[3] Lauretta Bender, "Childhood Schizophrenia: A Review," *Journal of the Hillside Hospital,* 16 (1), January 1967, pp. 10-20.

[4] Harold Garfinkel, *Studies in Ethnomethodology* (Englewood Cliffs, N. J.: Prentice-Hall, 1967), pp. 35-65

[5] E. A. Doll, "Recognition of Mental Retardation in the School-Age Child," in *Prevention and Treatment of Mental Retardation,* Ed. I. Philips (New York: Basic Books, 1966), p. 62.

[6] Garfinkel, *Studies in Ethnomethodology,* pp. 3-4.

[7] A statement made by Dr. Peter Bowman, Superintendent, Pineland Hospital and Training Center, Maine, in the *PCMR Message,* No. 11, April 1968, p. 1.

[8] B. Pasamanick, "Etiologic Factors in Early Infantile Autism and Childhood Schizophrenia," *Journal of the Hillside Hospital,* 16 (1), January 1967, pp. 42-52.

[9] William Goldfarb, "Corrective Socialization: A Rationale for the Treatment of Schizophrenic Children," *Journal of the Hillside Hospital,* 16 (1), January 1967, pp. 58-71.

[10] Robert B. Edgerton, *The Cloak of Competence* (Berkeley: University of California Press, 1967), p. 2.

[11] "Mental Retardation," reprinted from the *Journal of the American Medical Association,* Vol. 191, No. 3, January 18, 1965, p. 1.

[12] President's Panel on Mental Retardation, "A Proposed Program for National Action to Combat Mental Retardation" (Washington, D.C.: U. S. Government Printing Office, 1962), pp. 6-7. Also see "Mental Retardation," p. 1.

[13] The following excerpts are taken from the case history accounts of a large metropolitan clinic offering treatment and evaluation services for the mentally ill and mentally retarded. All names, dates, and places have been changed to insure the anonymity of the patients.

The Quack as Healer: A Study in Doctor-Patient Interaction

Carol Whitehurst

●●● The purpose of this paper will be to describe a Mexican border-
●●● town "clinic" which catered to American patients who suffered
●●■ from arthritis and other chronic diseases, and which has been
shown to have used dishonest medical practices. In such a setting both the
patients and the "clinic" personnel may be seen as "deviants," the personnel
for offering questionable medical care and the patients for seeking it.

Support for the contention that the patients and the clinic doctors were
doing something generally considered out of the ordinary, abnormal, or unac-
ceptable, from the point of view of established medicine, can be had from
several sources. First, a series of three articles in the local newspaper set out
to determine whether the doctors at the clinic (Dr. M. and his nephew,
Dr. C.) were really working miracles or if they were treating their patients

with something potentially dangerous. In the second of the three articles, the newspaper reported that although the doctors adamantly maintained that they prescribed no cortisone, a potentially dangerous drug, three pills were analyzed by a local laboratory and were found to contain hydrocortisone, a combination of prednisone and prednisolone (both derivatives of cortisone), and terramycin, a broad spectrum antibiotic that can be dangerous if not carefully controlled.[1]

Although this seemed proof enough that the clinic was a deviant enterprise, letters of inquiry were sent to the Mayo Clinic (with whom D. M. is reported by many patients to have connections) and to the American Medical Association. The Mayo Clinic answered promptly stating that Dr. M. was totally unknown to them and that they had received many requests for information about him in recent years. They also said that their staff was not aware of Dr. M.'s work ever having been reported in a medical or scientific journal.[2]

The letter from the American Medical Association stated that it was the belief of the Association that the medications prescribed by the clinic were extremely high doses of cortisone, although they had no proof of this. They went on to quote a representative of the Arthritis Foundation as saying, "I have talked with many, many very sad and disillusioned (and broke) arthritis sufferers who have been to him (Dr. M.) for his miracle treatment. Some have developed bleeding ulcers which required surgery."[3]

Finally, the author contacted the local branch of The Arthritis Foundation. Their representative stated that their position was essentially that of the investigating newspaper—that they would not recommend the clinic and believed that its patients were getting huge doses of cortisone. The representative said that hardly anyone ever called first to inquire about the clinic, and that she had talked to persons who had been there who had a very favorable opinion of it. She went on to say, however, that they knew of a patient at the clinic last year, a young woman in her early twenties with rheumatoid arthritis, who began experiencing some rather severe side effects of cortisone therapy. She stopped taking the prescribed medication and apparently began to have what the representative called "withdrawal symptoms" and other complications. The representative mentioned that Mexican doctors are not subject to the same controls and regulations as doctors in the United States, and are freer to "experiment" if they wish.[4]

The clinic in question and the doctors who ran it were not only perpetrating a fraud upon the public, but, as we shall see later, were observing only minimal medical and professional standards. This paper will offer some observations on the clinic setting, describe the persons who attended it, and sum up the general atmosphere of the clinic and the attitudes of the patients toward it. Finally, it will attempt to reach some conclusions about why a person chooses to patronize a "fringe" establishment rather than continue with "normal" treatment in a legitimate setting.

THE SETTING

As the new patient crosses the border and drives into Mexicali, hanging above the street he sees a large, simple, black and white marquee-type sign pointing the way to the office of Drs. M. and C., "one-half block left." By the time he has made the left turn he can see the medical building displaying a similar sign over its double glass doors. There is a large unpaved parking lot next to the "clinic" where for fifty cents one can park all day, and swarms of young, English-speaking Mexican boys will park your car and wash it if they can talk you into it. The boys say they work for the doctors; and since they give you a metered parking ticket, it is assumed that this could be another money-making venture for the clinic. In the parking lot there are mostly medium-sized, medium-priced cars, usually several years old. Small foreign cars and large, expensive, or flashy cars are conspicuously absent. Most of the cars seem to have California license plates, but there are a few from other states and some from Mexico. It was impossible to tell if all the cars in the lot belonged to clinic patients.

Upon entering the clinic one is struck by the modernity of the building and the contrast with most buildings in Mexicali. The interior is spacious and clean, well-lighted and airy. Near the entrance is a glassed-in section for the office girls, their filing cabinets, and adding machines. In front of their counter is a table with an electric urn of hot water, powdered coffee, sugar, and cups. There are two water coolers, one at each end of the room. The room is rather long and narrow, and around the walls and in the middle of the room are yellow upholstered benches with backs. Between the benches is a table stacked with magazines.

On one of the long walls there are two doors displaying the names of the doctors and leading to their offices. Between the doors is a large artificial rubber plant. On the walls there are two framed diplomas and two signs which read, in English, "No smoking." There are no other decorations. At the end of the room, there is a door leading to the only rest room.

The receptionists, or office girls, all spoke English and were well groomed, young and attractive. They also seemed to be entirely bored with their jobs and with the patients. I was struck on each visit by how indifferent the girls seemed, when compared to the usual medical receptionist. They were not actually rude, but their habit of keeping the patients waiting and never mitigating this with a smile or an apology made me feel that they were totally disinterested. There were no nurses in the clinic and none of the girls wore a uniform.

Upon coming to the clinic for the first time, the patient is asked to fill out a form giving his name, address, telephone number, and age. There is no medical history of any kind requested, nor is it necessary to state your complaint. The patient is then given a number and is asked to wait until the number is called. The wait is usually from two to three hours, depending on how busy the doctor is. It appears that the doctor generally sees from sixty to eighty patients each of the five days a week the clinic is open. (It also appears that Dr. C. is running the clinic almost alone; Dr. M. seems to be there only infrequently.)

When the patient is finally called, he enters one of the two offices and is seated in one of the deep, comfortable, gold vinyl-covered chairs in front of the doctor's huge desk. The office is furnished with a couch and a thick gold carpet, and generally gives an appearance of opulence. (A fuller description of the office is given in the field notes.)

The doctor, who has an extremely charming, if not ingratiating, manner, is young and attractive, and wears a white tunic over dark slacks. In a pleasant, almost lilting voice, he asks about the patient's complaint and any surgeries and enters this information on a 3 x 5 card (presumably the same card on which the office girl has entered the patient's name and other particulars). At this point, the patient is moved a few feet to the "examining room," which is an ill-equipped alcove, where the doctor quickly takes blood pressure and perfunctorily listens to the patient's heart without removing any of the patient's clothing. In my case, the medical evaluation proved completely inaccurate. (See the field notes for a more detailed description.)

The clinic uses printed cards and forms giving specific directions (all in English) to the only pharmacy in town where the doctor's prescriptions can be filled. The pharmacy, located fifteen blocks from the clinic and in a rather run-down section of town, was a modern glass-and-concrete building which, like the clinic, stood in sharp contrast to its shabby surroundings. (The pharmacy is rumored to be owned by the Drs. M. and C., but this has never been proved.) There is also a hospital nearby, at which the doctors perform surgery and admit their patients. The hospital was not under study.

The clinic seems to be a piece of America dropped in the midst of a poor Mexican border town. If one walks a block or two away from the clinic and enters a store that does not specifically sell to tourists, he will be lucky to find anyone who speaks English. In fact, apart from the clinic the town does not seem to cater to tourists to any extent. Many of the town's foreigners are clinic patients.

THE PATIENTS

The first thing that strikes one upon observing or conversing with the clinic's patients is that they tend to be working class, with little formal education, and relatively unsophisticated. Of the fifteen persons we were able to interview during our visits, all were classified by the author, on the basis of occupation (when known), dress, speech, and other indicators, as either working-class or lower-middle-class persons. Of these fifteen, eight were men and seven were women. This sex ratio seemed representative of the total clinic population—that is, there was probably an equal number of men and women present at any given time.

The age of the patients was heavily weighted toward the middle-aged and older. The age range was from about twenty-four to about seventy, with two persons in the under thirty-five group, seven in the thirty-six to fifty-nine group, and six in the sixty and over group. This seems to be a fair picture of the total clientele.

Although about ninety percent of the patients are white Americans, there were always a few Mexican patients waiting as well. In most cases, these people were not interviewed because they spoke only Spanish and the writer's Spanish is poor. In one case, an elderly Mexican lady from Tijuana was interviewed, although not very satisfactorily because of the language barrier. During all of our visits, we saw only one Negro family and no other minority group members.

The homes of fourteen of the total sample were learned. Seven patients came from Southern California (Anaheim, Victorville, Whittier, Yucaipa, San Jacinto, El Cajon, and Garden Grove), three from Northern California (Merced, Morro Bay, and San Francisco), two from Arizona (Phoenix and Yuma), one from Chicago, and one from Tijuana, Mexico. We were told by other patients of people who came from Kansas, New York, Alaska, Canada, and Louisiana.

The complaints of the patients interviewed included arthritis (twelve), emphysema or asthma (three), eczema or psoriasis (two), and miscellaneous complaints such as "heart problems" (one), neuritis (one), "bad spleen" (one), tumor on foot (one), and glandular problems (one). The number of ailments exceeds fifteen because some patients had multiple complaints. The sample was heavily weighted toward arthritis, which is probably true of the patient population in general, but probably not in as great a proportion as indicated by the sample. In general, the people seen at the clinic during the observations did not appear badly disabled. During the visits, we saw no one in a wheelchair, two people using crutches and walking with difficulty, one person using a cane, and several others walking unaided but with difficulty.

All of the patients interviewed said that they had heard about the clinic from family or friends who knew of some encouraging results. Eleven of the respondents said that their family and friends were happy to see them going to the clinic and were supportive; of the remaining four, one said her relatives were definitely against her going, one said her family did not try to stop her but did not believe it would help, one said she had had mixed reactions (some supporting and some definitely against), and one said most of his friends and relatives were skeptical.

Of the fifteen, two were first-timers, five had been coming to the clinic for a year or less, seven had been coming from two to four years, and one had been coming for seven years. Twelve of the respondents reported that they had been helped a great deal, two had not taken the pills yet, and one felt he had been helped a little. Five of the fifteen said they had heard adverse comments about the clinic, while the other ten said that they had heard nothing but good.

An attempt was made to discover whether trying "quack" cures might be a pattern with the patients, or whether this was the first experience outside normal medical channels. This information was only obtained from nine of the interviewees, either because the interview was cut short, or because the question was never worked into normal conversation. Of the nine, six could be characterized as susceptible to "quack" cures. Their behaviors included seeing a faith healer, trying special fad diets, becoming a fresh juice faddist, seeing chiropractors, and going on a twenty-nine-day fast. While the three remaining patients had spent a great deal of time and money on treatments and medicines with a series of doctors, they had not sought unorthodox treatment plans up until the time of their first clinic appointment.

All the information gathered about the patients was based on casual conversation between the interviewer and the patient, and ranged from about ten minutes to an hour, with most lasting about half an hour. Although the writer had a list of questions which were to be included, an attempt was made to work them into the conversation naturally. (See the field notes for the list of questions used in the interviews.) No notes were taken at the time, but all the interview material was written down privately as soon after the conversation as possible.

The respondents were not selected in any systematic way, but most often were persons sitting near the interviewer. I presented myself as a new patient who was interested in knowing about the respondent's experience in the clinic. I maintained throughout the interviews an attitude of positive interest, making no negative remarks about the doctors or the clinic, and in general allowing the respondent to talk on at length, injecting a comment or question only when conversation lagged or seemed to be getting away from the subject. Generally, respondents were not only willing but eager to discuss their health problems and the clinic at length. (The field notes give a fuller description of the interviews.)

THE ATMOSPHERE AND ATTITUDES

Having set the stage with regard to the setting and characters, we may now begin to describe the general atmosphere of the clinic. First, it seems that the patients were working within a "nothing unusual is happening" frame of reference. The atmosphere of the clinic can probably best be characterized as friendly, informal, and relaxed. The patients sit, patiently waiting, for hours, sometimes exchanging talk about symptoms with those nearby, occasionally getting up and walking around, and often chatting with others. Many take a number, then go downtown to shop or go sightseeing for an hour or so. The atmosphere is really not too different from the atmosphere of any doctor's office, except that there are more people in the clinic waiting room who generally have to wait longer, so that they usually end up talking to each other.

There were no indications that anyone was anxious, uneasy, or suspicious, but neither did anyone seem particularly exuberant. While it was quite possible to sit in complete silence, we found that once we began to talk to a patient, there was usually eagerness on his part to share his experiences. The attitude of newcomers seemed to be expectant and hopeful, while that of oldtimers was grateful and confident.

Friendliness, conversation, and the circulation of patients all seemed to increase with the number of people waiting. There were usually anywhere from twenty-five to thirty-five people sitting around the waiting room at any one time, but probably only one-third to one-half were patients, since everyone seems to come with a spouse, other relatives, or the whole family. In general, one gets the impression that for many of the patients (and their families) this has become a pleasant all-day or weekend outing (depending on how far they have come). Quite a few people seem to know each other from previous meetings at the clinic, and these people sometimes stage little reunions. Patients meeting someone from their area of the country often exchange addresses. They also exchange other information, such as the name of a book on nutrition, the location of some other kind of doctor, a recipe, or any other information they feel has been helpful to them.

In short, the atmosphere is generally friendly and open, and almost any patient in the clinic is completely willing to talk about his ailment, how much the clinic has helped him, and anything else one may want to know. Sharing of experiences seems to be a large part of the success of this establishment, since each person feels even more confident on hearing about the successful experiences of others.

The attitudes of the fifteen patients interviewed can best be summarized with respect to their answers to four queries. First, thirteen of the fifteen were asked about their attitudes toward American doctors. All of the thirteen felt they had never really been helped by American doctors; seven felt this was because of lack of knowledge on the part of the U. S. doctors, but three said they had never been of any help because they did not have access to the medicine dispensed by the clinic doctors. Two others claimed that American doctors were only interested in money, and not interested in helping the patient, because they wanted to keep him coming back. One respondent felt that American doctors were conscientious but cautious, and were not willing to take chances.

In contrast, patient reactions to Dr. C. and Dr. M. were positive. While most (eight) remarked directly on their own improvement or the fact that the doctors "get results," several others (six) said, "He knows what he's doing," or otherwise indicated that they were impressed with the doctor they were seeing. This second group made such remarks as "They're doing marvelous work," and "He's so good (Dr. C.) he can tell by just looking at you what's wrong with you." Only one respondent was not completely sold. He said he felt there was nothing special about the clinic, that he was just trying it be- cause he had tried everything else, and that none of the other treatments had helped much. He said that he felt the doctor was not performing any miracles but that "most people that come down here think he's the Messiah."

Of the fifteen, twelve were asked why they thought they could get this help in Mexico while it was not obtainable in the United States. Six felt it was because the Mexican doctors had much better medical knowledge and train- ing than American doctors, and were aware of more advanced techniques. Several mentioned that the doctors had studied in Europe, where their tech- niques and medicines were available and accepted. Three felt that the treat- ment was not available in the U. S. because the A.M.A. was against it and was fighting it. A fourth felt it was a plot of the American drug industry to keep the medicine out of the U. S. When asked why the A.M.A. should be so much against the drugs, most people had no explanation, although one said that the A.M.A. was simply resistant to change and refused to look into it. One man felt that the drug could not be distributed in the United States because there was not enough of it to go around, while another felt that the Mexican doctors knew nothing special, but simply felt laws governing the dispensing of drugs were freer in Mexico.

*Although this was not systematically asked, it came out in conversation
over and over again that no one had ever bothered to ask what the medication
was.* Several apparently had asked whether the pills contained cortisone; they
were assured by the doctor that they did not, and they asked no further
questions. This lack of curiosity led to many different and sometimes incredible stories about what the medicine was. One patient believed it was a natural
(or herbal) drug developed by Dr. M. himself and therefore a secret formula
available only to his patients; another believed that it was a regular synthetic
drug imported from Germany or Switzerland, and in wide use in Europe.
Although there were perhaps more people who believed the medicine to be a
personal secret formula of Dr. M., there were several who believed it to be an
accepted drug in use in Europe. One woman even said that the pills contained
every ingredient necessary to cure or relieve any possible ill of the human
body, so that no matter what you had, the pills would help.

The general attitudes of the fifteen patients can be separated into three
groups: those who were extremely enthusiastic and proselytizing (eight);
those who were positive, but expressed some reservations or seemed somewhat restrained in their praise (six); and the one gentleman who could be
classified as frankly skeptical. It would appear, from comparing the reactions
of the patients with their socio-economic status and social sophistication
(using the objective and subjective indicators previously referred to), that the
somewhat higher-status and more socially sophisticated respondents tended
to be somewhat less enthusiastic.

As an example, Mr. G. was very interested in nutrition and was an avid
reader of health magazines. He seemed fairly well-informed about many
aspects of medicine; and although he was positive about the clinic, he mentioned that the doctor's examination was pretty routine and brief, and that
he was not "putting all his eggs in one basket," since he continued to see a
nutritionist in Anaheim. Another example was a bright twenty-four year-old
woman who felt she had been helped tremendously by the treatment she had
received at the clinic, but had questions about the safety of the drug and its
possible side effects. She indicated that she had read an article somewhere
about the clinic which had cast doubt on their work. Her attitude was positive but not unreservedly so. She was both thankful and apprehensive.

The most positive people were the ones who almost invariably said they
had never heard one bad word about the doctors. In fact, among the eight
that have been classified as extremely positive, only one mentioned that she
had ever heard anything negative, while of the remaining seven not-so-positive
respondents, four had heard adverse comments. Whether the first group was
so positive because they had never heard anything negative, or whether they
avoided hearing anything negative to eliminate dissonance, is impossible to

know, but it seems clear that the people with some doubts had heard, and continued to hear, some negative comments. The only respondent in our sample who was definitely skeptical, Mr. O., seemed to have the most cautious appraisal of the situation. He felt that the pills prescribed by Drs. C. and M. could be cortisone, and that his doctor in San Francisco had asked him to bring him a sample. He was willing to try this clinic because he had not been helped any other way, and he felt at his age it was worth the risk if he was helped at all. He even mentioned that he had read a very negative article in the newspaper about the clinic and had asked the doctor about it. The doctor had laughed, showed him a drawer full of clippings, and said, "I've got lots more just like it."

Mr. O. expressed the opinion that many people go to the clinic as a last resort, and try it only when everything else has failed. This is probably a fair assessment of how the patient first comes to contact the clinic. However, from that point on, their treatment and the things they hear from others largely determine their overall attitudes toward the clinic. Those who are helped, who are somewhat gullible and looking for simple solutions, and who do not try to find out about the clinic or health care in general, will tend to be enthusiastic and completely sold on the clinic and believe the doctors capable of performing miracles. On the other hand, those people who see no dramatic change in themselves and tend toward considered opinions—those who read widely and talk with other fairly sophisticated people—will tend to have some reservations, and perhaps a "wait and see" attitude.

The study sample was quite homogeneous with respect to education, occupation and socioeconomic status—there was no one we felt had more than a high school education, there were no professionals or white collar workers, and there was no one we felt could be classified as middle class. Apparently, persons with a high degree of social sophistication (college education, professional status, or at least middle class membership) are not tempted to try a "fringe" establishment of this sort, nor do they believe that American doctors are malevolent or incompetent. There must be, then, something about the clinic and its personnel that tends to attract the less sophisticated. Some of the reasons why lower-class persons exclusively seem to attend the clinic will be dealt with below.

CONCLUSIONS

Let me preface the discussion that follows with a note by another researcher on the subject of quacks. Beatrix Cobb, in a study of cancer patients who turned to non-medical practitioners, described rationales which are strikingly similar to those of the respondents in our sample. For instance, Cobb

reports that one woman told her that the quack she visited was always courteous, did not frighten her by telling her she was in a certain stage of cancer,
and gave her medicine for anything that ailed her. Another patient said that
the quack did not merely say he would keep her alive, as the doctors had, but
gave her hope of recovering. The approach of the quack is a positive one: "I
can cure cancer; all I ask is the opportunity to prove it."[5]

The quack may also tell the patient that what he is giving him is a medicine that will allow the body to build up its own defense mechanisms. Although this is apparently not the approach used by Dr. M. or Dr. C., some
patients seem to interpret their treatment in this way. Cobb also mentions
religion and "faith" as being prominent features of quack treatment plans. As
far as we could determine, this was not a part of the clinic's approach, except
as it relates to item (5) below. We will indicate how many of the above forms
of reasoning were also used by the clinic's patients. In my opinion the reasons
for this "deviant" behavior can be at least partially explained as follows:

(1) The doctors *do* get results. It cannot be denied that people come to
the clinic in pain and discomfort and after short periods of treatment
feel much better. Even the most skeptical person has to be impressed
by the improvement he sees. There was only one person in our sample
who did not feel he had made dramatic improvement, and even he
admitted that he had improved somewhat. Regardless of any possible
negative long-range effects the patients may experience they were
able to function much better after coming to the clinic than before.

(2) The doctors are dealing in hope. Whereas other doctors usually have
told these patients that they will have to learn to live with their dis-
abilities because there is nothing that can be done, Dr. M. and Dr. C.
said to them, "You will be feeling better in three or four days." No
one who suffers from the terrible pain and the limitations of movement that come with arthritis wants to be told that there is no hope.
The clinic's doctors have hope for everyone; they would never tell
anyone that there was nothing really wrong, or that they could not
help a potential patient.

(3) The doctors are charming, courteous, and solicitous. Generally speaking, American doctors tend to be hurried, impersonal, and often
brusque. They have a tendency to think of their patients in terms of
their diseases and frequently do not take time to listen to the
patient's problems or his evaluation of them. Although Drs. M. and C.
spend only a short time with each patient, they give the impression
that they are tremendously glad to see the patient, that he is important as an individual, and that they are truly interested in helping him.

Dr. C. (the only doctor seen by this writer) is very gracious, smiles a great deal, and makes frequent tension relieving comments. His whole attitude is one of concern for the patient's welfare.

(4) The continued existence and success of the clinic "proves" to the patients that American doctors are incompetent. It also provides a means of writing off past treatment failures and establishes grounds for a new hope in the success of the clinic's treatment plan. Most of the patients have been frustrated by years of pain and the outlay of much time and money on regular doctors, with no improvement. Many come to feel almost paranoid because no one helps them, and they begin to think it is not because they cannot be helped, but because regular doctors are deliberately making no effort to do so. They become completely disillusioned with regular doctors and grasp at anything that offers relief from pain. When they come to the clinic and get relief right away, their suspicions are confirmed and they find an object on which they can project their hostilities.

(5) There seems to be an element of magical thinking involved which imbues the situation with an almost supernatural aura. Many patients repeated the theme that the doctor knows what is wrong with you just by looking at you, so that an extensive examination is not necessary. The doctor is not only credited with superior knowledge and abililty, but is somehow assigned superhuman powers. Because the patient's desire to believe in the doctor is so strong, there is a great deal of "selective perception" at work. The patient hears and sees what he needs to hear and see in order to believe, and discards the rest. (If one is skeptical, one would look on the doctor's superficial examination and unprofessional standards as evidence of his quackery, rather than as proof of his vast knowledge and power.)

The medicine prescribed by the clinic doctors is also often treated as if it were something magical; many patients feel it is a secret formula, developed by the doctors and known only to them, or that it somehow contains every ingredient necessary to cure all the ills of the human body. The very fact that almost no one ever asks the doctor what the pills are seems to support the idea that the patients view them as something mysterious or exotic, and that whatever they contain is all right, because the doctors can do no wrong.

Also, in this case, the fact that the clinic is distant and in a foreign country may lend a sort of enchantment, and serves to provide the patients with a plausible explanation for why the treatment is not available to them in their own communities. (For example, if the same treatment were available in the United States, the patients would not have the same arguments about the superior medical knowledge of Mexican doctors or the plotting of the A.M.A. to keep the medicine out of the country to explain why the treatment is not widely accepted.)

(6) Finally, there is always the possibility that middle-class and upper-class persons do not resort to unorthodox treatment plans as often as lower class patients because they have ready access to the best treatment that legitimate medicine has to offer, and therefore suffer less and are less desperate to "try anything."

Granting that there is no cure for arthritis, it is still true that middle-class and upper-class patients find the same therapuetic effects from items (3) and (5) (through their ready access to good and legitimate treatment plans) that lower-class patients finally found at the "clinic." The problem may be that the clinic patients did not have access through legitimate channels to patient, courteous, and sympathetic doctors or the better medical services provided to middle-class and upper-class patients. These would have, at the very least, helped to establish and perpetuate a feeling of hope.

Middle- and upper-class patients may not resort to the quack cures that the clinic patients resorted to because they had access to many of the same saving features through legitimate treatment plans—that is, a ready professional ear, faith (the doctor as priest), and the "placebo effect" that believing provides. These features are not characteristic of lower-class doctor-patient interactions.

The above analysis is based upon my own observations during a series of visits to the "clinic" as a "patient," and on informal interviews conducted with fifteen other clinic patients. We must bear in mind that the vast majority of the people attending the clinic were relatively uneducated, unsophisticated, and from working-class or lower-middle-class backgrounds. We must also remember that many of the patients have what are often classified as psychosomatic ailments, and all have chronic complaints of one sort or another for which little or nothing can be done with respect to effecting a cure. All of this works to make clinic patients much more susceptible to all kinds of quack cures than the average patient. With arthritis particularly, millions of dollars are spent each year on such things as copper bracelets, special pillows, fad diets, and gadgets designed to relieve pain and discomfort.

There may come a time when a cure is found for arthritis and other chronic ailments. Until that time, there will be pain and suffering, and where there is pain and suffering there will be despair. Despair has led and will continue to lead to desperate counter-measures to reestablish hope. In this regard, the quack can expect to continue to profit from the misfortunes of others, and, in a perverted way, may even help to heal some of his patients in the process.

FIELD NOTES

January 24, 1970

A friend and I arrived in Mexicali and found the clinic, but the doctor was away for the weekend at a medical convention. The building is modern, spacious, clean, and very Americanized (attempt at legitimization?). The office girl spoke good English, told us the office days and hours (she was not very helpful and had to be specifically asked for information about office hours, where the pharmacy was, and so on.) She gave us three pieces of paper, all printed in English, which gave all the holidays the office would be closed, directions to the pharmacy, and office days and hours. She finally told us that no appointments are made and we would have to come back and wait.

We walked around town and found that the stores in the area do not cater to Americans. In the regular department stores, hardly anyone spoke English and those who did were not helpful. In the novelty shops they spoke English and obviously catered to tourists.

We asked a policeman for directions to the doctor's office and he responded immediately with directions to the "clinic." He did not seem inclined to talk, so we did not find anything out from him.

We drove over to the pharmacy (fifteen blocks away), which is an ultra-modern, glass-and-concrete building in the middle of a fairly run-down old neighborhood. The clinic itself is located on Mexicali's main street, in the downtown business district, and is no more than two blocks from the border. It is very easy to find.

February 2, 1970

Monday. We crossed the border at about noon, and this time noticed the signs above the street (black and white marquee type) as soon as we entered Mexicali. They gave directions to the office, which is no more than a block and a half from there. We pulled into the unpaved parking lot next to the clinic and were besieged by several Mexican boys (aged about fourteen to sixteen) who took our car to park it for us for fifty cents. They also wanted to wash it but were dissuaded from that. A public parking lot seems to be a rare thing in Mexicali, but is undoubtedly a good business in this location. We looked at cars in the lot before going into the clinic, and noted that they tended to be medium-priced, medium-sized cars, several years old, with mostly California license plates. There were no very expensive cars or sports cars in the lot.

We went into the office and I spoke to the receptionist, who gave me a paper to fill out with my name, address, age, and phone number (no complaint or medical history). I was then given a number (58) and asked to wait. (The receptionist was not rude, but fairly brusque and rather blase. There was another girl with her behind the desk who seemed to be doing paperwork.) There are rows and rows of small filing cabinets of the type for 3 x 5 file cards. The girls type the information from the paper the patient fills out onto these cards and a file is kept.

On a table in front of the reception area there was a big electric urn with hot water, powdered coffee, cream, sugar, cups, and so forth. There were two water coolers, one at each end of the room. There were signs on the walls, all in English, saying "No Smoking." The office was very clean, well ventilated, and well lighted. There were no nurses, no weigh-in, nothing to make it seem like a doctor's office.

When we arrived, there were about 25 people sitting in the waiting room, 18 of whom were white Americans, the others Mexicans. Most of the people were middle aged or older, although there were some children who had apparently accompanied parents. There were also two Mexican girls, one of whom was a teenager and apparently the patient, and another girl of about 21 with no apparent health problem, who also saw the doctor. In most cases there was a couple, one of whom was seeing the doctor, although there were a few people alone, a mother-daughter combination, a mother with her children, and so on. At first, I was struck by the fact that everyone seemed so silent and somber. There was little or no talking going on, even between members of the same group. Later, however, a few people seemed to strike up conversations, discussing symptoms and exchanging information. Generally speaking, the group appeared to be working people. Almost everyone was dressed casually, many of the women wearing slacks, most of the men in work clothes (uniforms, boots and cowboy hat, denim jacket). Most of the people we saw while we waited seemed to be there for arthritis, although there were a few respiratory problems and a few unidentifiable ailments. There were probably more women patients than men, but not many more.

In all, the doctor saw about sixty patients that day, judging by my call number. Most of the patients has been there since about 9:00 A.M. and some were still waiting for their medicine at 2:00 P.M. The following are interview results from the patients I was able to talk to.

Mr. A: About 55, a dairy farmer from Merced, California, has had emphysema for four years, this was his first time at the clinic. He heard about Dr. C. through friends who had a friend who had been helped immensely by him and decided it was worth a try. His wife and grown children all seemed to be in favor of his trying the clinic. Apparently they had heard nothing unfavorable about the clinic. Mr. A. had gone to a "healer" in Ashland, Oregon, for a year; but although he says he has been helped, he is still not well. He said that he would "try anything once;" and after seeing specialists who told him he was incurable and should stop smoking, he decided to try Mexicali.

The A.'s feel that medicine in Mexico is much more advanced than that in the United States, and that the clinic simply has a wonder drug not yet available to U. S. physicians. They also feel California doctors are the "quacks," only out for money, and of no use at all.

Dr. C. told Mr. A. that Mr. A. did *not* have emphysema, but a bronchial infection, and gave him medicine and instructions to come back in a month. Dr. C. described Mr. A's symptoms "to a T" without asking a lot of questions, so Mr. A. is convinced that Dr. C. really knows what he's doing. He seemed to feel coming down here was the right thing to do, and definitely does not see his attending the clinic as a deviant enterprise. His general attitude is hopeful.

Mr. B.: About 50, occupation unknown but appeared to be more lower-middle-class than working class because of dress, appearance of wife, and so on. From Phoenix, Arizona, suffers from acute rheumatoid arthritis, his first visit to clinic. He heard about the clinic from a friend who was completely sold on it. His wife seemed to be all for his trying this, as apparently nothing else has helped much. He has been taking cortisone, but Dr. C. told him to quit taking it at once (despite the fact that Dr. C.'s pills have been analyzed and found to be cortisone derivatives.)

He feels that the reason the clinic's drugs are not available in the U. S. is that the big drug companies are keeping them from the public, since they would lose money on all the other drugs. Mr. B. seemed quite impressed with the doctor, was waiting for his medicine as we left. His attitude, also, was hopeful and expectant.

In general, the atmosphere of the office was not too different from that in any other doctor's office. There were no indications that anyone was uneasy, or anxious, or suspicious, but neither did they seem particularly exuberant. Once you began to talk, there seemed to be an attitude of eagerness to share experiences. Generally, the atmosphere might be described as being "expectant"; definitely there was a "nothing unusual is happening" frame of reference.

February 14, 1970

Arrived 11:30 A.M. at the clinic waiting room, which was teeming with people. After a wait at the reception desk a very unconcerned girl looked at me and I told her I wanted to see the doctor. She looked me up in the file (3 x 5 cards) and found I wasn't there. (The three girls in the office are all young and attractive.) I told here I had not been able to see the doctor the time before, and she said they throw away the information sheet if you didn't see the doctor. (This seemed to me a rather cavalier way to treat a prospective patient.) I filled out another information sheet and was given number 83. (The waiting room was crowded with people, who seemed to be talking and circulating a lot. The atmosphere was noisy, almost festive.)

The composition of the room was much like last time. There were lots of magazines available for patients, mostly American but some in Spanish. Some patients were having Blue Shield forms filled out by the receptionists (who do not, by the way, wear any sort of uniform). Sanitation standards are not terribly high; the restroom is not spotless, the fixtures are old, and there is only cold water. There was also a cockroach dead in the hall. I talked to the following people:

Mr. C.: About 50, occupation heavy equipment operator, from Santa Ana, California, has arthritis, is greatly overweight, has been coming to the clinic for seven years. He reports that he first heard about the clinic when he had to quit work seven years ago because of pain and inability to do heavy work. His foreman told him about the clinic and he began coming down once a month for the first year, then once every two months for the second year, and now only comes about once every four to six months. He reports he has been given medication all these years, but at present has taken none since July (1969). He was accompanied to the office by his adult son, who seemed to be in favor of the treatment, and he reported that he had never heard anything bad about Dr. M. or Dr. C. He has not told his doctor in Santa Ana that he comes to the clinic, but tries the new medications which that doctor prescribes as well as those from the clinic because he is "willing to try anything." He says he has tried everything over the years, including diets, but nothing has helped except Dr. C.'s medicines. He had surgery for removal of his kneecaps recommended by an American doctor, but after he started at the clinic he improved so much it wasn't necessary. He told me the medication costs about $20 to $30 per month. When asked what it was, he said he didn't know and had never asked; apparently he didn't consider it important. He mentioned that the doctors also do a lot of surgery at a nearby hospital. When asked why he felt this help was not available in the U. S., he said he supposed the medicine couldn't be sold in the U. S. He was very vague as to why not, but when pressed he said he felt that there was not enough of a supply of it to serve the millions of arthritis sufferers. (The prescription, then, is a secret formula, known only to Drs. M. and C.) He is completely sold on the doctors, feels that they can help anyone almost immediately, and urged that I follow directions carefully and that my friend, who was on crutches, see the doctor and she would be walking without her crutches in no time. He is a true believer.

Mrs. D.: 70 (looks much younger), housewife, husband retired, working class (husband dressed in work pants, shirt, cap, had worked with hands), from Yuma, has arthritis, heart trouble, asthma (husband, daughter, and great grandson also being treated at clinic). Her husband is being treated for arthritis, daughter for asthma, four-year-old great grandson for allergies and skin outbreaks. Daughter has been hemorrhaging for month and half, is now in the hospital and needs an operation (apparently this is not seen by the family as connected with the clinic treatment). She was accompanied to the office by her husband and two granddaughters. Has been coming to clinic for one year, about once every three months now. First heard about how great Dr. C. was from friends, after she had gone to many other doctors. She has never heard one bad word about him, all her family and friends think he's wonderful; she will convince everyone else how great he is and says he needs no advertising because his reputation is spread by word of mouth. She said when she started coming, her arm was frozen in a twisted position and she couldn't use it, and now she gestured with it in a normal fashion. He has also cured her asthma and her heart isn't bothering her. She has been to many other doctors and none of them ever did any good. Her explanation was that "American doctors don't want to cure arthritis—they want to keep you coming back." When asked why American doctors don't have the medicine and don't want to cure arthritis, she said that the clinic doctors had studied in Europe and Europeans know so much more about medicine. She says the pills have every ingredient necessary to cure all the ills of the human body. She also said that the doctor doesn't require that patients disrobe because "he's so good he can tell what's wrong with you just by looking at you." Her attitude is one of total acceptance of the doctor without question. Her manner was one of gushy enthusiasm. She looked fine, and seemed perfectly healthy for her age.

Mrs. E.: 62 (looks younger), working class, is going to retire on disability insurance, here from Chicago (plans to move out here to be near doctor), has arthritis and had severe neuritis as result of an accident, but when she came to the doctor here two months ago, he gave her twelve shots all at once and got rid of her neuritis completely. She first heard about Dr. C. from a niece who lives in California and decided to try him. Her niece (Mrs. F.) has been helped, too, so all the family is much in favor of her going to clinic. She has apparently heard only praise for the doctors, and thinks they are doing marvelous work. She feels she has been helped tremendously. She feels that the clinic doctors just know a great deal more than American doctors. She had nothing but praise for the clinic, felt they could work miracles in short order. She mentioned that Dr. M. had connections with the Mayo Clinic.

Mr. G.: 60 to 65, retired craftsman, working class, from Victorville, California, severe asthma, been coming to clinic for two years, about every three months; had three heavy doses of medication at first, now down to very light doses and no longer bothered by asthma to any extent; first heard about the clinic through friends, and his wife and friends think its great for him to be coming. He saw a chiropractor who sent him to nutritionists in Anaheim (he feels nutrition is very important). He says one of the doctors in Anaheim has no opinion about his going to the clinic, but the other one said that he would like to know what the pills are, and suspects cortisone. Mr. G. also said he knows there are quite a few people who are against Dr. M., but "he gets results, and you can't quarrel with results." Mr. G. reads nutrition magazines, seems to follow health fads. He has felt that regular doctors in the U. S. have never done him any good, but he continues to see off-beat sorts of doctors. When asked why the medicine was not distributed in the U. S., he said the A.M.A. was keeping it out and they were "a powerful group."

His attitude was somewhat more knowledgeable about health than many of the other patients, and he feels that other things are important as well, such as proper nutrition. He feels that the clinic is great, but he's not "putting all his eggs in one basket." He is not questioning of the doctors, but neither did he seem completely accepting.

Mr. H: 63, occupation unknown, but classified as lower-middle-class (according to dress, speech, grammar), from Whittier, California. Said when he started coming to the clinic "everything was wrong with me," including some arthritis in the spine and a "bad spleen." He has been coming for three years, but in the last two years he has been treated for arthritis in his feet, a condition which didn't exist when he first came to the clinic. He found out about the clinic from relatives after he had spent "a small fortune" (about $500) on regular U. S. doctors for complete checkups, but they could find nothing wrong. Mr. H. said that at the time, if he got down on the floor he couldn't get up again. Mr. H. and his wife (was was with him and did a lot of the talking) are fresh juice faddists. They own two juice machines, one of which cost $300. Mr. H. said he also had psoriasis, which he cleared up by drinking fresh juices.

Mr. and Mrs. H. feel that Mr. H. has been helped by Dr. M., and feel that American doctors are no good because they could not find anything wrong with Mr. H. His general attitude toward the clinic was very positive, proselytizing. He spent a good deal of time trying to convince one of my friends (who was with me) to see the doctor, and he apparently brings friends down whenever possible.

Mrs. I.: About 70, wrinkled and thin, occupation unknown but classified as lower class since she appeared to be quite poor (very old clothes, held together by safety pins), from Tijuana, Mexico, Spanish-speaking only, accompanied by a very young girl, probably a granddaughter or great-grand-daughter, who didn't speak English either. Mrs. I. said she had arthritis in her fingers, neck, and back, had seen seven doctors who had not helped her at all before coming to the clinic. She said she had been coming to the clinic for three weeks and is much better. She seemed to have a very positive attitude toward the clinic and Dr. C.

Mrs. J.: About 40, housewife, occupation of husband unknown but judged to be working class (husband did not accompany Mrs. J. to clinic, she was driven by her daughter and son-in-law); complained of some arthritis, a tumor on her foot, and a glandular problem (she was very much overweight). She was from Yucaipa, California; had heard about the clinic from a friend who really sold her on it; she had been to many doctors in the U. S. who did not help her at all; and she said she "wanted to try everything" before she gave up. Her children were very much against her going to the clinic but she was insistent, and said the very first time she saw Dr. C. she got shots and the swelling in her legs was reduced some immediately. She thinks little of U. S. doctors, is quite complimentary about Dr. C.

At 2:30 my number was called and I entered Dr. C.'s office, which was furnished with deep, comfortable, gold vinyl covered chairs, a matching couch, a huge desk, and a thick gold carpet. Along the wall behind the doctor's desk was a short row of medical books, some in English, some in Spanish, and several of the "popular" types, on diet, heart, arthritis, and so on. Above were two rows of small plaster-of-paris reproductions of classical sculpture, a colorful popular sculpture of a girl's head, and a Mexican dancing girl doll in a colorful costume. On the desk was a huge crystal vase, housing a gold clock, and filled with masses of long-stemmed gold metal roses.

Dr. C. was in the adjoining office, talking to the last patient, and he came in within about five minutes. He first asked if I were Carol Whitehurst, then approached me with a super-charming smile and a gracious manner and took my hand, which he pressed rather than shook. He is young (early thirties), rather attractive, and was wearing a white tunic over dark slacks. He then sat down at the desk and asked my age, whether I had had any surgeries, and how long I had had my present complaint, and entered this information on a 3 x 5 card, similar to the cards kept in the files in the reception area. He then asked me to tell him "all about my aches and pains" (he seemed at a loss at first to know what I was doing there). I told him a little and, apparently satisfied, he asked me to step into the adjoining examining room and seat myself on a stool. (This is not really a separate room but rather a small alcove off the main room. It is not well equipped with instruments, like those one is used to seeing in the examining rooms of American doctors.) He then took my blood pressure and listened to my heart in a perfunctory manner without having me disrobe, and manipulated each of my joints. On the *right* hip joint he poked hard enough to make me say "ouch," and this seemed to please him and confirm his feeling that my previous hip surgery had been unsuccessful—

surgery on my *left* hip. He also failed to comment on the bandages which encircled my right leg from ankle to knee. After this "exam," including the comment that my ankles were swollen, which no doctor has ever told me before, he asked me to return with him to his desk so we could "have a little talk." He then proceeded to tell me that he wished I had come in a long time ago, before my hip surgery, because they now know that the kind of surgery I had was not successful and that the technique he and Dr. M. were using (which was widely used in Europe and also by a doctor in San Francisco and by the Mayo Clinic) was much better and about 90 percent successful. He then proceeded to show me an x-ray of someone who had recently had hip surgery done by him. In the meantime, the receptionist came in and they talked to each other in rapid Spanish for a couple of minutes. Dr. C. wrote out something on a prescription form and gave it to her, telling her in English to take this whenever she had her headaches. There was more conversation in Spanish, a boy came in and they spoke in rapid Spanish, and finally all left. Dr. C. explained to me that one of his patients was being released from the hospital and he had to write her a prescription. The doctor then drew for me a drawing of the way in which his type of hip surgery was done, explaining that he cut the bone below the joint, pushed it over with a sort of plate, releasing the joint from the socket, and put muscle between the ball and the socket where there should have been cartilage. He said it would take about 95 years to wear out the muscle. (This procedure sounded incredible to me but I have no way of knowing if it was legitimate.) He then offered to give me the name of a patient who had had hip surgery and I accepted his offer. He called the desk and asked the girl to give me the name of a man in San Jacinto. He encouraged me to have my hip surgery redone by him.

The doctor also told me that he could take me off prednisone, which he said was of course damaging to my bones, and he proceeded to write out a prescription for three medications. (He told me to stop taking prednisone at once, which is supposed to be dangerous.) I asked him what the medications were, and he said one was an antibiotic, one "something to get rid of the calcium around your joints," and one a fluid pill to get rid of the swelling when I went off prednisone. (Note: normally you swell when taking prednisone, not when going off it.) He also commented that my ankles were swollen, which no doctor has ever done before; also, no other doctor has wanted to give me fluid pills. He gave me instructions for taking the medicine, saying I would be feeling fine within about four days; he asked that I come back in a month. He was very gracious, charming, and escorted me to the door. He seemed more interested in selling me a hip operation than in pushing the pills, and he certainly didn't tell me anything new or interesting.

On the wall of the waiting room, there was a certificate of completion from La Universidad Nacional Autonoma de Mexico, granted to Dr. C. in 1962.

After leaving Dr. C., I went to the desk, where I again was kept waiting for no apparent reason, paid $12, was given a receipt by an indifferent office girl, and made my exit past a teenage Mexican boy who appears to be employed by the clinic to shoo away beggars. The boys in the parking lot told us they worked for the doctors, although it is not known in what sense this is true. We left, and in crossing the border, told the officer we had been to see Dr. M. He said that thousands of people come to see him every year, some from as far as New York City. He said, "I don't know myself, but a lot of people swear by him."

February 16, 1970

Sent airmail letters to the Mayo Clinic and the A.M.A., asking the Mayo clinic whether Dr. M. had ever been associated with them and inquiring about the technique described to me. I asked the A.M.A. for any information they might have concerning the doctor's qualifications and the medicine they prescribed.

February 18, 1970

Some thoughts. Generally speaking, the patients aren't very disabled. I've only seen one person on crutches, none in wheelchairs or being carried in. Some seem to be hypochondriacal, many have psychosomatic ailments, probably all with chronic complaints of the type that nothing much can be done for.

The patients seem to assign superhuman powers to the doctors—they are not just credited with superior knowledge, but with the ability to tell what's wrong with you just by looking at you. I think many can be so carried away with wanting to believe it, the relationship becomes like that with a fortune-teller or a horoscope caster—you hear the part you want to hear, the part that has meaning for you, and forget the rest. If you're skeptical, you notice discrepancies and errors, and you look on the doctor's superficial exam as evidence of his "quackery," rather than evidence of his omniscience.

February 19, 1970

Called Mr. K., a middle-aged meat cutter from San Jacinto, who had a hip operation (he has osteoarthritis) last May 26; at that time, he was so badly crippled with pain in his hip that he had to stop working. He had been to several specialists in his area and in Long Beach and no one would do anything for him because of his generally poor condition. He first heard about the clinic from a friend who was going there. He went down just to get medication, but the doctor suggested surgery and he agreed to it. It cost $1,350; he was in the hospital thirteen days, he takes no medication, he has had no pain at all, but he has had his shoe built up and walks with a cane. He hasn't returned to work yet. He has been to the doctor three times since his surgery. He said the surgical technique was developed in England and wasn't accepted in the U. S. yet because our medicine is behind that of Europe. He said he decided to follow through because he'd "try anything." From the comments he made about a son and his wife, it appears that his family supports him all the way. He seemed to think Dr. C. was a nice guy, and said, "He really knows what he's doing." However, he didn't seem to be bursting with enthusiasm. His attitude was positive, but restrained.

February 21, 1970

Received a letter from the Mayo Clinic stating "I . . . do not find that he (Dr. M.) has ever been associated with the Mayo Clinic in any fashion, nor does he maintain any privileges here. He is totally unknown to us . . . We have received many letters in recent years requesting information about Dr. M . . . Our staff is not aware of Dr. M's work ever having been reported in a medical or scientific journal." Signed by M. G. Brataas, Administrator, Mayo Clinic, dated February 19, 1970.

March 5, 1970

Called the local branch of The Arthritis Foundation. The representative said that their stand is that of the local press; that they wouldn't recommend the clinic to anyone, although the representative has talked to people who have been there and are positive about it. The representative said that she feels they are getting huge doses of cortisone, which no American doctor will prescribe in those amounts, as they feel it must be carefully controlled and slowly withdrawn. They don't have the same controls and regulations in Mexico, according to this representative. She said the Foundation knew of one of Dr. M.'s patients last year, a girl in her early twenties with rheumatoid arthritis, who began having side effects of cortisone (swelling), and when she stopped taking it suffered from "withdrawal symptoms" and other complications. The representative said that hardly anyone ever calls the Foundation first, because they don't want to hear anything negative, they *want* to have something to believe in.

March 7, 1970

Arrived about noon. Waiting room not so crowded, mostly families together, atmosphere friendly, informal, people talking to each other. I was given number 66 and sat down to wait. Saw one woman leave on crutches—seemed very bad. There were several younger people including one teenage Mexican boy who looked sick and held his head in his hands. Mr. and Mrs. L. were the first people I spoke to, Mrs. L. being the patient today, although Mr. L. sees Dr. C. also for an unnamed ailment.

Mrs. L. is in her late forties; occupation of her husband is unknown. She is a housewife, apparently working class, from El Cajon (where they had moved inland from San Diego because of the effect of dampness on her health). She has arthritis in her hands and spine, and has been coming to the clinic for two years and four months. First heard about the clinic through a friend. She has ten brothers and sisters, all of whom have arthritis but none of whom will come down because they don't really think Dr. C. can help them, so the family is generally not supportive. She said her regular doctor in El Cajon knew she was seeing the doctors in Mexicali, disapproved, and said he was just waiting for the side effects. She said there had been none, except for purplish splotches on her arms that were a sort of bruising from broken blood vessels, but she would rather have bruises all up and down her arms than have the pain she had before. She said she was very much against cortisone, had never taken it, but had spent a lot of time and money on all kinds of doctors, treatments, shots, and chiropractors before she finally came here. She said she had been helped immediately at the clinic and continued to come every two months because this was the first relief from pain she had ever had. They emphasized that both Dr. C. and Dr. M. had said that the medicine was *not* cortisone, although others had voiced the opinion that that was what it was, including a nurse friend of theirs. They felt that the medicine was some formula developed by Dr. M. himself, and they told me that Dr. M. had written papers on his discovery and had tried to present them to the A.M.A., but the A.M.A. wouldn't look into it, just assumed it was cortisone. They had no explanation for why the A.M.A. refused to consider it, but simply seemed to feel the Association was not ready to accept innovations, was resistant to change. Their attitude toward American doctors was not as completely negative and rejecting as some, but they felt that U. S. doctors had not ever been able to help them simply because of lack of information. They apparently were no longer under an American doctor's care. They were sold on the clinic, and took the attitude that they didn't care what anybody said so long as they felt better. They felt the medicine was expensive but worth it. Their attitude in general was very positive; they were eager to share their experiences with me, and reassured me about the treatment. They tended to be proselytizing.

Mrs. M. was about 24, a housewife (husband's occupation unknown, but he was probably a skilled laborer, judging from his hands, which looked well worn). She appeared to be intelligent and articulate, perhaps with some

college experience. She comes from Morro Bay, California, has had severe
eczema since she was nine months old, and has been coming to clinic for
three years. First heard about Dr. M. from a friend of her mother-in-law,
apparently gets support from husband and mother-in-law, but a lot of argu-
ment from friends; said she has had many people tell her she was crazy to go
to Mexicali, said a lot of people don't think much of Mexican doctors, and
thought the long trip not worth it. She said she had read an article written by
someone affiliated with the A.M.A. saying that cancer had been linked to the
drug Dr. M. uses, but she didn't believe it because she generally distrusts the
A.M.A., and besides, "Why hasn't the story about cancer been spread all over
if it's true?" She said her eczema is caused by the fact that her body doesn't
assimilate foods right and they're turned into poisons which come out in
eczema. She has been to doctor after doctor, never with any real results; she
once went on a 29-day fast which cleared up her eczema, but as soon as she
started eating again, it returned. However, when she finally came to the clinic
the doctor gave her the prescription and within three days her eczema cleared
up. She now comes down only about once every five or six months to renew
her medication. A year and a half ago she got pregnant and worried that the
medicine might be harmful to the baby. She asked Dr. C. and he assured her
that it wouldn't, so she continued to take it, although she continued to
worry. However, the baby is eight months old now, and all right. When asked,
she said she didn't know what the medicine was and really didn't care so long
as it helped her. She said she had heard it was natural (herbal) but had asked
the doctor and he told her no, it was a synthetic drug. She thought the drug
was not the doctor's discovery, but something developed in Germany. She
said she had never had any side effects, took slightly less medicine than prescribed (two pills per day rather than three), remained slightly worried that
the drug could be harmful, but had been taking it for three years with such
wonderful results she intended to keep right on. She simply felt that she had
to come to the clinic because she couldn't get the drug in the U. S., and felt
that the A.M.A. was responsible for keeping the drug out although she didn't
understand why. She seemed to feel that the A.M.A. might feel differently if
they knew how many people came down there. She didn't seem to think
there was anything special about the doctors, and in fact mentioned that she
had never really been examined. The selling point for her was that they dispensed the medicine she needed. She didn't think American doctors were
quacks or indifferent or anything, but felt that they simply didn't have access
to the drugs. Her attitude toward the clinic in general was positive, and she
said when she saw people with arthritis or eczema she wanted to tell them
about it, and in fact had done so a couple of times but had been laughed at or
had her suggestion brushed off.

Mr. O.: About 60 to 65, retired fireman (on disability), from San Francisco, arthritis in knees as a result of a knee injury, and psoriasis. Has been coming to the clinic about two years; first heard about it through friends, but many of his relatives and friends very dubious about his going there. Has heard a lot of negative comments, read an adverse article in San Francisco newspaper, said his firemen friends told him he was being "took." His wife (who was along) supported him, but they were all skeptical, himself included. He also said he was seeing a regular doctor in San Francisco who opposes his coming to the clinic because he believes Dr. C. is prescribing cortisone—asked Mr. O. to bring him a pill. Mr. O. recently had a physical checkup and the doctor said he was showing too many white corpuscles. He apparently hadn't tried any other quack cures, but mentioned an interest in nutrition. He said he felt he had been helped "about a third," said he felt Dr. C. wasn't doing any miracles with him, but said, "Most people that come down here think he's the Messiah." In general, he didn't think there was anything special about the clinic, felt the medicine could very well be cortisone, but just felt he had been helped some (said he could still only walk a block). He felt that many people had doubts, but were just there to try it out since they hadn't found help any other way. He had no negative attitudes toward American doctors, just felt they were cautious, conservative, and wouldn't allow the treatments in the U. S. because they didn't want to take any chances. His general attitude toward the clinic was if they could help him even a little, it was worth it to him at his age even if it was dangerous. He said he had heard all the stories about the great successes, but hadn't experienced it himself, and he said, "We don't know about the ones that don't come back." His whole attitude was skeptical, and he said he had taken the prescription he got to a doctor friend who lives in Mexico and speaks Spanish, and the doctor couldn't read it. He also mentioned the adverse article to Dr. C., who laughed and pulled open a drawer, saying, "I've got lots more just like it."

March 3, 1970

Received a letter from the A.M.A. They said they didn't have specific information about the drugs used, but believed them to be extremely high doses of cortisone. They said they had a letter on file from Dr. M. stating that the medicine was called "X" and they found that a Mexican firm named "X" markets "Y," a cortical hormone, and "Z," a potent anabolic drug. They also quoted a representative of The Arthritis Foundation as having said that he had been told the doctor gives massive doses of cortisone and in prescribed regime gave tranquilizers, hormones, and codeine. They knew for a fact that one capsule dispensed contains hydrocortisone. "I have talked with many, many very sad and disillusioned (and broke) arthritis sufferers who have been to him for treatment. Some have developed stomach ulcers, some have bleeding ulcers which required surgery . . . The majority of people I have talked to feel that they actually are worse physically after they have discontinued their visits to Dr. M. than they were before." Letter signed by Oliver Field, Director of Research, Department of Investigation, American Medical Association, dated March 5, 1970.

Questions used in interviews

The following set of questions were worked unobtrusively into the formal conversations the author had with fifteen of the clinic's patients.

1. Where are you from?
2. What do you see the doctor for?
3. How did you find out about the clinic?
4. How long have you been coming here?
5. Have you been helped? How much?
6. How do your family and friends (and your doctor) feel about your coming here?
7. Have you ever heard anything bad about the doctors or the clinic?
8. What other kinds of things have you tried before?
9. What do you think of American doctors?
10. What do you think of Dr. C. (or Dr. M.)?
11. What do you think it is that these doctors have or know that American doctors don't have or know? And why do you think this treatment is not available in the United States?
12. What's your general attitude toward the clinic (or how do you feel about coming here)?

NOTES

[1] Will Thorne, *The Press,* Nov. 24, 1969, p. B-1.

[2] Personal correspondence from M. G. Brataas, Administrator, Mayo Clinic, dated February 19, 1970.

[3] Personal correspondence from Oliver Field, Director of Research, Department of Investigation, A.M.A., dated March 5, 1970.

[4] Personal conversation with a representative of The Arthritis Foundation, Riverside, California, chapter, March 5, 1969.

[5] Beatrix Cobb, "Why do people detour to quacks?" in E. Gartley Jaco, Ed., *Patients, Physicians, and Illness* (The Free Press, New York, 1958), pp. 283-287.